An Inquiry into the Philosophical Foundations of the Human Sciences

SAN FRANCISCO STATE UNIVERSITY
SERIES IN PHILOSOPHY

Anatole Anton
General Editor

Vol. 14

PETER LANG
New York • Washington, D.C./Baltimore • Bern
Frankfurt am Main • Berlin • Brussels • Vienna • Oxford

Alfred Claassen

An Inquiry into the Philosophical Foundations of the Human Sciences

WITH A FOREWORD BY
David Rubinstein

PETER LANG
New York • Washington, D.C./Baltimore • Bern
Frankfurt am Main • Berlin • Brussels • Vienna • Oxford

Library of Congress Cataloging-in-Publication Data

Claassen, Alfred.
An inquiry into the philosophical foundations of the human sciences /
Alfred Claassen; with a foreword by David Rubinstein.
p. cm. — (San Francisco State University series in philosophy; v. 14)
Includes bibliographical references and index.
1. Psychology. 2. Philosophy. 3. Social sciences—Philosophy.
I. Title. II. Series.
BF38.C53 001.01—dc22 2006000715
ISBN-13: 978-0-8204-8179-1
ISBN-10: 0-8204-8179-3
ISSN 1067-0017

Bibliographic information published by **Die Deutsche Bibliothek**.
Die Deutsche Bibliothek lists this publication in the "Deutsche
Nationalbibliografie"; detailed bibliographic data is available
on the Internet at http://dnb.ddb.de/.

Contents

Editor's Introduction

ANATOLE ANTON
THE SAN FRANCISCO STATE UNIVERSITY SERIES IN PHILOSOPHY

This series is designed to encourage philosophers to explore new directions in research, particularly directions that may lead to a reintegration of philosophy with the sciences, the humanities, and/or the arts. The series is guided by three premises: (1) The intellectual division of labor into distinct academic disciplines is a product of changing historical circumstances and conditions; (2) The current intellectual division of labor has outlived its usefulness in many ways; and (3) There is a pressing need to reintegrate the metaphysical and evaluative concerns of philosophy with current work in the sciences, humanities, and arts. Works in this series are intended to challenge social and philosophical preconceptions that block the reintegration of philosophy with other disciplines and at the same time maintain unquestionably high standards of scholarship.

The fourteenth volume in our series, *An Inquiry into the Philosophical Foundations of the Human Sciences* by Alfred Claassen, exemplifies our intentions perfectly. Professor Claassen, a sociologist by training, argues on philosophical grounds that the disarray and seeming inconsistencies among and within the various human sciences can be overcome and that a philosophically grounded conception of the unity of the human sciences can be achieved. Doing this, however, requires a shift in point of view from that of either positivism or phenomenology alone to that of a neo-Hegelianism that incorporates both of these partial points of view. The unity that Claassen envisions is of a dialectical nature, but one that is capable of reconciling the disparate intellectual traditions within and among the human sciences. Further, it shows the bearings of facts on values (both moral and aesthetic) and vice versa. Finally, it clarifies the practical role that social science as a whole can play in the world. Professor Claassen thus provides us with a conception of social science that is relevant at once to the great problems of history-making that present themselves to societies and the smaller problems of life-making that simultaneously present themselves to the individuals within them. (In making this latter point, I might add, he draws on his own original expanded view of Freudian psychology.)

Needless to say, such universalism is not intellectually fashionable today. Not only does it fly in the face of the teachings of postmodernism, but curiously, as Claassen argues, it offers a better account of the realities of the phenomena of postmodernity than do postmodernist theories. The fundamental shortcoming of previous metanarratives has not lain in their "totalizing" ambitions to grasp the social whole, according to Claassen, but in the inadequacy of their conceptual resources. Accordingly, Claassen lays out four basic dimensions along which to study human nature: (1) in terms of reflexivity and (2) along the polarities of the consummatory and the instrumental, (3) the real and the ideal, and (4) the individualist and the collectivist. Each of these dimensions, he claims, is essential, and failure to think all of them at once explains much of the incoherent state of the human sciences today. Claassen's humanism appears in his view that oppositions within the human sphere lend themselves, in the last analysis, to reconciliation, of both a theoretical and a practical nature. A full understanding of the dimensions of the human, he tells us, makes possible the overcoming of seemingly incommensurate frameworks. This in turn opens the path both to answering skeptical challenges to any such "totalizing" program and to reasserting the primary role of a dialectical philosophy in the ordering and mapping, as it were, of the human sciences. What he achieves is a framework that, arguably, is adequate to a thoroughly historical and comparative view of all aspects of all societies in all time periods. The boldness of Claassen's vision deserves praise aside from the interesting and innovative particulars and technical details of his program. Rather than skirting the incoherence of the contemporary human sciences, he is able to bring it into focus and to suggest a plausible solution.

The intellectual affinities of Claassen's work can probably best be located with what might be called the third generation of critical social theory, the generation that includes those of Habermas's students who have moved away from Habermas's Kantianism and back in the direction of Hegel. Such development requires a clear way of distinguishing Hegel's mode of overcoming oppositions and his linguistic framework from Marx's historical and dialectical materialism. Professor Claassen takes up this problem in Chapter 15, entitled "Dialectical Historicism." Hegelian/Marxist writers such as George Lukacs and Herbert Marcuse notwithstanding, Claassen argues that Marx's historical materialism goes wrong in its abandonment of holism and therefore of the possibilities for affirmation of and reconciliation with the very societies it seeks to understand and improve. Thus, in Claassen's judgment, Marx's radical conflictualism and inability to be at home in the modern social world are part and parcel of his antiholism. Ultimately, according to Claassen, this derives from both his inability to consider all dimensions of social being and his methodological insistence on the priority of negation and conflict over concern with the social whole. However, Hegel and Marx both remain exemplary, according to Claassen, for the central place they give to history and the way in which they address the whole sweep of history. Claassen follows them in this when he says, " . . . the central goal of the social sciences must be to construct a comprehensive comparative historical sociology of the world."

The secret to the failure of previous attempts to develop a comprehensive social theory is contained in another of Professor Claassen's remarks: "People and societies are not one- or two-dimensional *objects* to phenomenology but many dimensional *subjects*." He thus proposes a methodology that incorporates a very broadly defined descriptive phenomenology having its sources in the work of Nietzsche, Weber, Husserl, and Schutz, but he insists that this phenomenology have both macro- and microsides and that these be in constant dialectical interaction with one another. The line between knower and known, as in Hegelian thought generally, turns out to be a blurry one for Claassen. Both are required, and they are not independent of one another.

There is much in Claassen's work that I have not touched on in this introduction. I have not, for example, talked about his remarkable attempt to incorporate the entire field of aesthetics into social theory or of his direct confrontation with the specters of skepticism and radical relativism as they haunt social theory. However, I would fault him for overlooking Volume 6 of this very series. For in *The Concept of Object as the Foundation of Physics* Irv Stein demonstrates a sort of conceptual disunity in physics similar to the one that Professor Claassen associates exclusively with the human sciences. Nonetheless, Claassen's work is pathbreaking in many ways and will hopefully point the way forward to a truly reflexive and humanistic social theory that will open up myriad possibilities for us to be "at home in the world." This is no small accomplishment.

Foreword

DAVID RUBINSTEIN
PROFESSOR OF SOCIOLOGY, UNIVERSITY OF ILLINOIS AT CHICAGO

Sociologist Alfred Claassen's *An Inquiry into the Philosophical Foundations of the Human Sciences* is a bold, ambitious neo-Hegelian effort to ground, orient, and unify the human sciences. It offers a distinctive new approach to the subject that seeks to encourage comparative historical and developmental scholarship. The motif that carries through the book and could have served as its subtitle is "dimensions of the human." Having digested an impressive array of scholarly literature, the author organizes his ontology and epistemology around five dimensions underlying the most fundamental features of the human: the instrumental and consummatory, the reflexive and unreflexive, idealism and realism, individualism and collectivism, and universalism and sectoralism. These dimensions, along with the historical one, form the conceptual space within which Claassen proposes that we study the human. Believing that the contemporary human sciences have reached an impasse, he provides what he considers to be necessary for progress, a counterparadigm intended to underpin a resurgent harmonism—for the human sciences and ultimately for society as a whole.

The author's intellectual origins lie primarily in nineteenth and early twentieth century European social thought and philosophy, and his sociological touchstone is Max Weber. From the classical theorists he draws an insistence that where possible the human sciences be historical, comparative, and comprehensive in scope. Claassen also bears the influence of American sociologist Talcott Parsons who sought to synthesize the classical European tradition. Following Parsons, he seeks to ground and systematize that tradition, but he goes well beyond Parsons philosophically. Claassen's aim is to prepare the way for future work similar to that of the classical theorists that might one day cover the human sciences and explain the major phenomena and events of history.

The book's historical vision builds especially upon Marx, Weber, and Lenski. Claassen introduces what he terms "dialectical historicism" to overcome the opposition between Hegelian idealism and Marxian realism and generate the major questions of history in a comprehensive and balanced way. Like these thinkers, Claassen's view of history centers on stages of development. However, he departs from their periodizations by also distinguishing a global capitalist period that begins from the mid-1960s. What he envisions and seeks to support is work like that of Barrington Moore, Charles Tilly, and Perry Anderson, but carried through all social and cultural institutions, all kinds of societies, and all time periods.

An Inquiry builds its psychology primarily upon Freud, developing the latter's psychic functions and extending his character types. The provocative outcome is Claassen's postulation of the "superid," "super-superego," and other new aspects of the personality likely to be of considerable value to practicing human scientists. Claassen argues that these sectors of the personality, which also form home bases for character types, parallel corresponding sectors of society. Like Plato, he emphasizes the close analogies between sectors of the psyche and society, both of which he considers to be levels of the human.

As philosophy of human science, Claassen's book, like Dilthey's, Weber's, and, more recently, Runciman's methodological writings, aims to ground subsequent work of comparative historical scholarship. Like Foucault's *The Order of Things*, it emphasizes epochs that stamp themselves on diverse interrelated aspects of the human. Like Honneth and Joas's *Social Action and Human Nature*, it contains a philosophical anthropology. It has less in common with such philosophies of social science as those of Hollis, Lukes, and Elster, which tend to be organized topically. What most sets this book apart are its ambition and scope. Claassen architectonically lays out a fundamental paradigm for the human sciences and grounds it philosophically, for which purpose he develops an entire philosophical system. He does this in the belief that no existing tradition within the human sciences has the conceptual resources to break out of the current impasse.

An Inquiry's philosophical origins are primarily Hegelian. Its ontology resonates with Hegel, and it pursues Hegel's project of reconciliation throughout. In keeping with his dialecticality, Claassen strives to overcome basic oppositions rather than accepting one pole and rejecting the other. In that spirit he seeks to harmonize the opposition between liberalism and conservatism by recognizing that each is valid under certain circumstances. Less surprising is his embrace of both the instrumental and consummatory. His balancing of the reflexive and unreflexive is standard Hegelianism, although it is presented with exceptional clarity; while other syntheses, including those of the ideal and real and the universal and sectoral, are less familiar. In the same vein he argues compellingly for the complementarity of phenomenological/interpretive and positivist strands of research. An important part of what he does consists of "reactualizing" the core of Hegel's philosophy, much as Honneth has recently done for Hegel's political philosophy in his *Suffering from Indeterminacy*. However, Claassen's Hegelianism, like Kojève's but unlike most contemporary renderings, is a comparatively free one.

Claassen argues that there is so much Marxian but so little Hegelian human science primarily because Hegel is unclear in his depiction of the dimensions of the human. In Claassen's view, since these dimensions form the framework of the human sciences, having them laid out clearly is the most pressing need of these fields. His central aim in the book is to carry out this task. Thus, he basically follows Hegel's philosophy but attempts to recast and update its fundamental oppositions while correcting for its one-sided idealism. Claassen also absorbs the Kuhnian language of paradigms and paradigm shifts into Hegelian philosophy. The result is a neo-Hegelian synthesis of the deepest theoretical structures of the human sciences.

His unapologetic universalism and relentless synthesizing put Claassen sharply at odds with much that is postmodernist in the human sciences. He accepts postmodernism's inclusiveness and interpretivism, but where postmodernism is conflictualist, he is harmonist; where it is skeptical, he is not; where it divides, he unifies; where it venerates difference, he dialectically overcomes difference; where it specializes, he is interdisciplinary; where it abolishes the subject, he centers his work on the subject; and where it calls for an end to metanarratives, he calls for the metanarrative of all metanarratives. The key points of contention have to do with whether it is possible and desirable for collectivities and persons to overcome oppositions dialectically and, if so, whether it is possible for human scientists to study this reliably. Postmodernism takes the negative and Claassen the affirmative on both points. Claassen's approach will meet considerable opposition from those disciplines like contemporary sociology that have made conflict and power struggles the central reality of social order. It will provoke skepticism from those who, like David Hume, regard the scarcity of resources and limited altruism to be the fundamental realities of social existence. Nothing is potentially more valuable to the human sciences than laying out a new paradigm, and nothing is more predictable or healthier than that it will be at odds with many of the reigning verities. For decades postmodernism has encountered strong opposition at the popular level but relatively little at the philosophical level. Claassen's work is part of a small but growing opposition that draws on the thought of Leo Strauss.

The functionalism of the industrial era sought to avoid its provenience in traditional universalism and morality by means of scientism and biological analogies or systems language. It never acknowledged that what it was ulti-mately about was moral stewardship. Claassen has essentially moved to the larger philosophy that always lay behind functionalism, the holism dominant in the major traditional civilizations of the world, especially as rearticulated by Hegel. What the author carries back to the human sciences from his sojourn in philosophy is a new ontology and phenomenological analysis that have shed the spurious functionalist program of legitimation. The sectoral and nonmoral are fully treated in Claassen's analysis, but the universal and moral take center stage, although in a distinctly modern way. By openly reviving traditional forms of inquiry the book implicitly reestablishes ties with the hierarchical worlds that were their context. This reconnection with the tradi-tional is not carried out by fiat as in the popular conservatisms but via reason informed by knowledge of the human sciences. If we recall that the reigning paradigm of Anglo-American human science was a harmonist one in the form of functionalism not so long ago, and if we agree that no one should under-estimate the philosophical resources and cultural power that have lain dor-mant in Hegelianism, Claassen's embedding of a powerful new harmonist paradigm in this philosophy is of major significance.

The central themes of the book come together in the last two chapters in which Claassen argues respectively for the return of the absolute and for the reunification of the separate disciplines under philosophy. He concludes that both have become possible with the philosophy he has adapted and devel-oped. This is remarkable philosophy of human science but also a great deal more. Very little work of such seriousness and scope appears in any era, but especially in our own. Here the big questions are commandingly addressed. Ranging through the human sciences and philosophy, as well as art and liter-ature, this is an unusually erudite work. Few thinkers in the world today can move back and forth between so many fields as knowledgeably and fluently as Claassen.

Claassen's book provides a conceptual guide to the human sciences that helps place their many different schools, disciplines, specialties, and modes of inquiry amid the bewildering complexities of contemporary scholarship. When even Clifford Geertz (Ch. 7) as much as says he can no longer see where his work fits in relation to that of others, clarification of the larger pic-ture within which scholarly activity takes place is vital. More importantly, Claassen's conceptual mosaic helps us more easily see the fundamental com-plementarity of the varied strands of the human sciences and acknowledge the value of diverse scholarly work. The picture he offers is one of kindred disciplines, theories, and modes of inquiry working at different places and in different ways in a single vast enterprise. Like the architect who loves all building materials, his appreciation for the whole range of scholarship in the human sciences, evident throughout the book, helps support the sense of its complementarity. This may not persuade the postmodernist combatants to disarm, but it assists those who seek a better sense of the validity of sometimes bafflingly divergent approaches.

An Inquiry also has practical use as a scholarly reference resource. For those who use such concepts as the id, ego, or superego, or community, politics, or consensus, it will be invaluable to conveniently know what these are and their universe of related sectors. It will also be helpful to have at our disposal tight, convenient treatments of the nature of reflexivity and workings of individualism and collectivism, as well as the glossary's high-level definitions of the most elusive terms in the human sciences. The book includes an extremely useful presentation of the logic behind historical periodization, one that carries over to clarify the stages of psychological development. For those pursuing phenomenological/interpretive study, Claassen offers analysis of what their inquiry entails. For disciplinary specialists, there is no better brief discussion of the nature and logic of the limiting assumptions that must frame their inquiry.

An Inquiry into the Philosophical Foundations of the Human Sciences is also wellwritten and edited and treats difficult concepts with ease. One need not agree with all of the author's positions to appreciate the crispness and force with which he has laid out his argument. At occasional interludes during which he steps back and views human nature or the human condition from afar, his writing approaches a kind of philosophical poetry. There and throughout, Claassen stands out for his broad humanism, in which he recalls such scholars as Jacques Barzun and Pierre Hadot. The affinity arises not so much because of any overlapping content but because of a tone. Claassen's work, like theirs, is the product of a lifetime of contemplation.

Claassen's book matters to all who are concerned with the progress of the human sciences. Its audience is advanced undergraduate and graduate students in the human sciences and philosophy, professional human scientists and philosophers, and the educated public. In the manner of Richard Rorty's work, it is fresh and brings fundamental insights into the nature of our times. Like Thomas Kuhn's *Structure of Scientific Revolutions*, it may well be the kind of book that generations of undergraduate and graduate students in many fields find necessary to ponder. As does Habermas's and much of Bourdieu's work, it brings together philosophy and the human sciences, but this is a one-of-a-kind, paradigm-breaking and -setting book that deserves wide notice and close attention.

Bibliography

Geertz, C. 1983. *Local Knowledge*. New York: Basic Books.

Acknowledgments

I would like to express my heartfelt gratitude to Frank Bergon, James Bushman, John E. Cantelon, Cayenne Claassen-Luttner, Robert Dostal, Thomas Hiller, and John Tinker for reading and critiquing some or all of the manuscript in earlier draft form. This work has benefited greatly from their suggestions. I owe special thanks to Anatole Anton for his valuable editorial suggestions and series editor's introduction, to David Rubinstein for critiquing the manuscript and contributing the Foreword, and to Robert Claassen for his line-by-line critique of an early draft of the manuscript. I owe general thanks to Tom Hiller for the years of weekly lunches over which many of these ideas were discussed, and to my children Robert, Lisa, John, and Lucas who have been sources of encouragement and inspiration throughout the writing of this book. I owe more than I can express to my wife Ruth Ingeborg Weick—for her critique of the manuscript, for her support, and above all for the existential community within which this thought has in many ways jointly arisen.

Introduction

An impasse exists today in the human sciences (the social sciences, psychology, and cultural studies) in which we witness an extraordinary outpouring of interesting work but little consensus or direction. Having studied an immense number of societies and aspects of the human experience, the human sciences maintain chaotic warehouses of disparate theory and findings. So extreme is the jumble that practitioners cannot coherently describe what they or their fields are trying to study, how their research fits into broader developments in their fields, or what concrete achievements their fields are likely to make during their lifetimes. Responses to questions about such matters tend to be varied, confused, and somewhat embarrassed in the human sciences. By contrast, these tend to be consistent, clear, and excited in the natural sciences. Where the overall development of the natural sciences has been continuous and worldtransforming, that of the human sciences has been uneven and disappointing. It is fair to say that the progress of the human sciences pales by comparison with that of the natural sciences.

In my view, what is responsible for the relative absence of progress in the human sciences is conceptual—their foundations are in disarray. The human sciences stand prominently among those fields referred to by Husserl (1960, 4) as "hampered by obscurities in their foundations, in their fundamental concepts and methods." Because of the reigning conceptual disorder, each major step has meant lurching into an unfamiliar new perspective estranged from the last, disrupting continuity. This in turn has spawned rancorous preparadigmatic struggles between multiple partial approaches and theories. Since the mid-1960's, the human sciences have experienced a degree of cultural dissension without parallel in modern history—skepticism, relativism, cacophony, and turmoil so extraordinary that even the most seasoned warriors of the cultural battlefields have been unnerved at times. This is not to say that there can't be disagreement, only that the extreme discord in the human sciences is symptomatic of their predicament. However little else they agree upon, many in the human sciences agree that their fields are in crisis.

I maintain that all of the elements are in place for major development in the human sciences except the ontology. Yet almost no one in these fields has been viewing the world in terms of the most basic notions underlying the human. For all his greatness, Weber was averse to philosophical questions[1] and left no real legacy of foundations. In my view, the approach practiced by Weber and described by Schutz remains exemplary, but without conceptual grounding even the most valuable method can be of only limited use. The human sciences have tended to leave the foundation work to philosophers, for philosophers have been viewing the world ontologically. Human scientists, however, have not found their formulations particularly helpful, and these have so far had limited impact in the area.

The situation in some ways resembles that of chemistry in the seventeenth and early eighteenth centuries. Premodern chemistry was directionless. A large amount of dissimilar research had been conducted on alchemy, distillation, dyes, and other sundry topics, but without grounding or coherence. What had long been holding that field back was its lack of conceptual foundations. But the speculations of natural philosophers did not help much. The materialist notion of atoms was helpful though vague, but many others like pneuma, phlogiston, and vortices were not. Soon after the establishment of conceptual foundations by Newton and Lavoisier chemistry was able to begin sustained development (see Toulmin and Goodfield 1962).[2] Once provided with such basic notions as mass, immutability of atoms, conservation of matter, and force through a distance, chemistry was poised for takeoff. Not until natural scientists took ontology into their own hands was the bottleneck broken. Like chemistry before them, the human sciences are most in need of foundational theory.

I aim in this book to establish conceptual foundations for the human sciences. Where I begin is with the assessment that the reason for their disarray is related to the difficulty of adequately responding to an elusive feature of human nature. Human phenomena are manydimensional and radically interconnected, such that any significant change has rippling effects in all directions, producing a kaleidoscopic richness with which these fields have not yet been able to cope. If the human sciences are to gain control of the resulting complexity, they require a depiction of the elemental structure of human beings and societies. The basic dimensions of the human must be laid out and examined before the being described by their nexus—which is our own—can be productively approached. Only with comprehensive conceptual grounding can we order perspectives, reestablish direction, concert efforts, and again move forward in the human sciences. The natural sciences have long been doing their own ontology, and we have no choice but to conduct our own.

In this work I turn to philosophy as a means of solving the fundamental conceptual problems of the human sciences. A great deal of thinking of the utmost importance to the human sciences already exists in philosophy, although it is dispersed through many sources. What I do is largely to collect philosophy already in existence, arrange it in a coherent fashion, and put it in a form suitable for use in the human sciences.

But one does not extract the considerable philosophy needed for the human sciences from a distance. That process of interpretation, selection, and arrangement constitutes *doing* philosophy. Once assembled, the philosophy that grounds the human sciences at the same time constitutes a system spanning the range of major philosophical concerns with respect to the human. For most of these concerns have to do precisely with clarifying the nature of human nature and depicting the dimensions of the human. Orienting the human sciences and addressing the major questions of philosophy are essentially one and the same task. The grounding that gives orientation to the human sciences simultaneously provides the conceptual apparatus imparting determinacy to philosophy. Instead of addressing them piecemeal, this work takes up the problems of philosophy as a set.

Hegel holds an essential place in this enterprise, for his universalism provides its overarching structure and his dialectic infuses its spirit. Bringing perspectives large and small from many philosophers together with the accumulated experience of the human sciences, I have bought and occupied Hegel's property, so to speak. After long dwelling in and contemplating Hegel's architecture, I am setting out to thoroughly modernize it. What I want is a sounder, more focused, accessible, and capacious building with reinforced foundations, strengthened exterior walls, and redistributed interior space. Where the original structure put natural philosophy, this one places new wings devoted to the human; where it contained an ethics beholden to Rousseau and Kant, this one does not; and where it tampered with logic, this one does not. Hegel's system has harbored great potential, but Hegel only partially described the bedrock dimensionalism of our being and imperfectly overcame central oppositions. A good part of why Hegel's universalism has been unable to gain much pith and traction in the modern world is because of the resulting indeterminacy and imbalance. For all that Hegel got right and for all the continuing inspiration he brings, his abstractness and one-sidedness hindered the restoration of universalism his own situation demanded and ours does even more. This work initiates a renewal in Hegel's tradition from the ground up.

When properly redirected, philosophy returns to its Aristotelian and Hegelian role as general science providing the overarching integration of the special sciences. Philosophy at its boldest and most valuable has seen itself as the general aspect within the sciences. Philosophy assumes that posture here as the preliminary work is carried out to draw the human sciences together under it again. The foundations and framework that enable the human sciences to develop at the same time point toward their reunification. The numerous competing approaches and theories in the human sciences are not for the most part basically inconsistent but are framed incommensurately in ways this work makes it possible to overcome. Being but different perspectives on the same subject, the human sciences merge when their world is laid out coherently.

To solve the basic conceptual problems of the human sciences is not enough, however, for the chaotic status quo is also defended epistemologically by forces positioned against the kind of knowledge toward which this work points. We must contend with those who have created and who perpetuate the problems of the human sciences. On one front there is dissent from those with narrow and one-sided views of what constitutes human science. On another we face attacks from virulent postmodernist strains of skepticism and radical relativism that deny we can reliably know anything about the human and above all anything about what is universal with regard to it.

Accordingly, in addition to the ontological questions underlying the human sciences, I treat the central epistemic ones about human inquiry in order to clarify and justify the practice based upon these understandings. I introduce the dialectical historicism that generates the major questions to be addressed in interdisciplinary human science and hone the phenomenological method with which it is carried out. The interdisciplinary human science encouraged by this work employs all of the fundamental perspectives of the human systematically and simultaneously. I also take up the situation of disciplinary human science, emphasizing the importance of grounding its assumptions within and drawing its orientation from the same framework. Seeing phenomenological and rigorous disciplinary study as complementary to each other, I provide support for both major approaches to the conduct of human science. I go on to consider questions raised by the form of knowing found in the arts and by the incorporation of literary and art criticism into the human sciences. I then defend my approach against the challenges posed by skepticism and radical relativism.

This work brings important new phenomena into view. Two of the surprising and powerful notions it discovers are those of the superid and the super-superego (SSE). The superego is ubiquitous in the human sciences, but its nonrational analog, the superid, though no less important, has been overlooked by Freud and everyone since. Its recognition is basic and opens major opportunities in many directions. The SSE, the higher rational self-control of ordinary self-control, is the previously unanalyzed personality sector prevalent in the "gamesmen," the type and social class dominant in the postmodernist world. Without the concept of the SSE, we have not yet grasped the character of those whose leanings shape our era. By developing a determinate way of conceptualizing the universal, this work also enables the human sciences to study such universalistic phenomena as morality and leadership in direct, constructive, and sophisticated new ways. Additionally, it makes possible for the first time a powerful historical sociology and psychology of philosophy itself. It does so in part by clarifying how we may be at once both absolutist and relativist. With these neo-Hegelian foundations I believe we can and will soon break the current impasse and make rapid and sustained progress in the human sciences.

Part I describes the basic dimensions of human nature, one of which, reflexivity (i.e., self-consciousness and self-control), Hegel systematically utilized in a pathbreaking way, and three of which, the consummatory and instrumental, the ideal and real, and individualism and collectivism, he did not. The latter three dimensions, further elucidated by many philosophers and human scientists whose work I am bringing together, must be considered on a full par with reflexivity. These fundamental dimensions of the human, together with time, are all orthogonal to each other and are all indispensable. Part II delineates the complex dimension constituted by universalism versus sectoralism and explores the nature and forms of the universal. Part III addresses the epistemics of the human sciences while further characterizing the universal. I discuss the context of but do not go into economic theory. The Appendix contains a number of definitions of basic terms used throughout the book. The closest readers should read this before going to Chapter 1. All others should treat it as a glossary and consult it if needed. Let us now turn to the dimensions of the human, beginning with the basic ones.

Notes

1. See Marianne Weber's biography of her husband, *Max Weber: A Biography.*
2. This it did with the work of Dalton, although the process was somewhat delayed by a lack of experimental knowledge of gases.

Bibliography

Husserl, E. 1960. *Cartesian Meditations.* The Hague: Martinus Nijhoff.
Toulmin, S., and J. Goodfield. 1962. *The Architecture of Matter.* Chicago: University of Chicago Press.
Weber, Marianne. 1975. *Max Weber: A Biography.* New York: Wiley.

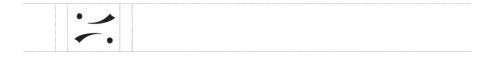

Part I. Sectoralism and the Basic Dimensions of the Human

1. The Consummatory and Instrumental

Four basic dimensions open up the existential space of the human or of mind.[1] These dimensions and the space they bring into being, together with time and a complex dimension I will introduce later, constitute the framework of human existence, spanning the field of all that is with respect to the human. Consciousness occurs and meaning arises within these dimensions. Existential space and time are the fundamental background against which the human is perceived, thought about, and acted upon. Human phenomena take their basic structure in relation to them. Much as most political questions reduce to matters of liberalism and conservatism, everything that pertains to the human itself comes down to positions on these dimensions. Let us take up our initial dimension.

****

All that we do and are is structured by a fundamental opposition between the consummatory and instrumental modes, the first being what is an end in itself, the second, what is a means to an end. This distinction has deep roots in social thought and philosophy. I take the distinction in particular from the sociological theorist, Talcott Parsons (1951a, 49, 80–88, 385, 401–3, 409–11; 1951b, 149, 208–12, 413), whose summary work considered it central, although he often spoke of it as the instrumental versus the expressive. Under various rubrics the distinction has also been a longstanding one in psychology, which drew it in part from Chinese and Indian philosophy. The consummatory versus the instrumental in what we do and are is the first basic dimension of the human.

The opposition between the consummatory and instrumental modes of the human has many manifestations. Most important, it lies behind the distinction between the emotional and the rational, for the emotional is consummatory and the rational is instrumental. What we do in proximity to ends in themselves tends to be relatively emotional; what we do at a distance from such ends tends to be relatively unemotional. The emotion associated with the consummatory is more direct and closer to the surface; that associated with the instrumental is more indirect and submerged. In the consummatory mode what we do is spontaneous; in the instrumental mode what we do is deliberate. The consummatory is inherently presentoriented and the instrumental inherently futureoriented.

The consummatory and instrumental modes must be seen as forming a systematic opposition, for of the two one or the other tends to dominate, generating a fundamental polarity in the human. By their natures persons and collectivities have two modes in all they do and are. These modes are variously termed their emotional and rational sides, their "hearts" and "heads," the yin and yang, or the "right-brain" and "left brain."[2] To emphasize the polarity here is to employ ideal types, a convenience that helps us keep in mind the basic concepts and their relationships, but it also dichotomizes what in actuality to a large degree forms a continuum.

Consummatory *perception,* with emotionality dominant, is natural and intuitive, a "seeing" of a pattern, a direct, effortless apprehension in which perception arises passively. On the other hand, instrumental perception, with rationality dominant, is artificial and purposive—an active, painstaking reconstruction of a pattern in which sensation is deliberately handled or gauged. In the one case we have fluent perception and in the other a considered detection of what is there. We may see at a glance that six people are in a room but must count or multiply to determine that thirty people are in a room. This is merely to point out different basic kinds of perception, not to make claims about their relative or absolute accuracy.

Consummatory *thought* is natural, spontaneous, and intuitive. One whistles tunes, tells stories, and creates art objects in the consummatory mode. In consummatory thinking, to which Freud referred as the "unconscious" mind, images strong and weak are spontaneously cast before us, sometimes intermittently and sometimes in steady streams. With the consummatory dominant a solution comes to mind passively, sometimes popping into it, sometimes slowly forming, but always just intuited. In the consummatory mode we think with emotions to the fore in the way most comfortable and natural to us. Indeed, the relevant sense of the word "natural," a major one, is as what is associated with the consummatory mode. Instrumental thinking is instead artificial, deliberate, procedural, and explicitly goal oriented. One can follow step-by-step what he or she is doing while engaged in it. Rational thinking in its more developed forms takes place with rules, heuristics, algorithms, or formulas, cognitive tools actively and methodically generating results. Among its most developed forms are formal logic, mathematics, natural science, and accounting. Consummatory thinking is from the specific to the general, instrumental thinking from the general to the specific.

As active as consummatory thinking gets is when one deliberately relaxes and opens himself to his nonrational mind (see Pieper 1963, 28–29). Where the rational mind engages in a taut and focused problem solving analogous to direct vision, the unconscious mind engages in relaxed and unfocused problem solving analogous to peripheral vision. The problems addressed by the consummatory are often mulled over "in the back of our minds." Yet the consummatory may sometimes perform feats that stymie the most advanced logics. The oft-remarked phenomenon of the scientific discovery that leaps into the researcher's mind while he is showering, walking, or taking the subway is a consummatory phenomenon. For its part, the rational mind thinks rigorously, systematically, and reliably in ways that make it indispensable to everyday life as well as to science and philosophy. Together consummatory perception and thinking comprise intuition.

As a manifestation of the larger divide under consideration, we also have two separate and distinct yet fully parallel consummatory and instrumental modes of *action*. One or the other tends to predominate in action according to whether the emotionality associated with caring or the rationality associated with effectuality comes to the fore. Much of what we do, such as visiting family members, talking with friends, traveling on vacation, playing games, or watching movies, is inherently and directly satisfying. However, much else that we do, such as earning a living, carrying out chores, or following instructions, is instead exherently and indirectly satisfying. Action that is consummatory is natural, spontaneous, an end in itself, and goes with our grains; action that is instrumental is artificial, deliberate, a means to something else, and goes against our grains. Consummatory action is presentoriented, instrumental action futureoriented. Where nonrational action is action oriented directly to ends, rational action is "action with known intermediate goals" (Schutz 1967, 61 [emphasis deleted]). In consummatory action one does what she wishes. In instrumental action one does what seems advantageous.

Central to their natures, the consummatory and instrumental are formed around sharply different motivational complexes, associated respectively with desires and interests. In consummatory action the cathected object is virtually present: goals lie immediately in front of the actor, and they directly impel. In instrumental action goals are removed, and their pull is extended through representational linkages. It is libido versus hustle, expectations with inherent pull versus expectations with exherent pull, ends in themselves versus means to something else. The time lag between the action and its associated satisfaction is correspondingly little in the one case and much in the other. Every thing, event, or state of which we are aware is evaluated in relation to both our desires and interests.

Tension necessarily accompanies the withdrawal of energy from consummatory action and its allocation to the instrumental—the more so the greater the magnitude of the undertaking. Instrumental motivation utilizes an attenuated energy taxed in the expectation that the ensuing benefit will outweigh its cost in sapped vitality. As the instrumental takes over, emotion becomes at once cramped and steadied. The more nervous energy is drawn by the person, the more dissatisfied he becomes vis-à-vis consummatory needs, but at the same time, all else equal, the better attended to are his prudential concerns. Because emotional stress goes against the grain of what one naturally wants to do, it is far more a by-product of instrumental than of consummatory action.

The human also *exists* in a consummatory or instrumental mode each time it moves to one or the other. Although we use both modes as we alternate from one aspect of what we do to the next, the things we do are ordinarily carried out with one mode dominant and the other subordinate. Yet the distribution of experience in one or the other depends upon circumstances, tending to make either the consummatory or instrumental the habitual way of being for particular persons and collectivities. We therefore normally go through life with one or the other mode dominant as an enduring trait of character, much as handedness tends to be an attribute of bodily behavior.

The consummatory-instrumental dimension even cuts through possessions, distinguishing between *treasures* and *tools*. Possessions held in the consummatory mode are treasures; those held in the instrumental mode are tools, respectively keepsakes we cherish and tools we use. Treasures have inherent value; tools have exherent value. Movable objects, buildings, land, and quarters of cities tend to be predominantly treasures or tools. Since representations are also possessions, a manifestation of our dimension is that the consummatory and instrumental perceive, think, and communicate respectively in images and concepts. Hence Rorty's (1979, 23–24 [emphasis deleted]) distinction between images and "thoughts" "as the paradigmatic mental entities." The languages of poetry, painting, and music are treasures; those of reason, logic, and mathematics are tools.

Although there are numerous kinds of perception, thought, and action we associate with either the consummatory or instrumental, almost any may be carried out in either mode, for it is the way we approach what we do, not the content, that distinguishes it as consummatory or instrumental. The same perception, thought, or action may also be carried out predominantly in different modes at different times. Thus, the instrumental often plays a more salient role early in our engagement in a certain perception, thought, or action while we learn to perform it. In time, however, the perception, thought, or action may become automatic and move to the consummatory.

With practice, what were once awkward, contrived, and "conscious"[3] instrumental perceptions, thoughts, and actions tend to become fluent, habitual, and "unconscious" consummatory ones. As much as possible, we tend to work what we do, making it habitual, natural, and effortless, thereby freeing ourselves to focus on other things. However, in some circumstances we have so much that is new and disruptive with which to contend that only some portion of what we engage in has the requisite conditions of stability.

Thus, the differing profiles of strength and weakness of the two modes in many respects complement each other, and we utilize both throughout life. Where rational routines reach their limits, intuitive ones take over, and vice-versa. In Gazzaniga and LeDoux's (1978, 72) words, the two modes "do not oppose each other but instead work together to maintain the integrity of mental functioning." As a yogic philosopher puts it, "[b]oth are essential to the completeness of the human reason" (quoted in Springer 1998, 293). However, Gazzaniga and LeDoux (1978, 150) also caution that "each with the capacity to produce behavior, and each with its own impulses for action . . . these systems are not necessarily conversant internally."

The consummatory and instrumental are very different, significantly independent modes that the human is only able to balance with difficulty. When one is strongly engaged, the other tends to perform weakly. Not only do consummatory perception, thinking, action, motivation, and being differ from their instrumental counterparts, but they are substantially barred entry by them. Rationality to some extent must be held in suspension in order that subtler intuitions come through, and play must cease that work may begin. A surprisingly large amount of the structural variation in personal and collective life is determined by the extent to which emotionality or rationality is salient in perception, thought, or action.

Notes

1. A dimension is a fundamental aspect of space-time.
2. Although there may be an anatomical basis for this distinction from contemporary psychology, precisely what that would be I leave to biologists to determine. In particular, by mentioning it I make no assertion that the actual hemispheres of the brain operate independently of each other or in a manner parallel to the opposition I am considering. My reference to the distinction is purely metaphysical and directed to the human.
3. This sense of the word "conscious" differs from the one that appears in the Glossary.

Bibliography

Gazzaniga, M. and J. LeDoux. 1978. *The Integrated Mind*. New York: Plenum Press.

Parsons, T. 1951a. *The Social System*. New York: Free Press.

———. 1951b. *Toward a General Theory of Action*. New York: Harper and Row.

Pieper, J. 1963. *Leisure: The Basis of Culture*. New York: New American Library.

Rorty, R. 1979. *Philosophy and the Mirror of Nature*. Princeton, NJ: Princeton University Press.

Schutz, A. 1967. *The Phenomenology of the Social World*. Evanston, IL: Northwestern University Press.

Springer, S. 1998. *Left-Brain, Right-Brain*. 5th ed. New York: W.H. Freeman.

2. Levels of Reflexivity

Reflexivity

The second basic dimension of existential space within which the human is arrayed is the level of reflexivity or self-referentiality of perception, thought, action, and other human phenomena. I take the fundamental notion of reflexivity from Hegel, although it has also by now been much used in the human sciences. In *The Phenomenology of Mind* (see e.g., 210–27) Hegel lays out the nature of reflexivity in a way that has powerfully influenced subsequent thought. Being capable in principle of forming representations of anything, the human is also capable of forming representations of itself. In all things human the aboutness or *intentionality* is oriented either externally or internally: we either perceive, think about, and act upon the world outside of us or do so with respect to ourselves. Perception and thought directed toward ourselves are self-consciousness,[1] and action directed toward ourselves is self-determination. Self-consciousness necessarily precedes self-determination, at least minimally.

Reflexivity begins with self-consciousness when, in time, the human develops awareness of the elusive subject of its experience. This awareness tends to take place incrementally at first, followed by relatively rapid consolidation as larger patterns are recognized. Merely regarding one's own or society's unreflexive mode in small, objective slices is but minimally reflexive because the unreflexive self that self-consciousness is about still only very partially appears in them. Later a view of the self or collectivity of sufficient scope may arise that cohering tracts of the unreflexive being before it come into view. Only then is the content sufficiently comprehensive to warrant the ideal type of *self*-consciousness. In other words, we must distinguish between minimal reflexivity and its fuller presence. When self-consciousness arises, a higher-level being is born in which significant separation exists between an unreflexive and reflexive mind. Hegel termed the former the "natural consciousness" or "ordinary mind." However, self-consciousness in and of itself does not yet move one reflexively.[2]

In self-determination the human goes beyond mere jumping to a reflexive perspective and takes the corresponding standpoint, enabling it to wield power internally. In self-determination, what one part of the human does is decided by another part having the power to communicate and enforce its decision. The one part promulgates a desired routine, and the other is prevailed upon to enact it. Whether the unreflexive or reflexive mode of a person or collectivity has the preponderant resources determines which prevails.[3]

In time, the reflexive element may move beyond mere self-determination to self-control, where the controller and controllee are distinct aspects of a single person or collectivity. The faculty of self-control is born as we begin regularly shaping ourselves in accordance with explicit or implicit routines, limits, parameters, goals, and/or images originating in self-consciousness. Personal or collective self-determination is consolidated and made ongoing in self-control. When self-control is in place, we may desire something very much, but, after deliberation and/or mulling over, choose not to pursue it. As self-control becomes institutionalized, one or more parts of the personality or collectivity go on to establish domination over one or more other parts.

Self-control in effect introduces a large loop in which we turn back from exercising control over our surroundings to exercising it over ourselves. Self-control introduces an intermediate step in the chain of causality in which instead of determining us directly in the unreflexive mode, external conditions come to do so indirectly via their effect on self-control, bringing about a more complex, organized, and coherent causation of our characteristics and doings. How extensive the self-control, how large the loop, varies from person to person and from collectivity to collectivity. To the extent which self-control is achieved, we have more coherence and our being is augmented.

Double Reflexivity

In addition to first-level, elementary reflexivity manifesting simple self-consciousness and self-control, we should distinguish a second-level higher reflexivity with self-consciousness of self-consciousness and self-control of self-control.[4] Still higher levels of reflexivity may also exist, in principle without limit. As with the consummatory and instrumental dimension, an inner contest of power occurs between levels of reflexivity at particular times and overall. Although the human goes back and forth between its different modes of reflexivity insofar as it has them, particular existential locations tend to prevail due to the reigning experience conferred by exposure to distinct circumstances. The degree to which the human is dominated by nonreflexivity, reflexivity, and double reflexivity becomes an enduring feature of the character of persons and collectivities. Only by grasping the manifestations of the different modes of reflexivity is it possible to understand the human. One of the basic dimensions of the human is a compound one: its many-leveled ladder of reflexivity.[5] This dimension lies behind many very important phenomena concerning the human.

The Hierarchy of Wants

With reflexivity the structure of motivation also becomes more complex. When a new level of awareness takes hold, associated wants begin asserting themselves, as when modern citizens begin critically examining their monarchies for the first time. Yet the wants from less reflexive standpoints continue to be felt. The more we dwell in an emergent perspective, the more the perspective becomes invested with feeling, competes for resources, and motivates us. The result is a hierarchy of wants (or needs in the sense of wants).

The nature of the human is such that as it solves large numbers of diverse problems on any given level of reflexivity and puts structures in place that sufficiently satisfy wants, it may then move toward greater reflexivity and begin reflecting upon itself in its own previous doings and satisfying the associated emergent wants. When lower (in the sense of less reflexive) needs are sufficiently well satisfied, they are still felt, but relatively stable routines for dealing with them are built in. They may therefore be taken for granted to a degree, freeing us to move to new and higher wants. But one can only get lower needs off her mind and attend to higher ones as she can securely meet the former. Reservoirs of rational and emotional competence must become large enough to stretch across major portions of our beings in order that there arise the realistic possibility of jumping to a higher perspective, from which self-conscious direction of what had been unreflexive may begin.

Lying between solved and unsolved problems is a motivational surface below which are ongoing expectations dependably met at the maintenance/containment level by available resources, providing a floor from which to ascend. On the surface lie the problems with which one is currently engaged. Above it lie those not yet encountered, about which we lack either the awareness or resources yet to concern ourselves. Need satisfaction is accompanied by degrees of risk in that solution pyramids manifest greater or lesser fragility and vulnerability (cf. Maslow 1954, 100–101). When wants are met but only insecurely so, the attention must remain fixed on them. It is not that some general need for security is itself a "prepotent" want or even a separate want at all; it is rather that we can't get beyond elementary needs if we continually fear the collapse of efforts to satisfy them (cf. Maslow 1968, ch. 4). Each new level up the metaprogression confers advantages only insofar as the lower levels are secure.

Reflexivity and Development

Movement up the ladder of reflexivity with its corresponding hierarchy of needs constitutes ontological differentiation and represents a very important and quite literal form of our development or unfolding. Neither the person nor the collectivity originates with self-consciousness and self-control. These remarkable faculties develop in Piagetian fashion in both. In early life and in foraging societies we yet possess only the simplest modes of being human—prior to which we were not actually fully human. In the course of life and of history those to undergo this form of ontological development move toward more reflexive forms of being.

However, as in the attainment of greater organizational complexity by large firms, that of ontological complexity by humans is not automatically advantageous. If people possess a sufficient reservoir of successful work at the lower level and sufficient ability to manage well the greater reflexivity, the latter promises a smoothness of performance and richness of satisfaction that benefit those who achieve it. In their absence, however, the heaviness of being that is the overhead cost of reflexivity weighs upon us. When people err in the direction of moving too far up the metaprogression, their overreaching is preempted by crisis control, and they soon tire of the cumbersomeness and slide back to the levels addressing their true problems. Thus, while it is human nature always to be able to step back and be reflexive with respect to previous levels of reflexivity—no matter how high—there are internal organizational costs of doing so that must be offset. These costs are why one need not become vertiginous about an infinite regress from ideas to ideas about ideas as Aristotle is in *Metaphysics* (1033b, 5–9). Even if it were possible, it would only be sensible to move to higher levels of reflexivity once the way were prepared, allowing the marginal benefits to exceed the marginal costs of doing so. Even where higher reflexivity will eventually prove advantageous, its earlier stages tend to be rough and arbitrary.

Nor do the levels of reflexivity automatically work together. The reflexive parts of us may treat the unreflexive parts badly, and/or the latter may attempt to ignore the former.

In ontologically unfolding, who and what we are are transformed even as we become more ourselves. When warranted, movement up the ladder of reflexivity brings an augmentation of being, along with greater power and satisfaction. Under the guidance of a more centralized inner effectuality, our newly concerted potential is redirected upon the world with redoubled force, while satisfaction of higher wants brings qualitative leaps in fulfillment. Persons and societies undergo epochal turns when they consolidate new levels of self-awareness and self-determination. Those existential resolves to take control of our selves or societies are of the utmost importance to both. The world of the human is one of suddenly jelling reflexive insights, resolutions, and passions that grow into momentous events, of intangible sparks that often prove decisive. Twenty-five centuries ago Heraclitus (fragment 45, quoted in Snell 1982, 19) gave us one of the earliest notes of this ontological development with the words: "The soul has a *logos* which increases itself."

Notes

1. This utilizes a sense of the word "conscious" as that pertaining to perception and thought, which will be clarified in Chapter 5.

2. My view of consciousness differs from Hegel's in one notable respect. Hegel believes, while I do not, that consciousness inherently entails self-consciousness. Thus, Hegel (1975, 47; see also Forster 1998, 116ff.) writes that "the spirit only has consciousness insofar as it is conscious of itself; in other words, I only know an object insofar as I know myself and my own determination through it, for whatever I am is also an object of my consciousness, and I am not just this, that or the other, but only what I know myself to be." Indeed, Hegel even makes "self-consciousness into the defining characteristic of spirit. . . ." (Beiser 1993, 285–86). This I object to. In my view, Hegel's acceptance of the understanding of human consciousness as inherently reflexive from Kant, Reinhold, and Fichte is misguided and a significant source of confusion and difficulty in his work. Why the assumption does not do even more damage to Hegel's philosophy than it does is because, despite subscribing to it abstractly, Hegel goes on to distinguish between and analyze particular structures of consciousness in which reflexivity, at least in the full sense, sometimes is and sometimes is not present.

3. The presence of reflexivity alters the ontology of action. Absent self-consciousness and self-determination, a cycle of doing, as noted in the Appendix, is composed of perception, thought, and action. But with self-consciousness, action becomes internally differentiated such that distinct subphases of intentionsetting and execution appear. Then in a complete cycle at a minimum something is perceived, thinking is done, a decision is made to act or avoid acting in a particular way under certain future circumstances, and the decision is executed when they occur. In the decisionmaking or intentionsetting subphase, which consists of generating alternatives and screening them, routines are placed online. Only later, when the circumstances arise, is the prior intent cued and the action fully carried out.

   Some mistakenly hold decisionmaking to be a separate fundamental moment of doing comparable to perceiving, thinking, and acting; for in the presence of reflexivity we act not directly but via the two steps of intentionsetting and a subsequent implementation. They take this implementation as action and the decisionmaking or intentionsetting to be a new phenomenon. But neither the earlier reflexive step that decides nor the later unreflexive one that executes should be seen as complete action by itself. When present, both are instead subphases of a single action phase. For consummatory action as well as for instrumental action, decisionmaking is a permutation, not a new basic element. By differentiating action the presence of reflexivity can affect all that action affects, including perception and thinking insofar as subordinate action plays a role in them. Thus, when reflexive judgment is brought to bear within perception, a separate intention or decision may be made to accept and go with certain perceptions and not others. Or, within thinking, a separate intention may be made to accept certain theories and not others, as in the careful, deliberate, and critical application of the scientific method with the assistance of the rational reflexive mind. Without self-consciousness the intention to act and its execution are joined. Action may or may not be reflexive and for that reason may or may not separate into intention-to-act and execution sub-phases. (This position seems to me to be close to Searle's (1983, 84, 95), notably departing from it only by highlighting the role of reflexivity.) Failure to grasp the basic nature of decisionmaking has caused much confusion among philosophers.

4.　For application of the notion of double reflexivity see Chapters 3, 4, and 13.

5.　The presence of double reflexivity again alters the ontology of action. Here, instead of action differentiating into intention-to-act and execution subphases, it further differentiates to include a higher decisionmaking. A higher-level intention is then made and placed on-line to engage in lower-level decisionmaking of particular kinds under certain general circumstances to put one or more lower-level intentions in place and on-line, which would then trip final execution when specific circumstances arise.

Bibliography

Aristotle. 1941. *Metaphysics*. In *The Basic Writings of Aristotle*, ed. R. McKeon. New York: Random House.

Beiser, F. 1993. "Hegel's Historicism." In *The Cambridge Companion to Hegel*, ed. F. Beiser. Cambridge: Cambridge University Press.

Forster, M. 1998. *Hegel's Idea of a Phenomenology of Spirit*. Chicago: University of Chicago Press.

Hegel, G. 1967. *The Phenomenology of Mind*. New York: Harper and Row.

———. 1975. *Lectures on the Philosophy of World History: Introduction*. Cambridge: Cambridge University Press.

Maslow, A. 1954. *Motivation and Personality*. New York: Harper and Row.

———. 1968. *Toward a Psychology of Being*. 2nd ed. New York: D. Van Nostrand.

Searle, J. 1983. *Intentionality: An Essay in the Philosophy of Mind*. Cambridge: Cambridge University Press.

Snell, B. 1982. *The Discovery of the Mind*. New York: Dover.

3. Id, Ego, Superid, and Superego

Once we view the consummatory-instrumental and reflexivity dimensions together, we are in a position to derive the elementary structure of the personality. The interplay of the two dimensions divides the personality into sectors constituting domains dominated by particular kinds of action. The resulting typology corresponds with Freud's division of the personality into the id, ego, and superego, one of his most central discoveries and widely used in the human sciences and by the educated public. With the philosophical tools at hand I will seek first to ground and then to expand Freud's tripartite division of the personality.

Id

I view the id as essentially consummatory, unreflexive action. The id, in other words, is spontaneous, emotional action in accord with the pleasure principle—action aimed at directly satisfying our basic wants. In its emotionality and spontaneity the id is present oriented. The id fantasizes about what it would like to do—often about sex and sometimes about aggression, but also often about food, drink, sociation, comfort, glory, relaxation, and other things inherently gratifying.[1]

Among the most central needs or wants of the id are the social-emotional ones for belongingness, conviviality, play, love, affection, nurturance, and large components of the needs for food, drink, and sex. (The last three needs are those of the id insofar as they are those of the human and physiological needs to the extent they are those of the body (cf. Fromm 1947, 184–86).) The need for sex may be the most intense need for many, but the needs for play, games, camaraderie, and rest and recuperation are also important in the id. The id prominently includes the need to enjoy the company of others. A major portion of the larger social-emotional need in more developed societies is fulfilled by friendship. The frustration of the broader social-emotional needs is alienation, the pain and joylessness of not being understood and accepted, and of not belonging.

However, the most profound need of the id in most people is a special need for oneness, first with parents, particularly those of the opposite sex, and later with spouses or partners. This is the ur-form of the need for love, acceptance, and belongingness, with the accompanying fear of abandonment. In the most primal portion of our ids we need to have emotional trust in those dear to us, and we are highly emotionally dependent on these significant others in our lives. As people come of age, it is natural (i.e., given human nature, we tend to be happiest and most fulfilled when the need is satisfied) that much of this need come to be associated with sexuality in a significant relationship. However, there is great variation in the forms it may take. This portion of the need for love is very deeply rooted genetically and psychically and represents the central foundation of the family—underpinning both the parent-child and the husband-wife relationship. Freud in his antibourgeois fabulism probed the need with his notion of the Oedipus complex. Proust refers to it in *Remembrance of Things Past* as "this terrible need of a person." The importance of secure fulfillment of this need for oneness is evident in the centrality of these closest relationships to our lives, the disequilibrium and frantic efforts to restore or replace the relationships built around this need when they are gone, and the extensive psychopathology that may result when the need is not fulfilled (see Maslow 1954, 89–90). That is true for adults when their significant relationships dissolve or are threatened and for children when they are not emotionally accepted by their parents or when they are separated from them. The id is substantially embedded in the group.

Although under ordinary conditions there is little trace of an inherent need for aggression in normal human beings, it *is* our nature that such a need should appear when we are frustrated, either episodically or chronically. While we have no basic or general need for aggression, we do have a situational need, when frustrated, to lash out at whomever or whatever we blame for the interference. When we do not successfully attain what we are seeking, anger tends to appear and with it a passing need for aggression. As anger intensifies, the relative power of the id grows in the psyche, as it does under sexual arousal. If the interference is chronic and debilitating, some develop a general, pathological need to aggress. Contrary to Freud, in everyday life only the disturbed and those in abnormally vexing circumstances are routinely angry.

Freud considerably distorts the id, beginning with his misunderstanding of aggression and his great exaggeration of our antisocialness. While he is right that the need for sex is important in the id and for many their most intense one, he fails to appreciate the extent to which it is psychosocial. Freud widely neglects the social needs, the needs for love, belongingness, sociality, and play. Such American psychologists as Sullivan and Murray come much closer to the mark by emphasizing that the id prominently includes these milder needs. The id is not *essentially* about sex and aggression, it is *especially* about sex, belongingness, and sociality—all of which are major contentments of civilization.

There is also another kind of need in the id that is very important but frequently overlooked, by Freud and many others. This is a need to do familiar things and to engage in habitual action. Much of the pleasure of our work is of this familiar, habitual sort. Habits settle into the id alongside what are for many only intermittently much stronger needs. Such needs may be mild by comparison with sex and aggression, but they *are* of the id and they dominate a large portion of our lives.

Ego

The ego is essentially instrumental, unreflexive action. Its rational coping is in accord with the reality principle, and it is future oriented. The ego's general need is for the ongoing provision of resources necessary for the satisfaction of all other needs. As Freud (1961a, 25) puts it, "[t]he ego represents what may be called reason and common sense, in contrast to the id, which contains the passions."

The most basic need of the ego is to assure survival. The need for physical security is so great that we ignore even sharp hunger and pain when it is threatened, although obtaining the minimum biological requirements of sustenance becomes indistinguishable from it in dire circumstances. Once the most immediate needs are satisfied, other less-pressing prudential needs may be addressed. The resources acquired by the ego include material tools as well as wealth, social connections, knowledge, skills, and the like.[2] However, in more complex societies money becomes paramount because it provides a general means of need satisfaction, beginning with the physiological ones. However, along with resource acquisition comes an additional important safety need, the need for security of property. Once this is relatively assured, the ego may resume busy concern with the acquisition and accumulation of resources. Under modern conditions, the ego's pursuit of resources is largely synonymous with the pursuit of economic interests. While everyone has an id, not everyone has significant development of an ego; very undeveloped people are almost all id and have next to no ego.

We often first develop entirely instrumental routines that for a long time remain cumbersome, but a very happy feature of human nature is that most of the actions we repeat over a prolonged period eventually become habitual and enjoyable for their own sake. As routines become increasingly habitual and comfortable, action initially undertaken in the ego tends to move slowly to the id. What was once the awkward and laborious action of the ego becomes the smooth and pleasurable activity of the id. In time, much of what we think of as primarily instrumental becomes consummatory. This does not mean that coal mining, labor arbitration, or bond trading becomes something we cannot live without doing—only that through years of practice many activities in the daily routines of most occupations eventually become automatic and inherently satisfying in a process that forms a major element of what mastery in a trade or profession entails. If the need for habitual activity did not reside in the id, it would be hard to explain how effortlessly and with what satisfaction we perform so much of our work.

Although we often find it very convenient to treat them separately, the id and ego interact intensively and depend on each other in many ways. Even in the midst of instrumental dealings both an ego-dominant Casbah trader and his customers need light moments that engage the id. During extended bargaining the id senses when and how it must break in, not to detract from the ego but to help it succeed. The merchant also requires his relaxing times of id dominance with friends and family. Similarly, without help from the ego, it is unlikely the id would ever arrange to meet a suitable partner or make the friends it needs or organize the party it wants.

Superego

The superego is essentially the same instrumental action as the ego, only reflexive and applied to control of ourselves rather than control of what is around us. In its kind of elementary self-control the superego operates with the use of a self-concept to which it is committed. The superego engages in rational decisionmaking with respect to the unselfconscious self, leading to the imposition of policies or rules upon the ego and/or id. The superego issues verbal or quasi-verbal commands to the lower-level self, such as to make a fortune before the age of thirty or to keep holy the Sabbath. The superego's commands may be prescriptive or proscriptive as well as general or specific. The policies and rules of the superego may be taken over from others or created by the person.

To the extent to which the superego dominates, its reign is one of self-discipline. Yet the superego's prior decisions are not carried out automatically; it must monitor, judge, and enforce compliance with its commands. Enforcement may include the reward and punishment of the self. A certain initial dominance of the superego over the id and/or ego is necessary to make a binding decision, and a continuing dominance is necessary to enforce it. If the balance of power changes, and it may as the id and ego come to feel with greater urgency, the superego's ability to enforce its preferences may dissolve. Hence the possibility of *akrasia*, an intention willed but not willed strongly enough to be enforced.

A superego begins with the appearance of self-consciousness in a rational person, which brings new reflexive problems into view requiring attention. If the person assumes responsibility for these problems, he will go on to address them with a developing superego. If he avoids self-consciousness and blames others for the unwanted conditions, he will instead flatter and indulge his recumbent unselfconscious self. Unselfconscious people have no superego.

Although it is usually substantially shaped by socialization, the superego may arise or consolidate power in a slowly dawning realization of the opportunities possible through steadiness and intelligence. Development of the superego frequently occurs as the person becomes aware that the ego cannot be consistent in its instrumental efforts without guidelines. Although future-oriented, the ego operates in a very ad hoc fashion, making it quite vulnerable to external pummeling. Tossed here and there by haphazard circumstances, the unregulated ego is less than fully reliable. With consolidation of a superego one may seek not only to gain resources but also to do so steadily, accumulating property—as is made possible when frugality and regular investment are applied to even a modest income. Instrumental action with respect to ourselves is as decisive an advantage for the ego as an effective political system is for an economy. Focusing and regulating the ego, the superego allows a higher personal efficacy and disciplined pursuit of interests. Without self-consciousness we often also overlook blatant instrumental errors and limit the effectiveness of our egos. The superego makes possible a significant increase in human potential and freedom, enabling a person to become more of a "destiny" in Nietzsche's expression. Frequently conferring dramatic advantages, the superego is anything but necessarily antagonistic to the ego.

The prominence of crisis and rebirth stories in the *Bildungsroman* and elsewhere reflects another well-traveled route to a strong superego, from excess or carelessness through dismay or fear to self-control. Consolidation of rational self-control may occur with dramatic quickness when the person receives a scare from a heart attack or encounters a dangerous side-effect of drinking, or when one suffers the dramatic reversal of bankruptcy or abandonment by a partner, although this must occur in conjunction with taking responsibility for the problem.

The need for order is the central need of the superego, not order in and for itself but order as the desire for consistency, delivering freedom from the id's outrageousness and ego's erraticism. To a prudent, self-conscious mind, the id poses dangers in all directions, giving rise to innumerable rational reasons to curb its excesses. The id's sexual and aggressive potential is explosive. It may also inadvertently harm its social relationships in countless ways of which it is oblivious. But the superego is also by no means necessarily antagonistic to the id and may even rationally help facilitate its satisfaction.

Like that of the ego, the motivation of the superego is indirect. In the superego the person determines or calculates that something is expedient or right, but he doesn't feel this in anything like the immediate or natural way he would the needs of the id. The superego is funded, so to speak, by resources levied upon one's energy for efforts that feel distant and spurious to the id, which, if successfully employed, may yet return disproportionate benefits. This indirectness introduces an artificiality that strains emotionally even as it rewards instrumentally. Self-respect is the positive emotion associated with the superego, guilt the negative emotion.[3]

In its control of the id's boisterousness and the ego's hustling the super-ego may be punitive or helpful. The rudimentary superego overpowers the unselfconscious self and peremptorily resolves to have things one way or another, issuing arbitrary fiats and cruelly disciplining the self to enforce them. Treating itself like an object and forcing itself to act as it wills, a tyrannical superego arbitrarily lays down the law to the ego to achieve or avoid this or that, or to the id to pursue or desist from this or that. But the more developed superego assumes leadership and resolves after consultation that things shall go in a certain way, arriving at reasonable and thoughtful policies and rules and then firmly but respectfully implementing them. The id and ego may be stormed in brutal assault by an imperious rudimentary superego, or they may be variously shepherded, maneuvered, co-opted, diverted, or channeled humanely by a mature one.

For all of the superego's advantages, a severe superego may wreak havoc on the self. On the one hand, it may generate terrible conflict with the id, causing the person to lurch back and forth, yielding first to the one sector then the other. Worse, the spirit may be broken by a cruel and unyielding superego. Such a superego may derive from fear—for example, of dissoluteness, disrepute, damnation, poverty, humiliation, or abandonment—giving it an air of desperation. Or in a battered and bitter person the need for punishment may become the cornerstone of an iron discipline in which the superego rules severely. In the pathological pattern unfairly attributed by Nietzsche in *On the Genealogy of Morals* to the superego in general, a punitive superego feeds sadistically on the very misery inflicted by its self-punishment. As such disturbed emotionality is added to the normal, salutary operation of guilt, the latter becomes twisted.

Contrary to Freud, the superego's rules and policies may or may not be moral. The superego may direct compliance variously with what the Golden Rule enjoins, what the Koran teaches, what Bentham holds, what civil law requires, what Franklin recommends, what social success mandates, what prevents hangovers, and what reduces insurance rates. The superego not only may be amoral, but it may be immoral—as in the case of a criminal who systematically sets up the rackets in a city. In addition to the prudential ones, there are dramatic moral advantages of the superego, particularly in the steady adherence to worthy moral principles it makes possible in a dynamic society.

Freud gives us the basic workings of the superego, though at the same time he confusingly attributes several other things to it. However, his identification of the superego with the moral and his belief that it is necessarily in conflict with the other constituents of the psyche seem difficult to defend. The superego may be moral, but frequently it is merely prudent. The superego may be harsh and punitive, but it may also be and often is moderate and considerate—if seldom by its own devices.

Superid

Elementary self-control, however, commonly takes a radically different form than the one exercised through the superego. I refer to this other form of self-control as the *superid*. The superid is essentially the same emotional action as that of the id, only reflexive. The superid is the consummatory analog to the superego. The superid imposes manners and styles of life on the id and ego. The superid operates by pursuing an attractive and avoiding an unattractive self-image, an image of how one might act or be. Like the superego, the superid is able to guide action to consistency, only here the consistency is aesthetic and imagebased rather than rational and conceptual. Under its power, ways become manners that coalesce into styles of life. The superid's emotional self-consciousness brings an attention to form that makes possible the refinement and gracing of action. Table 1 presents my view of the sectors of the personality.

Table 1. Two-Dimensional Model of the Personality

	Unreflexive, Absence of Self-Control	*Reflexive, Presence of Self-Control*	*Doubly Reflexive, Self-Control of Self-Control*
Instrumental	Ego	Superego	SSE (Super-superego)
Consummatory	Id	Superid	SSI (Super-superid)

Balzac's and Stendhal's novels are filled with examples of the superid. Various American celebrities from different eras also display robust superids: H.L. Mencken, Ernest Hemingway, Jesse Ventura, Jackie Kennedy, James Dean, George Plimpton, Muhammad Ali, Donald Trump, and Madonna. So do various world leaders in their quite different ways: John Kennedy, Winston Churchill, Charles de Gaulle, Vicente Fox, Adolf Hitler, Junichiro Koizumi, Margaret Thatcher, Gandhi, Mao Tse-Tung, Gamal Abdel Nasser, and Pierre Trudeau. Urbane European aristocrats with impeccable manners and elegant styles represent a classic expression of the superid. The superid also expresses itself in the crisp dignity and manners of Boston symphony audiences as they quietly talk during intermissions. The gently rhythmic gait and slightly angular carriage of Berliners as they stroll about their city reflect the superid, as does the proud meandering of Saturday evening promenaders in Siena. A superid of another sort is evident in the Harlem jazz clubs of the 1920s or the *cholo* style of many young Mexican Americans in the Southwest today. The superid tends to be relatively strong in aristocrats, celebrities, trendsetters, urban gays, and pimps, but relatively weak in the middle and working classes.

Nevertheless, the superid is an important part of everyday life for most people in developed countries. We are forming our children's superids when we insist that they eat with proper table manners. We are shaping their personal styles as we slowly impress on them the importance of acting in a certain way and treating others in a certain way, especially as reinforced by our own examples. It is the superid that nudges a young person, when she returns home from college, to express an indefinable new flair in playfully meeting and talking to hometown acquaintances. It is the superid that prompts one to carry himself in a certain manner at work, at home, in the gym, or at a party.

Where the superego is driven by resolve, the superid is drawn by passion. In the emotional self-control carried out by the superid the person follows her reflexive desires, attracted by an appealing style of life or repelled by a disgusting one. One who is self-conscious in the consummatory mode is reflexively aware of the inherent appeal of various forms of action. The superid guides the self while remaining as committed to the "pleasure principle" as the id. Where the superego makes a rational commitment to certain principles and policies, the superid makes an emotional identification with certain manners and a style. It is as if in the superego the person declares to herself, "I *will* do this or that," where in the superid she says to herself, "I *am* that kind of person." In the superego one pushes along with determination as commanded; in the superid one flows ahead in forms that intrinsically appeal. As a result, unlike prudently following policies or rules, acting with and around good form releases one into action. In it one flings herself into life because the source of the energy is what she deeply wants to do. Passion for a lifestyle is the analog to will power. Yet this is still self-control—intended effects are consistently produced in oneself when pursuing self-referential images as they are when applying policies or rules.[4] Those who can act with flair in their superids possess charisma and cause a stir.

Where a sense of pride in the form of self-respect is the positive emotion arising from conformity with the superego's commands, a sense of pride in the form of self-esteem is the positive emotion from successfully meeting the superid's expectations. Where guilt is the negative emotion accompanying violation of the superego's commands, self-disgust is the negative emotion accompanying violation of the superid's imperatives. In guilt one chastises himself for the wrong he has done. In self-disgust he turns away from himself for the tastelessness of his action. One is punished by guilt and sickened by self-disgust.

The superid's style and manners may be developed autonomously by the person or taken over from the milieu. Its content is most often formed in imitation of charismatic persons or groups as role models are observed directly or seen indirectly in the media. The advice Aristotle gives readers over and over again in the *Ethics* is, when uncertain, to watch how the best Athenian gentlemen conduct themselves and learn from their examples. Zola and Tarde (see 1962) in their different ways describe how powerfully imitation carries forms from one person to another.

The superid, like the superego, has both a rudimentary and a developed manifestation. The rudimentary superid is a little-worked self-control in which rigid manners or style of life transfix the person. To the extent to which the consummatory is salient in them, as preteens in the contemporary United States become self-conscious, they tend to develop a rudimentary superid around a few fixed forms visible in certain new gestures and ways of speaking and acting. The rudimentary superid can be reflected in a more overbearing way in cultlike phenomena. The rudimentary superid was dominant in the higher classes and especially the priestly classes of ancient Mesopotamia and Egypt, as in most archaic societies. The rigidity and frontalism that mark the visages on ancient Babylonian reliefs have an affinity to the aspects of cult members today, including those who are terrorists. The rudimentary superid was also found in the simple demeanor of many early Christians. As a more developed sense of form arises, the superid assumes the more flexible and refined patterns we begin to see in large agrarian societies. The characters of many of the more urban and developed members of the GrecoRoman and traditional Chinese aristocracies, for example, were dominated by mature superids.

Because the superid is consummatory, there is relatively little emotional conflict under its rule. If one is sensitive enough to hear the subtle beck of pure form, she will also hear the rambunctious call of the id. The superid is ordinarily on relatively good terms with the id, permitting it gratification to the extent of good form while guiding it in appropriate directions. If one's desire to be a certain kind of person or live a certain style of life is sufficiently strong, this simply out-pulls the more basic desires rather than stifling them. The superid—which grows out of the id as the superego grows out of the ego—doesn't *fight* desire when the id is lured by the distasteful or vicious, it merely turns away in disgust. The superid marginalizes the id when necessary but does not punish it. Where the superid tends to have more difficulty is with the ego. Easily offended by the ego's forms of action, the superid is oblivious to its logic and naturally profligate with resources. Where the excesses of the superego may bring emotional problems, those of the superid may bring financial problems. The theme of the stylish but impecunious aristocrat headed toward ruin, as in Flaubert's *Sentimental Education* or Chekhov's *Cherry Orchard,* is a great one in European literature.

The superid, like the superego, may be moral or amoral. A moral style of life is one of virtue. An immoral style of life is one of vice. The moral superid loves virtue and loathes vice. Aristotle's virtues are the noble ethical habits of the well-socialized superid-dominant agrarian aristocrat. With a moral superid there are no rules to recite, only moral beauty to emulate and perfect. An amoral superid devoted to the stylish without regard to morality is neither more nor less reprehensible than an amoral superego devoted to the accumulation of power in the absence of moral concern.[5] Self-esteem and self-disgust may be either moral or amoral.

Paralleling the case with unreflexive action, what was initially carried out in the superego slowly tends to migrate to the superid. Through practice and the force of habit, cumbersome personal rules and policies in time tend to be displaced by familiar manners and styles. What was once laborious and onerous self-discipline becomes smooth and effortless self-mastery. As part of this migration, moral rules tend to be succeeded through the life course by more fluent moral virtues consistent with them.

Like the id and ego, the superid and superego ultimately complement each other and frequently work together, with the efficacious augmented by the stylish, and vice versa. The superid's flair and sensitivity may prove useful to the superego's instrumental resolutions. The superego's steadiness and prudence may help facilitate the superid's reflexive playfulness. Thus the Christian moral rules were enhanced by the traditional lifestyle represented by such virtues as piety, faith, and charity.

The superid is the major elementary sector of the personality omitted by Freud. Recognition of the superid clarifies some of the inconsistencies and anomalies in Freud's analysis. To Freud the superego was composed of the conscience and the "ego ideal," the latter being an unverbalized image of what we would like to be. However, such an image is patently part of a consummatory function having everything in common with the id except reflex-ivity and nothing in common with the superego but reflexivity. Freud (see 1961b, 218) did anticipate portions of what belongs to the superid with his notions of the ego-ideal, sublimation, and the "narcissistic type" (in which, as he puts it, there is little tension between ego and superego but instead "per-sonality" and the capacity for vigorous action); but he never recognized a separate, reflexive, emotionallybased constituent and sector of the developed personality, and he had no inkling of its central importance. All of these ele-ments were instead lumped together incoherently with the superego.

Some might be tempted to see only narcissism in the superid, but narcis-sism is a narrower concept than that of the superid (see e.g., Kohut, 1985, 97–110). Narcissism is a pathological manifestation of individualism and amorality in which smugness, meaninglessness, and lack of emotional con-nection mingle in a prominent superid. But under such circumstances the superego is no healthier than the superid and manifests analogous disorders. Narcissism could no more be the essence of the superid than smug self-righteousness could be the essence of the superego. The superids of fifth cen-tury Greeks, Later Han Mandarins, or upper middle-class progressives in the early twentieth century United States tended to be significantly motivated by love of the larger community. Taking the superid to be synonymous with nar-cissism would be one level more convoluted than bourgeois disparagement of the id but equally one sided. When a relatively well-adjusted young person absorbs manners and lifestyle in emulation of the models around her or inde-pendently fashions them in a normal way, a superid, not narcissism, is devel-oped. The superid exercises a basic form of self-control, one that preceded the superego historically and one by no means inherently less healthy, worthy, or important than that of the superego. Understandably, some clinicians have emphasized related pathological forms, but the superid as a sector should not be impugned. Nor can narcissism itself be properly understood without grasping the nature of the superid and its place in the personality. Absent a distinction between the superego and superid, psychoanalysts have attempted to fit the phenomenon of narcissism into the superego, but in doing so they have muddled both concepts.

Without the notion of the superid neither the pattern of aristocratic life nor that of recent age, ethnic, and lifestyle minorities has been well under-stood by historians, sociologists, or psychologists. Elias's fascinating work, *The Civilizing Process,* for example, is seriously marred by conflated manifes-tations of the id, superego, and superid. One may begin conducting bodily functions in a more civilized way because he is shamed, disciplined, or refined into doing so, and these processes must be distinguished. There are indeed "stage[s] of restraint and control of emotions" as Elias (1978, 1:135) says, but there are also crucial kinds of the same that must be distinguished. Nor have philosophers well understood the phenomenon of virtue or its relationship to moral rules without the notion of the superid. The superid is a master concept of vital importance across the human sciences.[6]

Super-superego (SSE)

The super-superego or SSE is the core doubly reflexive instrumental sector of the personality. At very high levels of competence one may become self-conscious of his superego and/or superid, with which awareness there arises the possibility of and need for a higher self-control of self-control. If left alone, the superego and superid may tyrannize and romp over the unselfconscious self. Just as we learn to answer the old Roman question, "Who rules the rulers?" with constitutionalism, limited government, and the rule of law in the macroworld, we do so in the psyche with constitution-level governance by the SSE that regulates the scope and manner of rule by the superego and/or superid.

In the SSE one becomes a sophisticated student and higher-level supervisor of his own rational policy making and ruleuse and/or manners and style of life. Rationally viewing internal self-governance from above with a compound self-concept, those with a well developed SSE feel the need to hone their rational decisionmaking and self-control, at which they become *gamesmen*[7] who are not rulebound but higher strategybound. The gamesmen may nuance their self-control in furtherance of instrumental goals such as advancement in business, politics, or law, but doing so requires high levels of knowledge and particularly theoretical knowledge.

The SSE is evident in executive virtuosi at management who masterfully tailor their patterns of internal and external leadership as the situation demands. It is present in contemporary law where virtuosi at the rules nuance contracts or legal interpretation from a higher perspective. The SSE is there in the gifted innovators of finance who devise new derivatives more perfectly conforming to the Black-Scholes pricing model. It is there in the academic stars who deftly manage their research topics, publications, appointments, and promotions. The SSE is also widespread in the upper reaches of contemporary politics, media, advertising, and public relations where constructs of reality are effortlessly massaged to the requirements of task and audience. Gamesmen form the dominant class in highly developed global capitalist societies. They also form a small but growing and disproportionately influential presence in such rapidly developing countries as India and China.

The SSE may arise in the direct experience of young, very capable superego-dominants engaged in intensely competitive activities who learn that, in addition to outstanding ability, preparation, and effort, only with a higher reflexivity and nimbleness do they flourish in investment banks, consulting firms, or the halls of Congress. However, they were usually well on their way toward eventual consolidation of a strong SSE as they were being taught by upper middle-class parents to be self-conscious at a higher level, to think critically about the contexts and opportunities posed by the policies and rules around them, and to game their high school coursework, extracurricular activities, and testtaking for admission to top universities and colleges—if not in elite private schools where they were already earlier so disposed. In their highly effective educational settings, secondary, undergraduate, and graduate or professional, developing gamesmen acquire much of the competence base needed to support higher reflexivity.

The rest comes in well-placed early job experiences where savviness, steadiness, team play, and dedication are key. The apprentice gamesman learns to manage his time tightly on a personal digital assistant. He learns to fit in personal telephone calls at 11:00 P.M. while being driven home from work for example. He learns what he can still do and cannot do after two consecutive all-nighters.

The need addressed by the SSE is a higher need for order, one especially directed at the limitations of the superego. Ordinarily bound to restricted circumstances, the latter tends to become inflexibly attached to particular policies and rules. Without higher reflexivity and broad understanding even unusually flexible superego-dominants can only respond to new conditions in a relatively ad hoc fashion. That may suit the lower-level opportunities and responsibilities of simpler and less dynamic times, but it does not suit the higher-level opportunities and responsibilities of a rapidly changing context. No one approach to political leadership, corporate management, debt deals, or film production can work under such conditions—only the strategist at home in a wide range of techniques can meet the challenges. Performance on this level requires and calls forth high-level self-management. The SSE is far more adept and systematic at pursuing interests, hedging risks, and accumulating wealth and power than the superego. For all the rigors of consolidating one, the higher efficaciousness made possible by the SSE represents a major increase in human freedom. Its appearance is as epochal as was the rise of the superego five centuries ago.

The SSE may also introduce a higher management of the superid, although this tends to be not as intricate or developed as its direction of the superego. Under the SSE the advantages of the superid may be harnessed while the excesses of display or spending to which the latter is prone are curbed or modified for the higher strategic or tactical purposes of a career or social life. The gamesman, being self-aware and critical at a higher level, may revise or discard traditional manners and lifestyles (as well as rules). Hence the edge of bohemianism that also accompanies the profile, as was described by David Brooks in his excellent book, *Bobos in Paradise,* on what is essentially the gamesman type.

As with the singly reflexive sectors, the SSE's double reflexivity may be preceded by a negational rudimentary form of the SSE with a penchant for harshness and severity, in which some remain stuck. Abusive intellectual treatment of the superego and everything connected with it by Nietzsche, Freud, and many modernist intellectuals is of this sort. In their own higher harshness they associate the superego as a whole with its rudimentary form, replicating its injustice at a higher level. Unlike the dominant gamesmen of the postmodernist period, they were not yet able to work constructively from the SSE but employed it as a destructive platform.

Super-superid (SSI)

The super-superid or SSI is the analogous doubly reflexive consummatory sector. In the SSI one may become so self-aware of the superid's and/or superego's actions that she uses a higher aesthetic to hold them accountable, becoming a virtuoso "actor" drawing upon a diverse repertoire of styles, as a Marcel Marceau or Dustin Hoffman moves effortlessly between personae. The SSI is evident in a highly self-aware natural politician's adjustments of her television manner, an accomplished film actor's intuitive work on her method, or a serious club- or party-goer's modulation of her social performance. The SSI is richly developed in the highly reflexive, enigmatic subtleties of postmodernist literary figures' crafting of their public images. As the higher-level master of her own performance, the director of the film of her life, a person adjusts her aesthetic according to inspiration and whimsy in her SSI. In the fully developed SSI one no longer has particular manners or a single personal style she wishes to emulate or implement—she has a whole inner talent agency of superids at her command. The self-image becomes a compound one that may manifest itself in many different ways. As higher self-control becomes nuanced in the SSI and draws its forms from a whole panoply of possibilities, life becomes directorial.

The SSI, like the superid, is a consummatory sector that follows intrinsically appealing forms, and does so with a higher flexibility and playfulness. In the SSI the person follows her inherent desires, only these are now doubly reflexive. As consummatory self-consciousness of first-level self-control emerges and the psyche becomes aware of problems with respect to this self-consciousness, the motivation arises to shape it. In the SSE one is moved by resolve concerning higher policies and rules; in the SSI he is moved by passion with regard to higher-level style and manner. Like the lower-level sectors, the SSE and SSI are capable of becoming moralized, although this has not yet occurred.

Character Types

So profoundly different are the sectors of the personality that we tend to favor one over the others. Internal contests of power occur between sectors in which argument and emotion play significant roles, but differential experience lies behind their weights and is finally decisive for character. Experience wears tracks in our beings. The more experience one has residing in and engaging in the activities of a certain sector, the more power it comes to possess in our psyches. As Plato (1961, books 4 and 8) sees vividly, domination within the personality is analogous to and as real as the domination of one class by another, and both contribute mightily to who we are. Over and over again our minds come back to the perspectives and motivations with which we have spent a great deal of time. People's characters tend to settle accordingly into one sector or another as the relatively permanent institutional profile of their personalities, as their settled way of being. And this existential configuration marks them more fundamentally and pervasively than anything else about them.

The basic types of character are the id-, ego-, superid-, superego-, and SSE-dominant patterns.[8] The id-dominant person, exemplified by the traditional peasant, is characteristically under the influence of elementary unselfconscious, consummatory desires. The ego-dominant is characteristically the unself-conscious hustler, haggler, or scrambler. The superego-dominant is one who rigidly controls himself, much as the bourgeois directs his small business or a bureaucrat her office. The Puritan merchant of seventeenth-century Netherlands, England, or Massachusetts is an apt image often associated with the superego-dominant type. The superid-dominant is one habitually caught up in the style of life. The elegant aristocrat and landowner of eighteenth-century France epitomizes the superid-dominant type. The SSE-dominant is exemplified by the contemporary gamesman. The SSI-dominant is as yet too rare to consider. Just as only a limited understanding of bourgeois societies would be possible without grasping the notion of the superego, only a limited understanding of traditional agrarian societies is possible without the concept of the superid or of contemporary society without that of the SSE. While Fromm (e.g. 1947, 112–17) and others correctly emphasize that people are very often blends of the basic types, most people are dominated by a single sector. Moreover, we have no better way to understand the blends than by understanding the ideal types.[9]

The basic sectors of the personality represent distinct locations in existential space. Particular ways of being, sorts of motivation, and kinds of perceiving, thinking, and acting characterize each sector. The personality is synthetic, as Nietzsche (1967b, 200) says, preparing the way for Freud. The human I see resonates with Nietzsche's (1966, 26) metaphor of the person as "a social structure composed of many souls," which Minsky more succinctly puts as a "society of mind" in his book by that title. The basic sectors of the personality form an inner community with the richest and liveliest interaction.

Notes

1. Freud also characterizes the id as being associated with thinking "unconsciously" and the ego "consciously," an aspect of the distinction that will be examined in Chapter 5.
2. Maslow understands human wants or needs as "instinctoid" or vague biological urges without the programmed biological responses of instincts. While this is true of physiological needs, and partially so for those of the id, it is not at all true for any of the other human needs, beginning with those of the ego. What Maslow doesn't sufficiently consider is that, while the needs for food, clothing, and shelter are substantially physiological, they come to be routinely solved by consummatory and instrumental means, thereby becoming derived needs of the id and ego.
3. The instrumental sectors have emotions—these are just subordinate or recessive.
4. Understanding the superid makes clear how Hegel's (see 1956) hitherto controversial claim that prior to the sophists the Greeks had no conscience could be correct.
5. The moral forms associated with the superid and other sectors of the personality will be explored more fully in Chapter 11.
6. As this book goes to press, Aushra Augustinavichiute's work *Sotsionika: psikhotipy, testy* (Saint Petersburg: Terra Fantastica and Moscow: Izv-vo AST, 1998) has come to my attention in which she has independently developed what looks like a quite different concept of the superid.
7. I borrow the term from the insightful book *The Gamesman* by the psychoanalyst Michael Maccoby but use the term more broadly and with a somewhat different thrust than he.
8. This set of types subsumes Freud's (see 1961b) three types.
9. The concept of character will be further developed in Chapter 7.

Bibliography

Aristotle. 1953. *Ethics*. Harmondsworth, Middlesex: Penguin.

Brooks, D. 2000. *Bobos in Paradise: The New Upper Class and How They Got There*. New York: Simon and Schuster.

Elias, N. 1978. *The Civilizing Process*. 2 vols. New York: Pantheon.

Freud, S. 1961a. "The Ego and the Id." In *The Complete Psychological Works of Sigmund Freud*. Vol. 19. London: Hogarth Press.

———. 1961b. "Libidinal Types." In *The Complete Psychological Works of Sigmund Freud*. Vol. 21. London: Hogarth Press.

Fromm, E. 1947. *Man for Himself: An Inquiry into the Psychology of Ethics*. New York: Henry Holt.

Hegel, G. 1956. *The Philosophy of History.* New York: Dover Publications.
Kohut, H. 1985. *Self-Psychology and the Humanities: Reflections on a New Psychoanalytic Approach.* New York: W.W. Norton.
Maccoby, M. 1976. *The Gamesman.* New York: Simon and Schuster.
Maslow, A. 1954. *Motivation and Personality.* New York: Harper and Row.
Neitzsche, F. 1966. *Beyond Good and Evil.* New York: Random House.
———. 1967a. *On the Genealogy of Morals.* New York: Random House.
———. 1967b. *The Will to Power.* New York: Random House.
Plato. 1961. *Republic.* In *The Collected Dialogues of Plato,* ed. E. Hamilton and H. Cairns. Princeton, NJ: Princeton University Press.
Tarde, G. 1962. *The Laws of Imitation.* Gloucester, MA.: P. Smith.

4. Community, Association, Supercommunity, and Superassociation

The basic dimensions of the human intersect in collectivities as they do in persons. What the intersection of our first two dimensions describes at the macrolevel are the basic institutions of society, insofar as collectivity is sufficiently developed to manifest them. These are depicted in Table 2. The four basic social institutions are similar to those of Parsons, but the two doubly reflexive ones are new to social, if not to political thought. The elementary sectors of society reflect the same dimensions as the basic sectors of the personality and are strictly parallel to them. These close micro- and macro- parallels have never been systematically explored.

Community and association, the two most basic forms of collectivity, are the precise macroanalogs to the id and ego in persons. These notions go back to antiquity. In Aristotle's *Politics* (1261a, 10–30) "ethnos" and "state" respectively approximate community and association. The Roman legal distinction between *universitas* and *societas* (the latter in its broadest sense) also approximately corresponds to these expressions (see Oakeshott 1974, 199–200; Berger 1953, 708–9, 750–51; and Duff 1938, 35–48). Toennies (33–35), who introduces the terms community and association into modern social thought, sees them as linked respectively with the natural[1] and artificial, with "wants" and interests, and regards any collective task as able to be carried out by the informal social methods of the first or the formal economic ones of the second.[2]

Community is characterized by consummatory, unself-conscious action. In community one is attached to the group by emotional bonds. The ties are personal in the sense that what is important in community is who one is rather than what he does (see Durkheim 1933, 105, 123, 130–31). Fundamental to community is that one shares a common nature or essence with others in it (Husserl 1960, 120). This commonality is accompanied by a feeling of belonging together, a sense of community (Weber 1978, 40–42).

Table 2. Two-Dimensional Model of Society

	Unreflexive, Absence of Self-Control	Reflexive, Presence of Self-Control	Doubly Reflexive, Self-Control of Self-Control
Instrumental	Association (Economy)	Superassociation (Politics and law)	SSA (Constitutionalism and higher law)
Consummatory	Community	Supercommunity (Consensus and informal social control)	SSA (Higher consensus and informal social control)

Inherently personal, a relationship of bonding is characteristically communal. One identifies with those to whom he is so bound—insofar as he is such—and feels at home with them. The emotionality, fluency, and spontaneity of community necessarily being natural and effortless, it is also informal in and of itself. The basic drive behind community is the need for unself-conscious, spontaneous life with others in mutual caring and familiarity. When the need for community is well met, it brings joy to life. Frustration of the need for informal social relations brings alienation and loneliness, Durkheim's sense of the term "egoism." Community may be formed on any level—nuclear family, extended family, clan, club, city, region, nation, or world. It may also be composed on any axis or basis, such as kinship, friendship, class, occupation, avocation, religion, or ethnicity.

As habit is to the id, custom is to community. In its emotionality, naturalness, and spontaneity community tends to accumulate and treasure familiar ways or customs, for which reason in times of stability community tends to become custombound. However, the very fact that community, like the id, is both emotional and unreflexive means that, irrespective of how custombound it may sometimes become, it may also change suddenly, following the charisma of newly cathected forms, as it is prone to do in times of crisis.

Association is the form of collectivity characterized by instrumental, unself-conscious action. In association or the economy one is attached to the group by rational links, and what is to be gained from the relationship is to the fore. In association people deliberately act as tools for expedient purposes (Weber 1978, 41–42). In association people cooperate with others to achieve their interests and amass power. Inherently impersonal, the contractual relationship is characteristically associational (see Durkheim 1933, 123). In its rationality, deliberateness, and future orientation, association tends to accumulate policies, giving it a tendency to formality. The needs of association are those pertaining to the acquisition of scarce goods and services instrumental for the meeting of all other needs. Their frustration brings deprivation and dissatisfaction with economic performance. Like community, association may be formed on any level and for the promotion of any purpose.

All but the simplest collectivity has both community and association, and the two modes intricately intertwine, as do the id and ego in persons. In collectivities, also as in persons, one mode ordinarily tends to be dominant and the other subordinate. Yet each constantly depends upon the other, for even corporations require community with which to offset their formal rationality and more fully engage their members. Although a department store may be strongly association dominant, it might have a morale-boosting backroom party for employees on Christmas Eve, upon the convening of which, community may become rowdily ascendant as the last customer leaves, when a manager leaps onto a table to propose a toast. A corporate law firm that is intense business for sixty-hour workweeks still has its vital community—over lunch in the firm cafeteria, on the golf course in threesomes and foursomes, at deal-signing dinners, in offices or halls as attorneys banter or joke during a light moment, and on annual retreat weekends with spouses. On the other hand, the married couple that is usually entirely community may transform itself into efficient association for weathering a tax audit.

Like the id or ego, either community or association may be moral or amoral. A family, group of friends, nation, or community of nations may be either mindful or unmindful of its larger obligations. So too a company, *zaibatsu*, state, or military alliance.

Like persons, collectivities have two basic kinds of self-control, supercommunity or consensus and superassociation or politics. Supercommunity, the collective analog to the superid, engages in natural, spontaneous self-control, overseeing unselfconscious community and association. Supercommunity encompasses consensus decisionmaking concerning how economic and communal life are to be conducted, together with consensus endeavors to enforce it. Supercommunity entails earnest persuasive conversation and entreaties among community members toward consensus. Where the activity of the superid is the consulting of one's thoughts and feelings about her own life, that of supercommunity is the similar consultation by many different people of their thoughts and feelings about their life in common. Supercommunity entails a fluid process of caring communication in which members sincerely attempt to get at the forms that feel right for the community or association, emotionally airing and considering their differences. Supercommunity is a mulling over and working toward what feels right collectively. In supercommunity there is the spontaneous desire for activity with fellows that characterizes community, only now this is directed reflexively to the joint oversight and guidance of the collectivity. In supercommunity we pursue our natural collective representations and wants vis-à-vis community and association, just as the superid acts naturally in guiding the id and ego. The supercommunity's guidance is not by policies or rules but by intrinsically appealing images of how things ought to be.

As consensus is approached, those who had been at odds with the group's decision weaken in their certitude and defer to their fellows, swept up naturally by group feeling surrounding the decision. Thus Gadamer (1986, 329) speaks of how "opinion" always seeks to become consensus. Consensus is Rousseau's general will. The line of consensus is that at which obligation is assumed by members of the community, outside the pale of which is designated deviance. People ordinarily follow informal standards because, when the consensus process is complete, they have been freely persuaded of their appropriateness by the consensual power of their fellows. They wish to conform because others' opinions possess charisma and inspire emulation. Charisma is an emotional form of power that may be either excited and dramatically charged or calm and mildly so. As Tarde for his nineteenth-century Zolaesque milieu puts it, we live in a sort of hypnotic state of suggestibility in social life and draw from the models around us (Williams 1982, 346).

Those participating in the elementary informal socio-cultural supervision carried out by supercommunity form a consensual class. These informal leaders look over society, interact with each other, and set and enforce manners and style, which are then ordinarily freely followed. Those engaged in or carrying out collective self-control are not disciplining society to conform to a policy or law; they are yearning for a certain conduct in the community and feel impassioned to impress this collective self-image upon society. The ensuing consistency helps free the collectivity from vulnerability to the erratic or harmful performances of unguided community and association, and it does so in a way that goes with the grain, not against it.

Superassociation, the collective analogy to the superego in the person, is politics or the polity, collectivity engaged in rational self-control, supervising the unself-conscious community and association. Superassociation like association is extrinsically motivated activity, doing what it does for instrumental purposes, only it is reflexive. Thinking and acting expedientially, its collective decisions are made and enforced mechanically, and they are formally adjudicated and backed up by police or security forces. Following calculations of interests in contests of power, the decisionmaking of superassociation employs such artificial means as voting, adjudication, negotiation, arbitration, maneuvering, bribery, and *force majeure* to funnel preferences into authoritative decisions. Law is the branch of politics in which specialists authoritatively reconcile and apply present and past collective rational decisions. The need for politics is the need for an efficient formal apparatus directing the collectivity toward the consistent solution of its problems and accumulation of resources. Politics may be effected peacefully or violently, but, like economic activity, it always abrades to some degree, and distinctly more so in the case of amoral and/or coercive rule.

Those participating in the formal decisionmaking and implementation of superassociation form a political class whose members rationally enact and enforce binding policies and rules. The ensuing order makes possible a far more predictable and productive collectivity.

Supercommunity and superassociation are frequently interwoven. A parliament, which is predominantly political, at the same time depends in many ways upon consensus. Informal understandings constantly buffer the harsh mechanisms of voting and maneuvering under the rules. At the same time, what is predominantly supercommunity can occasionally be so time consuming or paralyzed that it requires a political mechanism to force a decision. Politics and consensus are not naturally in step with each other, but as politics becomes worked, it becomes increasingly embedded in the caring conversation of consensus. Like the other basic sectors, personal and collective, supercommunity or superassociation may or may not be in harmony and may or may not be moral.

Where collectivity is sufficiently well developed, it also develops higher- or constitution-level informal and/or formal self-control of first-level consensus and politics. In the super-supercommunity (SSC) higher consensus operates, within which higher informal self-control and legitimation of consensual and political regimes occur. In the super-superassociation (SSA) constitutional politics takes place overseeing and regulating supercommunity and superassociation. Respectively exemplifying the two, Britain's constitutionalism was traditionally relatively informal, the United States's relatively formal. In their different ways both may greatly stabilize and enhance first-level collective self-control. Politics without the restraint of constitutionalism can be arbitrary, violent, and disruptive. Informal social control without analogous oversight can be capricious, cruel, and divisive. The informal American higher consensus that gay people should not be discriminated against has been an SSC limit on the activities of consensus and politics. This prohibition is a higher informal standard as opposed to a rule. However, a movement is well under way to augment this norm with rulings by constitutional courts, which represent SSA.

As collectivities move up the ladder of reflexivity, they, like persons, move up a hierarchy of needs. If they can continue to meet lower needs while meeting previously unimagined emergent ones, they can greatly enhance overall performance and satisfaction, all else equal. Very important changes occur in the character of society as it moves from dominance by one to dominance by another collective sector.

Since collectivities are stacked in complex hierarchies of power with other collectivities, and since community and association are interdependent, the two are interspersed. Collectivities that are primarily communal supervise those that are primarily associational and viceversa. Thus, remembering that the emotional and intuitive normally has the last say, as the ultimate "Background" orienting rationality (see Wittgenstein 1969), an informal consensual class may and often does control a bureaucracy at the top while, many steps down the organizational ladder, control may be exercised by a functionary over an informal community service group.

****

Where Freud has been the thinker who has come the furthest in exploring the structure of the psyche, Parsons has done so for collectivity. His LIGA scheme, dating from the early 1950s, depicts all "social systems" as necessarily possessing institutions for coping with four basic functional needs or tasks: latent tension management and pattern maintenance, as exemplified by the family; "integration" or social control; "goal attainment" or the polity; and "adaptation" or the economy (see Parsons 1961, Parsons et al. 1953). Despite its imperfections, this model has been for over half a century the best general two-dimensional macroscheme available in the social sciences.

My approach departs from Parsons's broadly as follows: Where Parsons sees socialization and tension management, I see community. Socialization or pattern maintenance is conducted in all social institutions; it is not essentially bound to community. Tension management is one function carried out by community in advanced societies, but it need not exist to the same extent in all collectivities and is diminished in many simple societies. Additionally, Parsons is misled by his terms "polity" and "economy" into thinking governmentally administered programs are automatically political when most of them are part of the economy along with private business. Parsons lumps all social control together, failing to properly distinguish between informal and formal supervision. Nor does he include constitution-level politics and consensus. Moreover, all collectivities do not possess all four institutions. As the simplest human personalities are virtually all id, the simplest collectivities are virtually all community. Parsons also develops no workable parallel model of the psyche, and he does not develop the connection between his model and the dimensions I will introduce below. In short, Parsons' work is highly suggestive and filled with potential but much too uneven and little developed. Although modifying it to correct a number of errors, adding various features, and dropping its cumbersome terminology, I have essentially begun with Parsons.

Possessing the first two dimensions of the human has made it possible for us to lay out fundamental institutions of the personality and society. Doing so is crucial to the human sciences because it enables them to get about conceptually in their subject, systematically pursue important topics of study, and precisely demarcate fields of specialization. However, we have not yet distinguished between the cultural and social institutions or their parallels in the psyche. For that we must introduce another dimension, the ideal versus the real.

Notes

1. In the sense of the word utilized in Chapter 1.
2. By community and association I mean *Gemeinschaft* and *Gesellschaft*. The distinction must be grounded in these German words because no fully satisfactory substitutes exist for them in English. Community has been battered for so long in the English-speaking world that for all its remarkable strengths our language can no longer adequately describe informal human relations. What counts is that this fundamental distinction be accurate and sharp, and it is in German (again for historical reasons). It doesn't suffice to translate them as community and association in the usual senses because where the shallow sense of community as neighborhood or municipality is overriding in English, a profound, kinshiplike bonding is what must be brought out or at least reached into by the term, and it is by the German. A further manifestation of the weakness of English here is that it contains no convenient adjectival form of "community," although I use "communal" in this sense. "Association" is too limp a word to fully bear its side of the task either, but it is the best we have. The alliteration in the German terms confers an additional major advantage by indelibly conveying the linkage between the two. The concepts of organic and mechanical solidarity, also going back to Toennies, are hampered by oblique reference to the kinds of bonds used rather than to the character of the human (as well as by their confusing reversal in Durkheim). Status and contract, Maine's terms, have the same disadvantage and are narrower as well.

Bibliography

Aristotle. 1962. *Politics*. Harmondsworth, Middlesex: Penguin.

Berger, A. 1953. *Encyclopedic Dictionary of Roman Law*. Philadelphia: American Philosophical Society.

Duff, P. 1938. *Personality in Roman Private Law*. Cambridge: Cambridge University Press.

Durkheim, E. 1933. *The Division of Labor in Society*. New York: Free Press.

Gadamer, H. 1986. *Truth and Method*. New York: Crossroad Publishing.

Husserl, E. 1960. *Cartesian Meditations*. The Hague: Martinus Nijhoff.

Oakeshott, M. 1974. *Rationalism in Politics*. London: Methuen.

Parsons, T. 1961. "Outline of the Social System." In *Theories of Society*, ed. T. Parsons, E. Shils, K. Naegele, and J. Pitts. New York: Free Press.

———, R. Bales, and E. Shils. 1953. *Working Papers in the Theory of Action*. New York: Free Press.

Toennies, F. 1963. *Community and Society*. New York: Harper and Row.

Weber, M. 1978. *Economy and Society*. 2 vols. Berkeley and Los Angeles: University of California Press.

Williams, R. 1982. *Dream Worlds: Mass Consumption in Late Nineteenth-Century France*. Berkeley and Los Angeles: University of California Press.

Wittgenstein, L. 1969. *On Certainty*. Oxford: Blackwell.

5. *The Ideal and Real*

The third basic dimension of the human is the ideal and real. The ideal mode is what pertains to perception and thought, and the real mode what pertains to action in the cycle of doing. These senses are longstanding in ordinary language and frequently if inexactly used in the human sciences. The distinction between the ideal and the real represents an extension of Aristotle's between theoretical and practical knowledge. According to Aristotle in the *Metaphysics* (993b, 20–21), "the end of theoretical knowledge is the truth, while that of practical knowledge is action . . ." The difference between seeking the truth and putting it into practice is at the heart of this opposition. The difference also comes up in the *Ethics* (VI:5–8) in the distinction between theoretical wisdom (*sophia*) and practical wisdom (*phronesis*), as it does in that between the intellectual and practical virtues (see VI:1–2). The opposition parallels the central one between the locutionary and illocutionary in Austin and Searle's speech acts theory.[1] It also parallels, though it is broader than, the everyday distinctions between pure and applied fields and between the ivory tower and the real world.

In all that we do we go back and forth between perception, thought, and action, the three fundamental phases of doing. However, perception and thought frequently cluster together in opposition to action, and in that opposition one mode or the other tends to predominate. More precisely, where all action presumes some perception and thought, the extent to which people dwell on perception and thought versus action forms a continuum, albeit with a significant tendency toward the poles. In the ideal, action is present, but it is subservient to and in connection with perception and thought. It is directed toward satisfying the needs of perception or thought, as by obtaining a microscope or reading lamp for them. So too, in the real, perception and thought are present, but they are subordinate to and in connection with action. Perception and thought in the real are directed toward satisfying the needs of action, as in noticing what competing businesses are selling, or thinking about how to attract better employees. While every concrete action has both ideal and real aspects, necessarily drawing on perceiving and thinking and exercising power, the human has two large realms of greater or lesser concern with perceiving or thinking about the world versus acting in the world. Which moment of doing is *dominant* is the key, not whether something proximately constitutes one or the other. This focus on the relative weight of the ideal and real is parallel to those with respect to the consummatory-instrumental and reflexivity dimensions.

Perception, thought, and action are all present in particular instances of both the ideal and real, but they are not equally dominant or salient in them. A large scientific experiment or theoretical project respectively exemplifies overarching perception and thought within which a great deal of subordinate action may be found. Even smaller instances of perceiving and thinking, such as gazing at the stars from one's front yard or thinking about a movie one has recently seen, may be said to be predominantly ideal, although that incorporates subsidiary action. When we work in the garden or sell men's suits, perception and thought become intimately involved but subsidiary—there the concern is predominantly real. Perception and thought occurring in the midst of trading stocks or constructing an office building are again dominated by larger action.

In the ideal the action present is the special, rarified kind taking place within the restricted realm in which perception and thought are foregrounded. In the realm of the real the action is freer and more robust. However, there the perception and thought are the clipped sorts organized around action, not the autonomous and lingering sorts found in the ideal. Perception and thought are free in their own realm but curtailed in that of action, and viceversa.[2] Nevertheless, it is sometimes convenient to speak loosely of the real as the world of action and of the ideal as the world of perception and/or thought, even though, strictly, this is misleading.

These understandings enable us to distinguish between two vast areas of human activity, a realm of the ideal and a realm of the real. Where the ideal is dominant, we find crammed mental workshops with cluttered bits and pieces of concepts, propositions, and images lying about amid much special knowledge and many routines for working with them—accompanied by such neatly stacked cultural products as theories, models, interpretations, facts, and artworks. But where the ideal is dominant we find a sparse and little-used inventory of action-oriented knowledge and routines. Where the real is dominant, we find the opposite combination, spare ideal workshops but elaborately stocked real-world knowledge and routines. One or the other predominates according to whether the truth or making a difference is the greater concern.

We may also speak of possessions as being relatively ideal or real. Ordinarily bookstands are relatively ideal, howitzers relatively real. Ideal knowledge is relatively removed from action, as is the case with broad liberal arts knowledge. Real knowledge is instead how-to knowledge or know-how: routines and facts serving practice. It might include the knowledge of how to prepare and put on a Thanksgiving dinner or how to build a jet plane or control the business cycle. The practical knowledge in an insurance company of local market conditions lies entirely in the real world. Austin and Searle found its effects in language because the distinction between the ideal and real also applies to possessions.

All other alleged criteria of the ideal and real modes either reduce to my distinction (i.e., the slightly reformulated Aristotelian one) or are metaphorical of it. In the ideal the human uses representations to register what is; in the real world it uses representations as blueprints with which to bring about what it wants. The ideal is a taking in and the real a putting out.[3] The pure and theoretical mimic things; the applied and practical shape things. Accordingly, the goal of the ideal is to gain the truth; the goal of the real is to achieve anything else. The two basic sources of truth—perceiving and thinking—yield the complementarity of description and explanation and of research and theory.

Focus on the distinction between perception and thought versus action also yields the metaphor of *distance* that is so often found in distinguishing the phenomena of the ideal from those of the real. In the ideal the motivation is different; there is a distancing or detachment, and what that is *from* is concern with action and its consequences. One *withdraws* to the ideal, as it is often expressed in psychology. In the ideal mode, such needs as those of curiosity or aesthetic beauty might gently blow one along. In the real mode, economic or sociality needs manifestly push or pull one along. In that it is comparatively distant from action, the ideal may be said to be autonomous and for its own sake. Engaged in the world, the real is oriented toward making a difference; its consequences matter proximately and directly. Those of the ideal do not. Pure science matters only indirectly; applied science matters directly. So-called distance and minimality criteria can be helpful ways of expressing the basic distinction, but they add nothing substantive to the distinction; they merely season it metaphorically.

As with the other dimensions, the ideal and real often have difficulty conversing or coordinating with each other, and ordinarily one or the other is dominant, for which reason people tend to dwell either in the ideal or the real mode as an enduring feature of their characters. Those who dwell in the ideal tend to become absentminded vis-à-vis the real, reflecting their distance from it, but those who dwell in the real could as easily be considered absentminded vis-à-vis the ideal. In practice, ideal and real dominance are often associated with whether representations are brought forth or held by specialists in the ideal. Such persons characteristically dwell on perception and/or thought rather than on action. However, even those who are ordinarily lodged in the real are temporarily transported to the ideal when they concern themselves with religion, ideology, entertainment, and even, to a lesser degree, when in passing they concern themselves with their economic or technological understanding. While such persons may not be ideal dominant overall, they too have comparatively removed perceptions and thoughts. All humans have at least minimally developed ideal and real modes but not all have an institutionalized ideal with enough experience there for stable structures to have emerged. Neither ideal nor real dominance is inherently more developed than the other. Let us now turn to two pivotal concepts that may be grounded upon the distinction between the ideal and real.

The Concepts of Culture and Society

The centrality of the concepts of culture and society and their cognates across the modern human sciences, absent fixity or determination in their meaning, has presented a warning flare over these fields since their beginnings. Glaringly indicative of the reigning conceptual confusion is that they cannot even satisfactorily define their own fields of study without clarification of these terms, which have been employed in the most inchoate and jumbled ways. The standard anthropological conceptualization of culture as essentially the sum total of society's heritable mental possessions is unwieldy, though convenient.[4] Kindred is the dominant sociological conceptualization of culture as beliefs, attitudes, and values. (Psychology comparatively seldom employs the concept of culture, but its ubiquitous concepts of beliefs and attitudes stand in its place no more satisfactorily.) Anthropology's and sociology's senses of the word "culture" trace back via much winnowing to the nineteenth-century German *Kultur* through Tylor.[5]

For most purposes a crisper understanding of culture is as the realm of the ideal, with the corresponding sense of "society" being the realm of the real. My chief sense of the word culture also descends from the German, much of it instead via Arnold in *Culture and Anarchy* (5), who brought in something closer to the original Latin, defining culture as the "pursuit of our total perfection by means of getting to know . . . the best which has been thought and said in the world. . . ." Arnold's use of the earlier sense became established in the humanities where it underwent needed broadening, though retaining a focus on the ideal. Literary theorists, bearing that tradition, also tend to use the term culture as do I, in opposition to the real (see e.g. Jameson 1991, 277). As to the important corresponding adjectival forms, the cultural is the ideal, the social the real. Where culture and particularly society often also suggest that they are of an independent collective entity, especially one with sovereignty, cultural and social have the advantages of ordinarily not doing so, though "societal" does.[6]

The Cultural Institutions

Grounding the distinction between culture and society in that between the ideal and the real enables us to clearly distinguish between the cultural and the social institutions and to make the parallel distinction within the personality. The sectors distinguished in Chapters 3 and 4 were exclusively those of the real world. Each has a cultural parallel that must now be described. The ideal or cultural analog to each real-world institution will be described as its *pre*version. The *pre*version of each sector is cultural; the unprefixed version is social or its psychological analog. One may envision a figure with the ideal or *pre*version above the corresponding real-world sector, for the person as well as for the collectivity. The centrality of the notions of culture and society in the social sciences is a strong indication that something parallel to them and equally rooted in the distinction between the ideal and the real modes also needs to be of major importance to psychology. What this something is is one's personal culture and society. Let me describe each ideal-world sector and then return to the concept of culture.

The id, ego, superid, superego, and their higher-level analogs then must all be seen as but the real-world cases in a two-dimensional matrix which, if not so restricted, would otherwise conflate the ideal and the real. Being in the real world, all of those sectors and their collective analogs seek to make a difference. Yet, as Schumpeter (1950, 259n11) says, "[r]ationality of thought and rationality of action are two different things"—as are reflexivity of perception or thought and reflexivity of action. Distinguishing between the ideal and real modes enables us to address the three-dimensional sectors of the human, yielding a fuller, richer and more powerful typology. Paralleling each real-world sector of the psyche is an ideal-world one with the same location vis-à-vis the consummatory-instrumental and reflexivity dimensions. Each of these, to mint a series of terms, is described as the *pre*version of the corresponding two-dimensional sector, as the idea is father to the action.

Consummatory and unselfconscious, the pre-id then is the ideal analog to the id. The pre-id thinks naturally and figuratively, in images rather than concepts. With its passive version of the pleasure principle the dominant need of the pre-id is the slack unselfconscious one for entertainment, diversion, and amusement. Folk music, simple stories, and amusing lore catered to the needs of the pre-id in an earlier era as the mass media do today. The truth to which the pre-id is oriented is folksy and platitudinous.

As the id in ordinary times is the site of much habitual action, so the pre-id in such times is the setting of familiar and reassuring images, in repetitive decoration and formulaic stories and plays. The desire for pleasantly deco-rated tents, clothes, blankets, pottery, homes, and offices is part of the same complex as that for background music. While the pre-id may be engaged by such tepid content, it may also be engaged by bear-baiting, action films, or sports events. Moreover, in extraordinary times the mesmerism of powerful new images may assert itself in the pre-id, upending long-established pat-terns. Irrespective of the times, to the extent which the images of the pre-id lose their distance from the world, they become the fantasies of the id.

When the rationality of the ego is raised up to the ideal and undertaken for its own sake in curiosity, one has the autonomous pre-ego. Instead of thinking freely like the pre-id, however, the pre-ego thinks deliberately and step-by-step. The pre-ego's inherent need is to know and understand the world rationally and unselfconsciously. The exact scientist, and particularly the natural scientist, dwells primarily in her pre-ego. To the extent to which the pre-ego's concepts and propositions lose their distance from the world, they become subordinate to the technologies of the ego.

However, if a scientist fully immerses herself in her calling for long peri-ods and her rational activity becomes so fluent and masterful that she eats, sleeps, and dreams her work, her activity moves from the pre-ego into the pre-id. What had been step-by-step becomes a fluid play of images. The images that course through the pre-id may be dream-like fancy, but they may also contain the solutions to problems in mathematics, physics, or econo-metrics. When a basically rational, logical mind like Einstein or Szilard's, after rigorous education and long immersion in science, eases into contemplation, it "sees" the deep structure of reality if a theorist, or the solutions to experi-mental problems if a researcher. As what had been pre-ego moves into the pre-id, intuition and effortlessness displace method, and the scientist swims in her informal Wittgensteinian "Background" of tacit knowledge (see Wittgen-stein 1969 and Polanyi 1966).

The pre-superid, the ideal counterpart of the superid, is the home site of figurative self-knowledge. It contains the autonomous self-image, consisting of a very large set of figurative images of different doings actually or poten-tially engaged in by the self but detached from the practical. In its self-consciousness the pre-superid needs aesthetic beauty rather than entertainment or decoration. Its is the pure joy of self-consciously creating and contemplating form for its own sake, at a distance from the object. Those whose pre-superids are able to create the forms that capture us have aesthetic power.

As the real consequences of aesthetic painting, sculpting, or bodily move-ment come to the fore, one moves from the pre-superid into the superid where patterns originating in the former may be used but are no longer dwelled upon for their own sake. When one has a flourishing pre-superid and his own aesthetic, he has the resources with which to shape and refine the forms of the superid. Whether a person's consummatory action is routed by patterns he himself has created or by those he has picked up in the manner of Aristotle or Confucius's gentlemen from the social milieu, all flair and style have their ultimate source in the pre-superid or analogous higher functions.

The pre-superego, the ideal analog to the superego, houses the person's autonomous rational self-knowledge. The pre-superego contains a portion of the self-concept, the aggregate of the person's detached, discursive, singly reflexive knowledge about himself and his action. In the pre-superego lies the intrinsic, curiosity-driven need to know ourselves rationally. The applied portion of the basic self-concept and rational self-knowledge belongs to the superego. The superego may utilize the pre-superego's knowledge as it builds or modifies practical personal policies and rules, evaluates and selects them from others, or enforces them.

Still higher lie the constitution-level personal cultural sectors of the consummatory and instrumental modes, the pre-SSI and pre-SSE, which may variously influence the respective forms of higher self-control. The pre-SSI, the ideal counterpart to the SSI, possesses detached higher consummatory awareness of first-level reflexivity. The pre-SSE, the ideal analog to the SSE, contains detached higher instrumental awareness of first-level reflexivity. As we become self-conscious of our elementary reflexivity in a detached way, the doubly reflexive cultural sectors come into being, again with the distinct needs for their respective kinds of truth.

The macro cultural institutions are also yielded by our first three dimensions. Pre-community, the product of intuition directed freely to the external world, natural and social, is collective informal or popular culture, the ur-source from which all culture originates. Pre-community is made up in traditional societies of unreflexive, entertaining legends, myths, tales, curiosities, and lore, and in modern societies of mass media content. Where community is natural action in concert with others with whom we are comfortable, pre-community is natural perceiving and thinking with which we are comfortable. The nature of this unreflexive, informal culture is nicely captured in Levi-Strauss's (1963, 89) famous description as that which is "good to think." Insofar as what had once been rational knowledge comes to take the form of lore, it too becomes entertaining in its tepid and familiar ways, rendered funny or surprising or put in beat, jingles, rhyme, or riddles. In lore pertaining to the external world, as in all consummatory forms of collective knowledge, we are in touch with collective feelings. At least for the consumer, entertainment doesn't finally matter; the need it serves is only that of diversion.

Consuming popular culture, as in watching television sitcoms that churn amusing representations remote from consequences, is predominantly ideal.

But when the plot becomes intense, as in action films, the real becomes more pronounced, though ordinarily not predominating. Pornographic films, however, which manifestly engage prurient desires, become predominantly real. For most, watching a bullfight is also very engaging, perhaps even predominantly real. Nevertheless, for an Ernest Hemingway, watching it may remain quite detached and ideal.

Producing popular culture, on the other hand, at least in a developed society, is typically real-world activity. The main concern is making a profit. However, within a music company the creative artists and those close to them go in the direction of the ideal mode while executives, accountants, and janitors, among others, go far in the direction of the real. Similarly, while producing a reference book may take place in the real world, its end use may be in the ideal one. Producing popular culture in a traditional society, on the other hand, tends to be relatively ideal. However, to the extent to which even the medieval minstrel's or storyteller's action was aimed not at entertainment for itself but at achieving royal favor, romantic success, or moral reform, it too was in the real mode.

Watching sports events is again ordinarily relatively ideal dominant—the viewer is dwelling on it for its own sake or for the sake of distant considerations, and he or she is not predominantly acting but being entertained. However, the more the sports fan takes the contest as a symbol of local pride or engages in sociality with those around or heckles opposing team members, the more real what occurs. Game playing, as opposed to watching games, is real, for here there is engagement rather than distance.

This understanding of pre-community excludes real-world activities that frequently have been blurred with ideal ones in the traditional conceptualization of popular culture, particularly in that it excludes engagement in games and play (but not their vicarious enjoyment), because they are predominantly social and real. Participating in games is community (though association if professional) while watching them is pre-community. Of course, the two can and do shade into each other since all such distinctions are *ideal typical*.[7] The truths proffered by popular culture, such as they are, are simple, unselfconscious, amusing, trite, and formulaic.

Science is careful, systematic, rational thought and empirical research carried on in consultation with each other. Pre-association is pure science, natural and human, insofar as the latter is unreflexive—for all natural science is unreflexive but only some human science. Unreflexive science is parallel to the economy in that it regards both material items and people unselfconsciously, rationally, and as objects. As science gains self-consciousness, it becomes reflexive human science. Pre-association, as pure science, is ideal dominant and remote from application. As science loses its pureness, it becomes applied and part of the economy. The cognitive formulas of unreflexive science are analogous to the emotional formulas of popular culture. As unreflexive science loses its rationality, it becomes lore and popular culture.

In addition to its ontological requirements, science proper is under a technical requirement to rise to minimum accepted standards of carefulness and systematicity. If inquiry is directed toward nature or the human that is not careful and systematic, it fails as human science, precisely as bad art fails as art. It still meets the ontological but not the technical requirements of science. Although for convenience the sector may be referred to simply as natural science, other important activity also takes place here.

Pre-supercommunity is the arts, collective informal, self-conscious contemplation and fanciful perception, thought, and play with form. The arts, figuratively reflecting upon the world of the human in the consummatory mode are the natural home of society's detached, collective, poetic self-awareness. The need for the arts is the need to understand ourselves—and the world insofar as it relates to us—in this distinct way.[8]

Relatively remote from concern with making a difference, the representations embodied in traditional European literature and art were predominantly ideal, although they manifested a range in this regard. Michelangelo's *Pieta* is far removed from the real. However, baroque paintings commissioned by powerful patrons sometimes made interested statements about the nobility and grandeur of the patron or her class, rendering them less ideal. Wordsworth's "Prelude" was again extremely ideal. Dickens's novels remained in balance predominantly ideal but sometimes only barely, so actively involved were they in the issues of the day. Proust, however, is at the ideal pole. Socialist realist art could become so heavy-handedly engaged that it tipped predominantly into the real. Tightly subordinating aestheticism to economic purposes, an advertising agency is also thoroughly ensconced in the real, however arty its work might appear. Not so the aficionados of commercials who collect and replay them. French workers singing *La Marseillaise* in a May Day parade are engaging in the real action of expressing class solidarity. In a marriage ceremony the real effects are also ordinarily overwhelmingly dominant, yet some who attend may be quite engaged aesthetically by the form or content of the service—and, for those who are, such ideal aspects may outweigh the efficacy of the ritual.

If lovers are apart and exchange letters, there is a very strong real element to the thought expressed in their missives. Even poems they include could be very real in that they might be sent as part of an actual exchange intended to have and having a significant effect on the relationship. A century later, however, the correspondence might have overwhelmingly ideal import as descendents donate the letters to a library for their literary value. Even within the framework of their later ideal significance, however, there would be the real aspects of cataloguing, storing, and accessing them.

Pre-superassociation, the instrumental analog to the arts and the ideal analog to politics, is pure, reflexive social science, psychology, and criticism, seeking to understand the human rationally and self-consciously. The purview of the human sciences is society's rational self-understanding in all its ramified aspects and for its own sake.[9]

To the extent to which the human sciences address the consequences of action, their concern with them remains detached from any application. When scholars report abstruse theoretical distinctions or minor archeological findings, the real mode may nearly disappear. However, if they argue in a book or on television that there is much or little poverty in America, they simultaneously make representations about reality, enter a real political contest, and participate in collective action leading toward the determination of social and economic forms. Depending upon the relative balance of pure analysis and political import, either the ideal or real may dominate. Across the line in a real direction from human science lie politics, ideology, and policy research. When scholarly attention is directed to the distant past, it tends to be particularly ideal dominant, but even then today's issues may intrude with political implications for us of ancient structures driving analysis.

Reading a presidential biography is ordinarily an almost entirely ideal-dominant activity made up of autonomous perception and thought remote from action. However, if a sitting president reads it, he does so in a different mode, attentive to every clue as to how what he learns from the reading may be applied. Reading an archived transcript of a meeting held by the earlier president is again ordinarily ideal-dominant. A child's watching of the same meeting while standing to the side, however, may be fairly real dominant with salient consequences, in that for him it may be the thrill and story of a lifetime still to be repeated many decades later.

Finally, there are the pre-SSC in which higher aestheticism reflects upon and poetically represents first-level reflexivity, and the corresponding pre-SSA in which higher political and social thought reflects rationally upon that elementary reflexivity. The first is a more sophisticated, doubly reflexive art that is self-conscious about the phenomena of first-level reflexivity, including over the range of ordinary reflexive art. The second is doubly reflexive study of reflexive politics, consensus, art, and human science, namely political theory, social constructionist sociology, literary theory, and so forth. In the realm of the ideal, as of the real, any sector, personal or collective, may be moral or amoral, as will be clarified in Chapter 11.

****

Grasping the dimension of the ideal and real is vital to all who would understand the human experience. For the West, ancient Greece had a relatively high overall degree of idealism. Today we have an extremely low degree. Again for the West, twelfth-century France was relatively idealist overall, while seventeenth-century Holland was relatively realist. Among world religions, the Asian religions have been very idealist and the Middle Eastern religions generally realist; although, among the latter, Judaism and Islam have been relatively realist and Christianity relatively idealist. Among traditional Asian civilizations, the Indians were relatively idealist, the Chinese relatively realist. In the industrial era American universities were fairly idealist; in the postmodernist period they have been considerably less so. In my sense, Saint Francis was relatively idealist, Martin Luther relatively realist. Hegel was relatively idealist, Marx realist, Woodrow Wilson relatively idealist, Richard Nixon realist. Professors tend to be idealist, industrialists realist, artists idealist, attorneys realist. None of these differences can be understood without the dimension of the ideal and real.

In the world of the human the ideal and real, like emotionality and rationality, are interwoven to silken fineness, as Austin and Searle explore at length for the case of speech acts. Elements of both are always present in what the human does. All action, whether ideal or real, necessarily exercises some power and carries some influence. Even the most abstract art and theory were created in action and bear consequences. If consequences are subordinate in the ideal world, they are not necessarily less extensive there than in the real one. Sometimes the consequences may be even greater in the ideal—for in the twentieth century we learned well the truth of the adage, "ideas have real consequences"—although frequently they are vanishingly small.

In spite of their interdependence, few who specialize in either the ideal or real are also adept at and sympathetic to the other, and misunderstanding and friction between the ideal and real are frequent. Witness for example the difficulties of church and state relations in many societies, the prevalence of town and gown conflict over the centuries, or the severe alienation of Western artists and intellectuals during the modernist period.

Each sector within our three-dimensional existential space is the site of a potential institution, each with its distinct perspective and needs. The institutions of persons and collectivities build up in the locations formed by the intersection of the first three dimensions of the human. Thus the standard sociological definition of a social institution as "a distinctive complex of social actions" (Berger 1963, 87). The collective cultural and social institutions and ideal and real ones of the psyche are analogous. Community or constitutional polity, popular culture or human science, ego or superid, institutions are the clusters of distinctive patterns of perceiving, thinking, feeling, acting, and being that characterize the fundamental existential locations of the human. Before sufficient action and experience occur at such a site for settled structure to have arisen, institutionalization has not yet occurred there. We easily and naturally reify these existential regions, but they are defined by nothing more than the coordinates of the existential space within which they are suspended.

Grounding and depicting the cultural and social institutions is very useful to the human sciences. One way or another almost all disciplinary and interdisciplinary work in these sciences depends upon it. There is no more coherent way of mapping the contours of the human and getting around conceptually in existential space than with these first three dimensions. The distinction between the ideal and real modes is an essential one. There remains, however, one additional basic dimension of the human.

Notes

1. Speech acts theory (see Austin, *Doing Things with Words;* Searle, *Speech Acts* and *Expression and Meaning*) derives from Wittgenstein's linguistic turn and resuscitation of the practical and the real in philosophy. In broad strokes, the crux of speech acts theory is the notion that we do different things with words. Austin and Searle mean in general terms by the "locutionary" (with which I associate the ideal) the referential use of language; they mean by the illocutionary (with which I associate the real) the effectual use of language. (Austin and Searle differ on the details of their distinction [see Searle, Austin on Locutionary and Illocutionary Acts].) Austin and Searle note that the distinction manifests itself in a certain *directionality:* in the locutionary case the world influences words, so to speak, and in the illocutionary case words influence the world. For example, if ornithology students sit in a meadow and record what bird species they observe, that is descriptive and locutionary. If an authorized minister says at a wedding to the appropriate couple standing before him at the appropriate time, "I pronounce you husband and wife," that doesn't describe what is there but makes it so. Austin and Searle have essentially applied an old distinction to language and partially anchored it ontologically. Their distinction has been carefully probed and widely used by philosophers. When broadened to all that pertains to the human, Aristotle and Austin and Searle's distinction is more aptly described as that between the ideal and real, making use of the stable and familiar meaning in everyday senses of the ideal and real.

2. Representations, once constructed, are either held *off-line* and in storage at the ideal or real level, or placed *on-line.* In the latter case they are brought into the accepted plan and placed in the train of routines, facts, and other ideal possessions ready-at-hand as tools and treasures to be utilized in perception, thought, and action. When on-line, we count on using them as needed, taking them to be true, reliable, or at least in working order. For representations to be put on-line is for them to be taken-for-granted. When action utilizing representations fails or is disappointing on their account, our reaction is always at least momentary bewilderment. We must stop what we were doing, move up to the ideal and question and revise putative facts, assumptions, theories, routines, images, and stories before resuming real action. This process is comparable to what happens

when equipment upon which we were relying breaks down (cf. Wittgenstein 1969, e.g., para. 355). Stopping to perceive or think is the opposite of using representations. However, one doesn't always have to cease what he is doing; he may just go into automatic pilot, running lower maintenance routines while solving the ideal problem with a portion of his attention.

3. Not only does Austin and Searle's "directionality" still hold for the ideal and real as it does in speech acts theory, but here it is no longer ad hoc—for the opposition between perception and thought on the one hand and action on the other yields the directionality associated with the ideal and real.

4. In Geertz's (1973, 89) version, for example, culture is "an historically transmitted pattern of meanings embodied in symbols, a system of inherited conceptions expressed in symbolic forms by means of which men communicate, perpetuate and develop their knowledge about and attitudes toward life."

5. Tylor's (1958, 1) omnibus definition as the "complex whole which includes knowledge, belief, art, morals, law, custom, and any other capabilities and habits acquired by man as a member of society," however, is extremely incoherent, throwing together disparate, vague, and incomplete categories, blurring the ideal and real modes. The late eighteenth-century German word imported the original Latin sense of cultivation. Tylor then borrowed a newer and more democratic sense that had soon evolved, from the German ethnographer Klemm (Kroeber and Kluckhohn 1963, 14, 32, 44–46, 67).

6. When we reduce the contemporary anthropological definition of culture as society's heritable mental possessions to its basic constituents, we arrive at a definition of the cultural as that which is of, pertaining to, or associated with representation per se, and particularly the representations possessed by a society. If the sociological understanding of culture is broadened and pushed to its foundations, one comes to the same definition. In light of this, let us call the general approach, which includes the prevailing anthropological and sociological definitions and the fundamental one to which they both point, the representational view of the cultural. Remarkably, the representational conceptualization articulates with a different longstanding sense of the ideal than the one I predominantly use. In this construal the ideal is that which is concerned with representation in and of itself. The representational sense of the ideal is often contrasted with a corresponding sense of the real as that which exists as a thing, or, in effect, everything other than representation, and particularly that which is represented. In this *reductio* of the representational approach, the ideal or cultural would be that in which representation itself was relatively salient, the real or social by implication that in which the substantive or represented was relatively salient.

Where my conceptualization focuses on the human proper and particularly its ideal and real modes, the representational approach focuses on representational possessions. The two approaches and their respective senses of the word culture are therefore ultimately complementary. It is of value for human scientists to study the manifestations of the ideal and the real in the human itself as well as in its representations and other possessions, although it is important that the two not be confused. Nevertheless, the more central concern of the human sciences must be the core dimension that divides modes of the human—with "man" as the term was traditionally used in anthropology—not with possessions. My concept of culture redirects our focus to the human.

7.   An ideal type—using a different sense of the word ideal—is one pole of a dichotomized opposition, particularly of a fundamental one, employed for clarifying theoretical relationships.
8.   See Chapter 17 for further detail.
9.   See Chapter 16 for further detail.

Bibliography

Aristotle. 1941. *Metaphysics*. In *The Basic Writings of Aristotle*, ed. R. McKeon. New York: Random House.

———. 1953. *Ethics*. Harmondsworth, Middlesex: Penguin.

Arnold, M. 1994. *Culture and Anarchy*. New Haven, CN: Yale University Press.

Austin, J. 1975. *How to Do Things with Words*. Cambridge, MA: Harvard University Press.

Berger, P. 1963. *Invitation to Sociology: A Humanistic Perspective*. Garden City, NJ: Anchor Books.

Geertz, C. 1973. *The Interpretation of Cultures*. New York: Basic Books.

Jameson, F. 1991. *Postmodernism: Or the Cultural Logic of Late Capitalism*. Durham, NC: Duke University Press.

Kroeber, A. and C. Kluckhohn. 1963. *Culture: A Critical Review of Concepts and Definitions*. New York: Vintage Books.

Levi-Strauss, C. 1963. *Totemism*. Boston: Beacon Press.

Polanyi, M. 1966. *The Tacit Dimension*. New York: Doubleday.

Schumpeter, J. 1950. *Capitalism, Socialism and Democracy*. 3rd ed. New York: Harper and Row.

Searle, J. 1968. "Austin on Locutionary and Illocutionary Acts." *Philosophical Review* 57.

———. 1969. *Speech Acts: An Essay in the Philosophy of Language*. Cambridge: Cambridge University Press.

———. 1979. *Expression and Meaning*. Cambridge: Cambridge University Press.

Tylor, E. 1958. *The Origins of Culture*. New York: Harper and Row.

Wittgenstein, L. 1969. *On Certainty*. Oxford: Blackwell.

6. *Individualism and Collectivism*

The Distinction

The fourth basic dimension of the human is individualism versus collectivism, which is to say, orientation toward the personal and orientation toward the collective respectively. In both persons and collectivities, individualist forms are those oriented to personal independence and autonomy while collectivist forms are those oriented to dependence and heteronomy. The dimension of individualism versus collectivism does not pertain to persons or collectivities per se but to the predominant influence of one or the other on the forms of both. In the one the personal is dominant; in the other the collective is dominant. However, just as the consummatory never entirely disappears, even in very instrumentally oriented human forms, so individualism never entirely disappears, even in what is very collectivist, and conversely.

To say that we sometimes perceive, think, act, and desire autonomously and sometimes heteronomously means that we sometimes do so as *individuals* and sometimes as *members*. When in the individualist mode, we are alert to more aspects of what we are doing personally. When in the collectivist mode, we cede attention to others about many things, restricting our concern. Accordingly, when we perceive in the individualist mode, we notice more aspects of the world around us. When we perceive in the collectivist mode, we take for granted much that others perceive. When we think in the individualist mode, we think for ourselves. When we think in the collectivist mode, we take for granted much that others think. When we act in the individualist mode, we do so as individuals. When we act in the collectivist mode, we do so as members. When we want in the individualist mode, we are oriented to our own aims and needs. When we do so in the collectivist mode, we are oriented to the aims and needs of others.

While people all have some capacity to perceive, think, and act on their own and as parts of collectivities, they tend to lean naturally to the individualist or collectivist mode as a fundamental trait of character and thus may ordinarily be said to be either *individuals* or *members*. The individual is characteristically self-oriented. Marking herself off relatively distinctly and holding back from those around her, the individual needs autonomy and privacy and tends to be more comfortable on her own. The individual tends to be more resourceful and effective on her own than in a group and is self-motivated. The member is characteristically otheroriented. The member tends to merge existentially with others, thinking of herself as part of a group. She needs heteronomy, has little need of privacy, and tends to be more comfortable around others. The member tends to be more resourceful and effective in a group than on her own and is group motivated.[1]

Markets are the collective forms adapted to individuals, hierarchies the collective forms adapted to members.[2] Markets are collectivities that allow or facilitate voluntary action by persons or other collectivities. The New York Stock Exchange and Chicago Board of Trade are markets, but the definition is broader than that. The American political system is also a market. In it political organizations, activists, and diverse voters compete to make collective decisions within a framework. In the realm of community, singles dating scenes may be considered to be markets, as may friendships in a schoolyard playground. The free exchange of ideas in the academic world is widely and aptly viewed as a market. In markets such things as material goods, power, friendship, ideas, and aesthetics are exchanged in free competition subject to the laws of supply and demand. Markets are inherently competitive, with problem solving undertaken from below. Market-like organizations give relatively minimal direction to persons and collectivities under their control. Those subject to them act within broad guidelines, relying substantially on their own resourcefulness.

Hierarchies are collectivities within which action by persons or collectivities is coordinated by command. Hierarchies operate on orders, with problem solving monopolized and undertaken from above. They wield more intrusive and thoroughgoing control over their members. The economy of North Korea is hierarchical and monopolized. Collective decisionmaking was hierarchical in the France of Louis XIV, as it is today in the Roman Catholic Church. Autocracy is a political hierarchy. In most foraging and horticultural village societies marriage was arranged hierarchically. Older or more powerful relatives or clan members typically determined matches, often according to elaborate rules. When contemporary families forbid or strictly regulate media access by their children, select the books to which they are exposed, or place them in private schools, they are creating small-scale, partial cultural hierarchies within a larger cultural market.

Markets are essentially minimally structured organizational voids or holes, to use Burt's (1992) expression, as members might be considered personal voids or holes. Hierarchies are fully *there,* but markets are not; individuals are fully *there,* but members are not. The more room collectivities leave to the discretion of subsidiary collectivities and persons, the more marketlike they are. The more they regulate subsidiary collectivities and persons, the more hierarchical they are. Hierarchy may be seen as the internalization of what was once external. Thus, Coase (1988, 339) says of business, "[a] firm becomes larger as additional transactions (which could be exchange transactions coordinated through the price mechanism) are organized by the entrepreneur and becomes smaller as he abandons the organization of such transactions." The same could be said of political, communal, and cultural entities for the sorts of transactions in which they engage. Their degree of individualism versus collectivism deeply marks and has profound implications for both persons and collectivities.

This said, the simple dichotomization of individualism and collectivism can be misleading, for the ideal types cannot do full justice to the richness of this compound dimension's forms. There is actually a continuum with many gradations between individuals and members and between markets and hierarchies. Moreover, for collectivities the in-betweens here are comparatively stable, with a more clear-cut individualism or collectivism tending to emerge only in the long run. We should also remember that the collective actually manifests a vast range of overarching layers of collectivities within collectivities. Sometimes the concern is not with a simple opposition between the personal and collective but with what multiple levels are salient—with where the lights are on and the influence is strong up and down the array from the person to the highest level of collectivity.

Individualist and Collectivist Sectors

The individualism-collectivism dimension again crosscuts each of the other fundamental dimensions of the human. Each institution of the personality or collectivity laid out in the preceding chapters has individualist and collectivist modes, although these are now subinstitutional.

When it is helpful to distinguish them, the id may therefore be broken into an individualist id and a collectivist or social id. The individualist id either seeks private pleasures such as those from food, alcohol, and drugs, or it seeks pleasures that inherently involve others but does so in a self-centered way. The collectivist or social id, the more socially oriented side of the id, seeks enjoyment in the company of others and engages in joint activities in a more other-oriented manner. Sexual activity may be carried on in either the individualist or collectivist id. Aggression too may be relatively individualist or collectivist, according to whether the interference or affront is to the person or collectivity and whether the aggression is carried out solitarily or with the participation of others. The id-dominant individual is the slave of his personal desires. The id-dominant member, such as the traditional agrarian peasant, is deeply embedded in the group, cares about its opinions, and is needful of its acceptance.[3] The individualist ego tends to perceive, think, and act instrumentally on its own, the collectivist ego to perceive, think, and act instrumentally as a member of a team. Those with strong individualist egos are cognitively and emotionally independent of others in their instrumental efforts, where those with strong collectivist or social egos are relatively dependent upon others in them. The individualist superid pursues its independent style of life, and the collectivist superid follows the prevailing one. The individualist superid's self-image and style of life also focus on itself as apart from others; those of the collectivist superid focus more on the person as a piece of a larger mosaic. The individualist superego goes by its own policies and rules where the collectivist superego adheres to the established policies and rules of the group. The content of the superego's policies and rules will also tend to focus on the self as an individual or member according to whether it is an individual or social superego.[4]

In the person's cultural level, individualist and collectivist sectors of each institution are again found. The individualist pre-id leans to such solitary activities as reading popular novels or watching videos. The collectivist pre-id prefers such communal entertainments as traditional village storytelling or watching sports events with friends. The individualist pre-ego is exemplified by the lone chemist isolated in his early-modern laboratory or Darwin during his solo outings on the Galapagos Islands. The collectivist pre-ego is exemplified by today's team participants in big science. The individualist pre-superid is prominent in the solitary artist in the studio, the collectivist pre-superid in dancers in a ballet school, spending most of their waking hours together and highly sensitive to each other's aesthetic forms. The individualist pre-superego is again a lone one where the person independently comes to a detached, rational understanding of himself and his situation. In the collectivist pre-superego he reaches these understandings together with or adapts them from others.

As it does for persons, individualism versus collectivism also divides each collective institution into market and command sectors. Complex societies have sectors of each major institution that are relatively individualist and others that are relatively collectivist. Accordingly, individualist community is spare and respectful of personal privacy, as is contemporary British society; collectivist, hierarchical community is intrusive and all consuming, as was that of traditional China. Individualist association is the lean and minimalist capitalist economy, collectivist association the weighty and maximalist command economy. Individualist supercommunity or consensus allows informal standards to rise from the grass roots; collectivist supercommunity lays down blankets of informal standards from above. Individualist superassociation is democracy, a free market in political influence. Collectivist superassociation is autocracy or, more loosely, authoritarianism, a monopoly in political influence.

In the collectivity's cultural sphere, individualist pre-community is an open market in popular culture, such as exists in the developed and free countries of the world—any entertainment is available, most but not all at a price. Collectivist pre-community is a relatively closed and controlled hierarchy in popular culture as existed in traditional villages, Maoist China, or early-revolutionary Iran. Individualist pre-association is an open market in scientific inquiry, i.e., modern science, which slowly opened up in early-modern Europe. Collectivist science is hierarchical science, as under the medieval church or in the Stalinist U.S.S.R. Like large corporations in the capitalist economy, big science in the West today represents hierarchical lumps within a larger free market. Individualist pre-supercommunity is a free market in the arts. Collectivist pre-supercommunity is the arts under hierarchical control, as was typical in traditional societies. Individualist and collectivist pre-superassociation is respectively an open and a closed market in human science.

The Dynamics of the Human

Unlike any other dimension of the human, individualism versus collectivism plays a unique dynamic role in our personal and collective lives—for it constitutes the gas-pedal governing rates of development and therefore of progress in both psyche and society. Development entails working and successful problem solving that may be conducted more or less rapidly.

Rates of working and development are determined by the extent to which persons and collectivities are exposed to or protected from competition of all kinds, which is to say, by the balance between individualism and collectivism. The more a person or collectivity is exposed to markets of any kind, the more individualist it becomes, and the more sheltered from them, the more collectivist. This occurs because the more open a person or collectivity, the more it must rely on its own resources; and the more closed, the more it must depend upon others. In any institution collectivism means personal and collective comfort, security, and lower motivation, while individualism means personal discomfort, insecurity, and higher motivation. Markets of all kinds both permit and require more of the persons and collectivities subject to them. Competitive pressures accentuate the positive consequences of vigilance and striving, as well as the negative consequences of relaxing. The various markets open business, politics, community, consensus, science, entertainment, art, or religion to competitive forces. This principle has profound implications for the course of our lives and for the shape of history.

The human is forever pulled in two contrary ways, toward exposure and risktaking and toward shelter and security. At the macrolevel, this yields a Schumpeterian (1934) view of all markets, economic or any other, in which they are seen to bring surging creativity but also painful destruction. Otto Rank (1936, ch. 10) captures the personal analog poetically as the struggle between the fear of dying and the fear of living. We all know the fear of stultification in careers, relationships, or cultural development, and we also know the fear of getting in over our heads. The response is an inner Rankian openness or closedness of the person, boldly approaching or timidly shying away from challenge and development. The more one exposes himself to educational markets far from home, to diverse social groups or vigorous economic competition, the more rapidly he develops himself, but also the more risk he runs of dramatic reversal. In persons and societies the outcome of the struggle between the yearning for challenge and that for security across the sectors of the human substantially affects rates of development and movement up the hierarchy of needs.

The participants in all markets tend to vacillate between dominant emotions of confidence and fear, sometimes with enough regularity to speak approximately of cycles. As significant growth takes place, it tends to be accompanied in time by imbalances in the presence of which, at a certain point, fear is sparked, bringing retrenchment and contraction. The expansionary phase is profligate and the contractionary one careful with resources. In expansion the human is dominated by confidence that its important needs are going to be met. In contraction it is dominated by fear that one or more important needs are not going to be met. In an atmosphere of insecurity, pessimism, consolidation, and focus, new resources are directed to the endangered area, along with some previously invested in other activities. In time the retrenchment does its work, balance is restored, fear dissolves, and expansion resumes. The business cycle is but the economic manifestation of a universal human phenomenon.

Reflecting the operational centrality of the individualism-collectivism dimension, a great deal of human action is about determining the degree of openness or closedness in the institutions of persons and collectivities. Many choices in all institutions come down to degrees of liberalism and conservatism. Where possible, I use the terms as Milton Friedman does, in their traditional European senses, namely as leanings toward the markets and against hierarchies, or the reverse—across all sectors of the human. In collectivities and in persons degrees of liberalism and conservatism regulate the rates of working. For almost any issue, a liberal position is a stance for more open markets, a conservative position one for more closed markets. Liberals want to accelerate working, conservatives to decelerate it. Liberals want to encounter and work difference, conservatives to cling to the forms and solutions of the past. The many different senses of liberalism and conservatism are generated by the varying features of markets and hierarchies as one moves through the sectors of the human. People often take very different positions depending upon which type is under consideration.

The terms "liberalism" and "conservatism" are less familiar but equally applicable with respect to personal issues. In each personal institution some open themselves to what is around them, and others close themselves off. In the psyche ebullience and overconfidence during the expansionary phase lead eventually to imbalance and reversal. In the ensuing contractionary phase, scrambling to restore equilibrium may be accompanied by psychological depression.[5] All forms of growth and progress, whether in collectivities or persons, are functions of relationships to markets, and therefore of degrees of individualism versus collectivism.

Although it is the more common way, conservatism is only one way of departing from the working of markets and thereby from individualism. There is also radicalism with its efforts to leap out of the markets and into a secure stasis away from them. Radicalism's efforts to displace markets by boldly imposing new hierarchies and structures is the precise analog to conservatism's efforts to forestall markets by timidly clinging to old ones. Radical change is large and architectural, by design rather than from small, incremental acts. Indeed radicals are often in effect charismatic, preemptive conservatives; they too seek stasis, only one projected into the future. The new position, if realized, soon enough becomes the basis of future conservatives' obstructions of the markets. Liberals, on the other hand, stand for progressive neutrality by flexibly supporting free give and take between actors on all issues and accepting whatever outcome is so derived. Resisted intransigently by the one and pushed peremptorily by the other, upheaval is nevertheless the change equally wrought by conservatives and radicals. With their natural competitive problem solving, the change of liberals instead tends to be incremental.

As on the other dimensions, the phenomena of individualism and collectivism are not easily harmonized. Persons and collectivities that are predominantly one or the other tend to lack insight into and empathy with their opposites, a pattern all too apparent in contemporary American politics.

Paradoxically, all else equal (and it seldom is equal), collectivism is nevertheless finally more developed than individualism[6]—much as higher self-control is more developed than first-level self control. Being more oriented to higher collectivity constitutes development because, as it is able, the human works from individualism toward collectivism and from markets toward hierarchy. Despite the inner tug-of-war, the collective and secure are the human's natural home, toward which it works and to which it eventually returns. The long process of collectivization is always at least somewhat uneven, with some sectors further along than others, but as societies become better developed, subsidiary layers of collectivity are slowly worked into artic- ulation with higher ones and individuals slowly into members. Over time, orientation moves up the hierarchy of collectivity, facilitating cooperation over a progressively broader reach. Degrees of individualism and collectivism reflect where the human lies in this historical movement.

The human condition is such that we confront diverse internal and exter- nal impediments to the attainment of our goals. Our action indefatigably addresses these in a ceaseless working of problems and laying in of solutions reminiscent of a devoted horticulturalist's tending of his garden. Although reversals may occur, over time problems are solved, solutions become estab- lished, and progress is made. Governing the rate at which working occurs, the phenomena of individualism and collectivism are pivotal to a great deal of explanation in the human sciences. Scholars well know how vital the relative salience of markets and hierarchies across all sectors of the human is for the understanding of history. Whatever the institutional area, these phenomena describe central features of society and culture. Their microlevel manifesta- tions are equally central to the psyche.

Who *we* are turns out to be far from a simple matter. Only rarely are we discrete, isolated beings—hermit prospectors in the desert, tribes on lost Micronesian islands, or single embattled nations in utterly conflicted settings. In all but such exceptional cases, we are simultaneously our individual selves and ourselves as members of nuclear families, extended families, neighbor- hoods, businesses, cities, provinces, countries, regions, and the world. The needs of these overarching entities are our needs and ours are theirs as mem- ber persons and collectivities. The orientations across this great manifold are always central to our beings, and it is frequently very useful to reduce these to individualism and collectivism.

Notes

1. My distinction between individuals and members differs from Hegel's (see Hardimon 1994, 146ff.).
2. I arrive at this view of markets and hierarchies largely by combining the insights of Schumpeter (1934), Coase (1988), Williamson (1975), and Burt (1992) into the nature of markets and hierarchies with the tendency of Becker (1976) to apply economic analysis throughout the human sciences.
3. Freud in his radical individualism was oblivious to the collectivist id, seeing only the individualist id. Mead (1962) in his collectivism emphasized the collectivist id.
4. I leave it to the reader to distinguish the doubly reflexive forms.

5. While moderate experience of such cycles is common and relatively normal if unfortunate, bipolar disorder exhibits a genetically based propensity to severe personal cycles.

6. All else is seldom equal in this respect because for a more collectivist concrete structure to be further developed overall, it must lie in a suitable context. If the collectivism is forced, as it was in Stalin's industrial policy of 1928 that replaced Lenin's New Economic Program, it is more developed only in the narrow technical sense, not overall. England's Industrial Revolution, as superbly described by Landes in *The Unbound Prometheus*, was a far more natural affair. If it is to be truly more developed, collectivism must be worked toward naturally and not forced. However, this gets ahead of issues that will be discussed in subsequent chapters.

Bibliography

Becker, G. 1976. *The Economic Approach to Human Behavior.* Chicago: University of Chicago Press.

Burt, R. 1992. *Structural Holes.* Cambridge, MA: Harvard University Press.

Coase, R. 1988. "The Nature of the Firm." In *The Firm, the Market and the Law,* ed. R. Coase. Chicago: University of Chicago Press.

Hardimon, M. 1994. *Hegel's Social Philosophy: The Project of Reconciliation.* Cambridge: Cambridge University Press.

Landes, D. 1970. *The Unbound Prometheus: Technological Change and Industrial Development in Western Europe from 1750 to the Present.* Cambridge: Cambridge University Press.

Mead, G. 1962. *Mind, Self and Society.* Chicago: University of Chicago Press.

Rank, O. 1936. *Will Therapy.* New York: Alfred A. Knopf.

Schumpeter, J. 1934. *Theory of Economic Development.* London: Oxford University Press.

Williamson, O. 1975. *Markets and Hierarchies: Analysis and Antitrust Implications.* New York: Free Press.

7. Consciousness, Character, Space, and Time

The Flow of Consciousness

Consciousness is a vast, changing, kaleidoscopic gestalt of meaning framed by the dimensions of existence. A prolonged series of flashes of perception, thinking, feeling, and acting, consciousness arises in abstracting configurations from flows of representation and motivation in existential space. Consciousness in essence is nothing more than the huge symphonic form of the mental activity taking place across all of our dimensions at once. The human is what emerges when myriads of representations and motivations are arrayed through these dimensions.

Each personal or collective being brings its flickering, many-sided consciousness to the great assembly of all others as textured layers of overarching collectivity rise above it in a vast canvas of being. What consciousness comes down to in any given instant and person is a confined but extremely acute, rich, and agile attention. It can keep actively in mind only a very few things but can perform amazing feats with these while drawing passively upon inexhaustibly many more. Although attention tends to be carried on in any given instant primarily in a single sector, it may spill over into others, as in peripheral concern with the higher organization of its flow of activities or with after-hours diversion. In such cases attention is parceled.

A striking feature of consciousness is its darting in and out of perspectives at the blink of an eye. After a moment in one sector's task or enjoyment, the attention leaps to another and almost instantaneously begins operating there. We become our superid for a moment, then in a flash our pre-superego and our SSE. Consciousness tirelessly leaps from perspective to perspective and task to task. What we ultimately are is incessantly shimmering beings with kaleidoscopic perspectives. Our minds are like a basketball team in which a single, lightening-fast player simultaneously coaches herself and plays all positions—passing the ball and then leaping to another position a split second later to catch it. Although one person, we ceaselessly fly back and forth through our network of higher and lower sectors in practiced fluency.

Our motivations are not as electronically quick as our representations, but feeling flows pneumatically in and around whatever we represent and cathects it. Soon after we take a perspective we feel the accompanying chemistry, making our minds roving engines of desire as much as kaleidoscopes of perspective. Surges of distinctive energy accompany every angle from which we see.

In their flickering back and forth among perspectives collectivities are nearly as plastic as we. In the activities of a traditional Japanese clan, as it moved between concern with rice planting, propitiating the spirits, selecting spouses for young people, and caring for elderly widows, there were innumerable oscillations between rational and emotional elements, all in a predominantly consummatory context. In a very different setting, if an infantry platoon is told to march, it does so. If it is told to do crowd control under the military police, to perform staff work for the adjutant general, or to relax on a beach, it does so. If a corporation or university is pressed into service on national problems while carrying on its central missions, it too does so. Each such engagement brings different constellations of perception, thought, action, and motivation for the collectivity.

A collectivity or portion of one goes in and out of session just as does any sector of a person. The subtlest link to collectivity instantly activates it. Our connection with one collectivity or another is as nimble as our internal shimmering. A consultant switches from being part of one organization to part of another as rapidly as she clicks from one e-mail to the next. Collectivity comes fully alive as members lose themselves at work or among friends. A business firm adjourns as the doors close, and its members disarticulate, morphing themselves back into separate persons for a return commute, again to aggregate as family members upon reaching home—or sooner as thoughts or cell calls reach there. Or a team of auctioneers assembles for a few days in one part of the country to liquidate real estate developments, disbands, and then rejoins ten days later in another. We move from one being to another as quickly as we take up the concerns of one collectivity or another, which is as quickly as we pass from one perspective to another.

As the person becomes practiced, he performs this exquisite dance in and out of his own and collective perspectives as deftly as a great mime moves between personae. As he takes the point of view of his family at the breakfast table, thinking of collective tasks or enjoyments, he is not his individual self but part of the group. As he goes through the newspaper, he is alternately a citizen of his world, nation, region, city, or neighborhood while reacting to one article or another. As he thinks of his work while driving there, he is again a member of his company, division, department, or office faction when his perspective cuts from one to the other. In each of these perspectives, to the extent which he pools *intentionality* with the collectivity, he ceases to be his personal self. Only when he takes his own personal perspective as removed from all others, is he an individual—and for thoroughgoing members that may be hardly at all.

Arrays of personal and collective beings, each with its lambent consciousness and pulsing action, are interspersed within, around, over, and under each other. The life of the human courses on an immense scale—an ascending series of hills and mountains in a vast, golden landscape.

It is because in forming collectivities persons specialize and do together so many of the same things they previously had done by themselves that the same dimensions are there for collectivities as for persons. An internal conversation between parts, the person's inner structure is not so different from society's. We can speak with equal aptness of the society of mind and the mind of society.

Character and Social Structure

Even though they use them all, human beings seldom equally favor their sectors. Instead they have pronounced leanings toward one sector or another. Without orientation, the human's endless flight from sector to sector would leave it dizzy and bewildered. Finding a comfortable abode in existential space and residing there is the simplest way of managing the problem of orientation in existential space. Doing so is a natural way of being that was captured amusingly in 1976 by Saul Steinberg in the *New Yorker* map of the world as seen from New York City's Ninth Avenue. From his familiar existential home the person may move confidently through other perspectives without disorientation. Distinctive of my approach to the human is the way in which, working from the central oppositions of existential space, it accords a central role to dominance and subordinance of perspective.

Who we are is above all where we habitually reside in existential space. How experience is distributed among sectors of the human largely determines their relative prominence. As in the social world, so in the personal one: abilities are strengthened or weakened, inner arguments are made or not made, habitual slants are formed or not formed largely according to the predominant experience of everyday life. Those of our internal functions that are more dazzling or logically compelling in the inner dialogue come to the fore. Yet the sheer repetition of arguments, facts, lessons, or images deriving from prevailing experience most often carries the day and determines character or the structure of the personality.

A person's character is her enduring tendency to be in a particular existential place and perceive, think, and act accordingly. Character is a cast in existential space having a given slant that arises from its habitual perspective in the manifold of consciousness. To be right- or left-brain dominant, unreflexive or reflexive, ideal or real dominant, and individualist or collectivist is to dwell habitually in a particular existential location and find familiar horizons and regnant needs there. The perspective and needs of a dominant sector spill over to influence patterns in all other sectors. As Plato (1961, book 4) understood long ago, the most profound way of approaching social class is as the set of those bearing a certain character impressed on them by a common social location and experience.

Character is the decisive determinant of the forms of perception, thought, and action. "Character for man is destiny," as Heraclitus (fragment 119, in Hyland 1973, 170) says. Or as Schopenhauer (1969, 1:292) puts it, "every individual action must come about in accordance with the character. . . ." One's character is her existential address, without knowing which, most of what she perceives, thinks, feels, or does remains forever a mystery. The central differences between people lie in their characters or personalities.

Social structure in the related sense is then the character of collectivity, its relatively settled configurations on the dimensions of the human, and its enduring power relations between sectors.[1] Social structure reflects various degrees of the consummatory and instrumental, nonreflexive and reflexive, ideal and real, markets and hierarchies. As these nevertheless change, social structure changes. This understanding rectifies the remarkable absence hitherto, considering the concept's ubiquity and centrality, of consistent definitions of social structure in the human sciences (see Rubinstein, 1981, 49ff.).

Consideration of social structure places character in a fuller light, for to a large extent character is the product of social structure. Insofar as we wish to influence character, we may emphasize its voluntariness, but it is overwhelmingly the product of social experience. As collectivities take their forms, they slowly bring with them the fundamental beings of their members. Yet the converse is also true.

Existential Space and Time

Four basic dimensions along with one more we will consider make up existential space. All fundamental differences of form in the human—differences of perception, thought, motivation, and action—stem from differential location vis-à-vis the dimensions of the human, as, less directly, do such differences in power and satisfaction. Like all space and time, existential space and time possess "point-horizon" structures (see Merleau-Ponty 1962, 102). Things exist against a spatio-temporal background.

In the physical world far less-sophisticated dimensionalisms of space than Descartes' or Riemann's still allow crude or restricted popular conceptions of the physical world that bear some resemblance to the former. In the world of the human far less advanced dimensionalisms of existential space than this one also allow human phenomena to be conceived roughly and truncately in everyday life. However, these cannot be represented powerfully without at least tacit or partial dimensionalization along the lines I propose. All rational and nonrational means of representing existential space reduce to these dimensions to the extent which they comprehensively, coherently, and accurately represent the human (cf. Kant 1965, 68). Hence the utter centrality of these dimensions to the human sciences.

The regions of existential space and consciousness formed by the intersection of the first four dimensions represent the elementary kinds of being and doing of which we are capable. Each position in this space yields a personal or social location from which the world may be approached. The most basic of these locations form the institutions of society and the personality. Because our interconnectedness is such that every concrete manifestation of each basic dimension affects those on all other dimensions, to understand these dimensions and the human is above all to understand the perspectives accompanying experience in the distinct positions they describe. The development of perspectives in persons and collectivities frames and lies behind all other kinds of development. The essence of elementary personal and collective life is captured by this existential topography.[2] So central to inquiry are space and time that the physical sciences may be defined as the study of the distribution of matter-energy in physical space and time, and the human sciences as the study of the distribution of the human in existential space and time.

Existential time joins the dimensions of existential space to complete the framework of the human. The world of the human is superimposed upon and takes place within that of physical space and time. Because the human is itself ultimately a property of the material world, it cannot perceive, think, act, or exist outside the material world. Nevertheless, as we do to physical space, we have a most plastic relationship to physical time. The tempo of our action could be very different from what we know today—much faster or much slower. Our world could be speeded up if we were run on better hardware or slowed down if we communicated over light-years, but action could not take place outside of time because that would defy the laws of nature as we understand them. Physical time also radically impinges on us because the bodies in which we happen to be housed, given the states of physics and medicine, are so inexorably running down.[3] For what we are, however, there is no reason why we could not be beamed to another galaxy, deactivated for millions of years, and then resume a conversation as if no time had gone by. Yet this transit, storage, and conversation would all necessarily take time. Having a past, present, and future, the human traverses back and forth in what it does. Having motivation that inherently involves time, it is deeply embedded in physical time. We are fundamentally temporal and historical beings, yet our existential time is different from physical time as our existential space is different from physical space.

Existential time is the meaningful differentiation of time into stages and the interregna between them. Unlike physical time, human time is necessarily discontinuous, for character, though relatively enduring, does change—in development even if at no other time. The time of one's life or society assumes a series of epochs arrayed between a coming into being and a ceasing to be. With the human long periods of relative groundedness are punctuated by brief times of being at sea. A tilting on certain dimensions of the human dislodges much that had been firmly attached, often producing disorienting movement on other dimensions as well. At points in our lives and societies in which we are adrift, the framework is shifting—we have broken free of one gestalt, another has not yet formed, and all seems chaos. When the dominant character of persons and societies changes, human nature itself seems to change (though it doesn't), for in each sector of existential space who we are appears to be radically different. Existential time is therefore another compound dimension. However, actually specifying where the breaks in historical and personal development lie is a more proximately empirical matter that must emerge from research.[4]

We may agree with Kant (1965, 79) that time is "something real," yet hold that it is not so much "the condition of all our experiences" as the sequential field within which events empirically occur, including our own. How the human is distributed in existential space and time is the central question about it and the key to all other questions about it.

****

We make a large leap toward clarity with respect to the human when we soundly conceptualize its basic dimensionality. Descartes' three-dimensional framework allowed the physical world to come into focus with a sharpness that greatly facilitated the progress of the natural sciences. I sketch here the very different dimensionality of the existential that is no less essential to grasping the world of the human. As one cannot talk broadly and intelligibly about politics without the concepts of liberalism and conservatism or their equivalents, she cannot talk broadly and intelligibly about the human without all of the basic dimensions of the human or their equivalents.

To Hegel, a philosophical system achieves its systematicity primarily by being deduced from the nature of logic. His stronger standards of systematicity are not attainable given what we know today about logic. This work instead aims at a weaker systematicity achieved primarily through clearly defining and arranging the empirically derived dimensions of the human as the strongest attainable.[5] Hegel noted each of the basic oppositions that I treat in this work, though in some cases he did not reduce their different manifestations to core dualisms,[6] but before the rise of the modern human sciences he could not have refined these into dimensions and crisscrossed them to obtain the determinate sectors of the human. Taking these steps constitutes a progressive problemshift within the Hegelian tradition. But alas! The sectors of the human ordinarily become stamped on character in a way that poses major problems that must now be explored.

Notes

1. One should not conflate this sense of the word "social" (with its corresponding sense of social structure) as opposed to the psychological, with those treated in Chapter 5, which opposed it to the cultural. There is no need to banish different senses of the word social, only to be mindful of which is in play.

2. My approach to space remains in the neighborhood of Kant's (71) when he says of physical space that it is "nothing but the form of all appearances of outer sense," but the dimensions of the human that frame existential space are not synthetic a priori conditions of thinking about the human, as Kant might put it—for there are no synthetic a prioris. These dimensions form the empirical range of the human's most fundamental variations. It is not that we cannot otherwise think of the human but that the human would not otherwise be what it is.

3. This may appear Cartesian or even Platonic, but it is not. See "bodies" in the Appendix/Glossary as well as in fn. 9 there.

4. See Chapter 15.

5. This way of looking at the relationship between the two systems was suggested in conversation by Michael Forster.

6. See Forster (1998, 23–60) regarding the basic oppositions or dualisms with which Hegel worked.

Bibliography

Forster, M. 1998. *Hegel's Idea of a Phenomenology of Spirit.* Chicago: University of Chicago Press.

Hyland, D. 1973. *The Origins of Philosophy.* New York: G.P. Putnam's Sons.

Kant, I. 1965. *Critique of Pure Reason.* New York: St. Martin's Press.

Merleau-Ponty. M. 1962, *Phenomenology of Perception.* London: Routledge & Kegan Paul.

Plato. 1961. *Republic.* In *The Collected Dialogues of Plato,* ed. E. Hamilton and H. Cairns. Princeton, NJ: Princeton University Press.

Rubinstein, D. 1981. *Marx and Wittgenstein: Social Praxis and Social Explanation.* London: Routledge & Kegan Paul.

Schopenhauer, A. 1969. *The World as Will and Representation.* Vol. 1. New York: Dover Publications.

8. *The Impasse of Sectoralism*

In examining the basic dimensions of the human, I have noted that on each dimension people have difficulty balancing between the various polar or nodal positions and tend to favor one or another of them. For this reason, even though they use them all, people's perspectives tend to settle habitually into that of a single sector from which life is predominantly experienced by their social class or group. Perceiving, thinking, acting, and being predominantly from one particular locus or another, people ordinarily take for granted that their perspective is eternally true and what others would also see if they but opened their eyes. Yet, by itself, each perspective is misleading, since it views the world from only one angle integral to the human.

Sectoralism is the mode and way of life in which personal and collective life is organized around polar or nodal positions on the basic dimensions of the human. Dwelling in a secure home in a single dominant location enables the sectoral to restrict their horizons, fix their assumptions, have their necessary stability, and view the world in a simple way. We have long understood ideological extremism of the left or right normally to be an arbitrary and even desperate imposition of simplicity upon what is complex, but all sectoralism obtains its existential moorings in similarly one-sided and problematic ways.

Lambent though it be, sectoralism knows only peremptory fiat from its characteristic position, leaving no way of harmonizing between sectors. Under pure sectoralism every other perspective seems out of kilter and radically alien. Under sectoralism there is no way of properly respecting the needs of other, subordinate sectors of the psyche or society. Inherently provincial, pure sectoralism can never convincingly maintain that any representation is more valid than any other or that any need is more pressing than any other.

For a while, the sectoralist has its run with a comfortable mix of polar positions and builds upon its one-sided foundations. Although it may remain stable for periods, from time to time the many-dimensional matrix is rotated. This rotation occurs as tension grows from the mismatch between character and circumstances, for while the direct and indirect experience by which persons and collectivities learn is ordinarily mediated through their enduring characters, imbalances inevitably accrue as other sides of life and society are neglected or slighted. Eventually the accumulated weight of experience tips the balance and the existential edifice topples, setting off a many-dimensional shift realigning the horizons. When sectoralists are forced by circumstances to change fundamentally, they lurch violently into another position as extreme as the last. The sectoral recoils from its most recent folly only to embark upon the next.

In all sectors cyclical phenomena can be significant. These are associated with markets, although markets need not be dominant for them to occur. In slow motion the sectoral careens in one direction then the next. The superego is in charge, then the id. Morals are enforced, then not. Markets are out, then in. Immigrants are in, then out. The ideal is in, then out. Panic reigns, then complacency. Over the long run, the performance of pure sectoralists tends to be as erratic as their orientation. On its own, the sectoral is locked into particular twists of the n-dimensional Rubik's Cube, from which crisis alone can knock it into a new configuration. Unable to integrate different times, sectoralism is unable to avoid destructive oscillations, and we yearn for sustained growth.

Even more worrisomely, the sectoral finds itself in interminable conflict with others whose coordinates are different. Pure sectoralism, clutching its rigid, many-dimensional position, uncomprehendingly inveighs and batters against others in different positions. When able, the sectoral sees no reason not to tyrannize over others or itself. Human discord is deeply rooted in sectoralism.

A central determinant of conflict is the negational perception of essential difference, the perception of others or what is associated with them as disorientingly different, as strange or foreign. The human's first encounter with the other is a difficult conflictual one. As any sector can provide a place of residence, any can yield the perception of essential difference—of mutual exclusiveness of community or association, norms or laws, entertainment or theory, religion or philosophy.[1]

The perception of essential difference of identity is a radical discontinuity in community across which rejection occurs. The drawing of emotional lines between human beings is a key source of conflict insofar as the conflict is between communities or id dominance reigns. To the extent which people are consummatory and communityoriented, the perception of essential difference tends to generate animus and expressive aggression, and particularly when there is interference with goals. Such perception of not at all belonging together in effect denies or shuts its eyes to the larger community of which both are parts. Much of what is commonly referred to as prejudice may be described as emotional negation hovering about the sense of radical otherness. In a similar way the specious perception of inner difference as strange or foreign lies at the root of a great deal of psychological conflict.

The perception of essential difference of interest is a radical discontinuity in association across which rejection occurs. This rational analog to the emotional perception of essential group difference is the drawing of instrumental lines between people in the belief that the relationship with the other is a zero- or negative-sum one. To the extent which people are instrumentally oriented, perception of essential difference of interest tends to draw blame, particularly under conditions of frustration. The perception of mutual exclusiveness of interests may accompany anything from competition between states for scarce territory to competition between ethnic groups for employment. Wherever markets exist, irrespective of their nature, competition exists along with some degree of actual difference of interests, thus providing the potential for blame. On behalf of their product, policy, people, or ideology, different parties favor different possible outcomes for economic, political, communal, or cultural choices. Wherever resources are held by another, it is possible to conclude that an essential conflict of interest is present. Such a perception is in effect to draw a line between rational actors or collectivities and contravenes or ignores larger association in which both might share and benefit. In the analogous inner process the psyche may also rationally reject as fundamentally inimical to its interests some other aspect of itself, again with psychological conflict the result.

But differences of all kinds, not only those of community or association, may seem essential to and provoke conflict among sectoralists. Conflict is always about perceived mutual exclusiveness, nonreflexive or reflexive, cultural or social, individual or collective, as well as emotional or rational. How serious and numerous the matters over which the parties perceive essential difference contributes importantly to the likelihood and intensity of conflict between them.

It is not just the apparent essential difference that matters but also how close the difference that matters. All else equal, the greater the proximity, the greater the importance of difference. Difference that may be unbearable between husband and wife may be perfectly acceptable between colleagues. Separation buffers difference. Hence, all else equal, being thrown together by improved transportation and communication or urbanization increases contact and interdependence, spurring conflicts of identity, interest, rules, styles, religion, etc. Different island perspectives, when juxtaposed, can seem to represent only negations of each other. At the same time, proximity increases the ability of differing parties to inflict damage upon each other. When it occurs, conflict itself then tends to aggravate the enmities and misunderstandings, leaving a more profound sense of difference.

Pure sectoralism in its one-sidedness leads directly to general conflict within and between the society and psyche. Each sectoral provenience with its particular experience and setting generates its presumptive difference and nettled estrangement from every other. In a world of pure sectoralism every social class and ethnic group detests every other, eras of history denounce other eras, generations forsake other generations, those in one life stage condemn those in other life stages, the ideal disowns the real, the superego spurns the id, and the superid affronts the ego. Each remains ensconced in its singular fortification in the ontological latticework of the human. The sectoral refuses the other in its many forms—all in the name of the temporary metaphysical bearings to which it clings in the paralytic fear of an existential dizziness that it nonetheless cannot avoid. For in any event the flimsy existential bungalow that the sectoral calls home is going to be abandoned periodically as its denizens again frantically flee one abode for another. Nor is the peaceful sectoral working that is the great pride of the sectoral any solace, for it will soon be upended by conflict in a purely sectoral world. Unable to rise above different existential locations, sectoralism cannot avoid destructive conflict in a complex world.

All forms of inhumanity trace back to sectoralism. The human propensity to one-sidedness has produced an enormous share of the great catastrophes of history: grotesque persecutions, devastating wars, and the extinctions of entire societies. In and of itself, the sectoralist is amoral, clueless, and absurd and strews chaos and ruin in all directions—such are the perils of sectoralism. For all its dazzling precocity, pure sectoralism is a dead end.

* * * *

Most people and societies in important ways come close enough to the ideal type of sectoralism for the concept to shed profound light on their situations, yet many are able to find mixed or moderate positions that avoid the worst problems of sectoralism, and some do far better than that. People and collectivities often do manage to dampen destructive cycles and overcome conflict. What makes this possible, however, is outside the scope of the basic dimensions of the human. With the latter, we understand the range of the fundamental human perspectives, but we cannot yet understand how these may be reconciled to the extent they often are. Given such diverse perspectives and leanings, how does the psyche or society ever overcome difference to act in a harmonious or balanced way? We require existential anchoring, but there are such severe drawbacks to obtaining it via sectoralist arbitrariness that some other means of finding our bearings must be found, especially in a dynamic and pluralist world. The topic of Part II is the ontology of the universal by which the human rises above and overcomes the sectoral, providing humankind a much preferable means of orienting itself.

Note

1. My notion of essential difference is equivalent to Hegel's notion of the "ultimately other" (see Hardimon 1994, 112ff.).

Bibliography

Hardimon, M. 1994. *Hegel's Social Philosophy: The Project of Reconciliation*. Cambridge: Cambridge University Press.

Part II. Universalism and the Complex Dimensions of the Human

9. The Rational Universal

The Dialectic

Development beyond sectoralism means movement toward perceiving, thinking, and acting not one-sidedly but with the whole. Doing so is something many people and collectivities actually achieve to varying degrees. Determinately grasping how this is possible requires a framework allowing one to conceptualize fundamental dimensions and a means of overcoming (*aufheben*) oppositions on them. The first is contained in Part I. The second, in my view, is best exemplified by the dialectic, the method and language of the whole developed by Heraclitus, Chuang Tzu, Hegel, and other philosophers over millennia. From what I have argued about sectoralism, as well as for reasons that will be presented below and in subsequent chapters, I take it to be self-evident that we not only want to use the dialectic to understand how persons and collectivities overcome sectoralism but to apply it in our own lives and societies.

The operating principle of dialectics, as I conceive it, is expressed by the rule that where one has a basic position, she may look for the opposite position negating it, and then rise above the two, overcoming their opposition. The central feature of dialectics is the overcoming or sublating of oppositions, particularly fundamental ones. This consists of a two-step process, first recognizing the different fundamental sides of the human and then reconciling them. The recognition entails self-conscious acknowledgment of the opposed positions. Being able to overcome oppositions requires not merely stepping out of the single perspectives in which people naturally reside—that comes as a matter of course—but learning to dwell in and consult other perspectives, taking their horizons as our own. When a single mind, like a particle in quantum mechanics, dwells simultaneously in two or more opposing positions, it arrives at a more complex position reconciling them, one that overcomes the particular in the universal. The dialectic goes beyond self-conscious respect for plural aspects of the human to their incorporation within a single, larger one harmonizing and making cohere what had previously been at odds. The outcome may often be described as a balance between polar or nodal perspectives. In this balance the person accepts a certain proportion between the two positions or perspectives and the lead by each according to circumstances. With the dialectic it is both/and rather than either/or.

All fundamental oppositions may be overcome with the dialectic. The dialectic transcends the deepest, most seemingly intractable differences of experience, leaning, and assumption. A dialectical problem, even in Aristotle's (1941, 104b) comparatively loose sense, is one in which there are differences of opinion, reasonings conflict, or "we have no argument because they are so vast, and we find it difficult to give our reasons." The dialectic is a powerful means of laying bare false conflicts and rising above them to a level in which opposed positions are reconciled. Dialecticality is deeply rooted in the dimensionalism of human nature. It is part of people's many-sided nature that they always retain the potential to negate the assumptions upon which they or those around them have been acting, and then, with sufficient learning about or experience of one-sidedness, to overcome the opposition and grant each its place and due. Although such overcoming often occurs without the language of dialectics, that language is a very helpful way of describing what takes place in sublation generally.

Many who have used dialectics have taken it to be a kind of formal logic—indeed Hegel often presents and treats dialectics as if it were, although employing it various ways—but it is logic only metaphorically. Never mechanical or rigid, the core of the dialectic, as properly conceived, is merely an informal rule of thumb facilitating the overcoming of oppositions and, derivatively, a language facilitating discussion of what spans the whole. The dialectic is bound by the same rules of logic as any other intellectual endeavor.

Much of Hegel's use of the dialectic may be divided into speculative and nonspeculative employment. The speculative role of the dialectic is its employment as a formal logical engine for developing philosophy conceptually, for building up a system. Hegel (1967a, 101n) refers to this more ambitious use of the dialectic when he says that "*dialectic* in the strict sense . . . [is] the pulsating drive of speculative inquiry." This is the role Taylor (1975, 138) describes when he says that, using the dialectic, Hegel goes through the different forms of human consciousness more and more abstractly until arriving "at a concept that can maintain itself against contradiction." Forster (1993, 135–41) points out that this use of the dialectic is central to Hegel's system, indeed that Hegel would seem to believe it to be the major source of systematicity in his philosophy. Speculative use of the dialectic, however, tends to be arbitrary. The basic concepts, though they need to be ordered and made coherent, should emerge from and be developed in relation to empirical study, not be generated independently by metaphysical speculation. Dialectics, as properly understood, assumes prior reduction of phenomena to their ontological foundations and particularly their basic dimensions, a task that can only be properly carried out in intimate familiarity with the sciences. I am not persuaded by Hegel's speculative use of the dialectic, and I see other more valuable sources of systematicity in his philosophy. Nor, as properly understood, does the dialectic entail paradox or contradiction, for there is neither in balancing conflicting aspects of our lives or societies.[1]

My use of the dialectic restricts it to two other nonspeculative Hegelian roles: 1) the dialectic as the basic means by which humans overcome one-sidedness and rise above difference in the whole, and 2) as a special way of describing relationships vis-à-vis the whole to facilitate their determinate description. In both of these roles the dialectic may be applied either to real or to ideal problems, for the overcoming respectively of practical and theoretical oppositions. In both of these roles the dialectic is also less methodical than it is in the discarded speculative role. Whenever one rationally addresses the whole with determinacy, she is in a world of dialectics (or the equivalent) with its grasp of relationships between fundamental perspectives. Vague, abstract holisms in which the fundamental dimensions and sectors of the human are not explicitly brought out remain indeterminate.

To illustrate its core sublative use,[2] let us consider what is perhaps Hegel's most vivid application of the dialectic, the rather mythic discussion of masters and slaves from *The Phenomenology of Mind* (1967b, 229–40) in which he overcomes the opposition between levels of reflexivity. Whether master and slave are modes within ourselves or within society, the more-reflexive sector need not be allowed to tyrannize over the less-reflexive one. In the presence of the dialectic the oppositions are brought face-to-face, so to speak, to engage in open conversation leading to a relationship of mutual respect. The perspective of each is carefully consulted. Under the oversight of the dialectic the opposites encounter each other, and the relationship is transformed from an exploitative one into a humane one satisfying the needs of both. Yet the dialectical meeting need not be so dramatic; it may simply involve a fine-tuning of already relatively adjusted modes, which tells us to ease up our efforts or allocations at one level of reflexivity and move higher or lower.

The dialectic may be used to overcome the opposition between the consummatory and instrumental in a similar way. Again one dwells in and appreciates both sides, opting for a certain balance between the two. In that spirit, for example, both id and ego come to be valued, and a changing mix of the two is seen to be appropriate. So too, one accepts rather than rejects movement from community to association and viceversa, although she may moderate the shift, depending upon conditions.

With the dialectic one sublates the relationship between the ideal and real by viewing the world from both modes, balancing between them as warranted, and respecting equally an endeavor, life, or society in which one or the other is dominant. One could imagine another Hegelian story not so different from masters and slaves entitled "Intellectuals and Leaders." Daniel Patrick Moynihan and Willi Brandt represent examples of this opposition's thoroughgoing sublation at the personal level, and Confucian China and the Eastern European *shtetl* do at the collective level.

Among her overcomings, she with the dialectic also sublates the opposition between individualism and collectivism. In so doing, she reconciles liberalism and conservatism, determining how rapidly it would be wise to change collectively and personally. She overcomes liberalism and conservatism by identifying with the whole profile of changing needs associated with different positions. The dialectician is herself liberal under some conditions and conservative under others—in all sectors and for reasons that are universal rather than particular. The mixed economies of industrial capitalist countries in the postwar years may be considered the result of such overcomings. They utilized market and command principles side by side within welfare- and regulatory-state frameworks that allowed valuable contributions by both. (Marx and Ayn Rand negated the opposing forms and refused this sublation, which was achieved despite them.) Aristotle's overcoming of the three narrower forms of class rule under his polity, which includes each within a larger system respecting the principles of all, represents a different kind of sublation of market and hierarchy, this time with respect to political regimes.

Given that working is continually in process through all sectors of society, significant control over degrees of liberalism and conservatism might seem to be in place already in a sectoral world, and with it the capacity to regulate the rates at which processing occurs in markets. Under sectoralism, however, individualism and collectivism, market and hierarchy, ordinarily constitute taken-for-granted frameworks—as do positions on the other dimensions—predilection for or against markets being overwhelmingly a matter of fixed character. Sectoralists are locked into their liberal or conservative leanings and unable to use the markets as flexible rudders with which to steer persons or societies. Universalists, however, are not liberal or conservative for all times but only one or the other vis-à-vis a given situation with a particular degree of workedness; precisely as Aristotle tells us that the form of its political regime must suit a city's situation, not an arbitrary mold with which we have bonded. Sectoralists are so far from fathoming universalism that they can only think misguidedly of such flexibility as immoral.

The universal overcomes the opposition between radicalism and each of the other stances as well. It understands that radicalism is inappropriate in normal times during which certain orienting assumptions need to be in place. Incremental change is the universal's normal mode. However, in extraordinary times, when the assumptions have to change, the universal itself becomes radical and helps usher in the necessary shifts of paradigm. Because incremental working from time to time results in the need for large structural adjustment, intermittent architectonic change also has its place. In managing social and self-development, the universal's many-sided balance between liberalism and conservatism is complemented by its balance between moderation and radicalism. The dialectic of normal times of smooth incremental working and crisis times of bold transformation follows the natural rhythm of experience. Each has its place.

As should be clear from the foregoing, the balance on a dimension does not necessarily mean a moderate position between the poles. The balance in the broadest view is what is fitting, considering all sides of the matter. Extremism may ordinarily be unwise, but there are occasions when it is required. I have in mind such cases as Caesar's crossing of the Rubicon, Meiji's reforms in late nineteenth-century Japan, Nixon's China policy, and the U.S. civil rights protests of the 1950s and early 1960s. The dialectic's is a creative tension between the poles free of any fixed position. Nevertheless, especially in the normal circumstances of everyday life and politics, plain moderation is an important form of universalism.

He with the dialectic also dwells in no one time, instead embracing all times, as Heidegger compellingly establishes in his partial extension of the Hegelian tradition. The dialectician courses back and forth through existential time as he does through existential space and overcomes oppositions between epochs, generations, and life stages. Overcoming history by removing himself from the sectoral time of the present, he understands and empathizes with all eras and balances their perspectives, needs, and lessons. Temporally restricted and complacent, sectoralist persons and collectivities are trapped in growth and development sinks. The dialectician neither ignores tomorrow nor oppresses today for its sake; he treats the two as worthy equals and moves toward optimal development.[3] Wherever the dialectic is employed, however, a new perspective comes into view. We begin to examine the ontology of the dialectic in conjunction with a crucial extension of it.

The Perspective of the Rational Universal

Having argued that with the dialectic it is possible to overcome the polar positions on any basic dimension, I now propose that it is possible to do so on all dimensions at once, and that actually doing so constitutes a fundamental perspective without the understanding of which one cannot grasp central human phenomena. Let us call this perspective—the one held by the human using the dialectic or its equivalent—that of the rational universal.

The perspective of the rational universal is the complex one within which all other fundamental perspectives are held in mind and reconciled simultaneously. In the universal, people rise above the sectoral perspectives randomly fallen into by accidents of birth and happenstance, profoundly and self-consciously taking in the full set of perspectives, enabling them to perceive, think, and act with the whole. The universal is the complex sector above all other sectors, the sector that is a-sectoral. People only slowly and with effort develop fluency in and sympathy with all fundamental perspectives, acquiring the range to be at home and harmonize oppositions anywhere in the world of the human. It goes without saying that the notion of a universal in which all major oppositions are fully overcome can never be more than an ideal type not completely reached even in the best developed persons and societies—so difficult is it for all residual bias to be overcome. Moreover, to simplify, we must ordinarily ignore the many important partial universals that typically represent people's finest efforts. The concept of the universal is specifically Hegel's and more generally the common property of numerous philosophers from the major traditions of the world. My value-added and my systematicity come in large part from the way in which I build up to the rational universal and impart determinacy and power to it by clarifying and arranging the basic dimensions emerging from the human sciences.

Where the universal is a sector—an additional part of the whole with respect to the human—universal*ism* is a mode of the human and a way of life of perceiving, thinking, acting, and being with the whole. Universalism is the opposite of sectoralism. Their opposition forms the last fundamental dimension of the human—one that hinges on the degree to which persons or collectivities dwell in the simultaneous overcoming of oppositions on all other dimensions in the whole, or view the world from provincial sets of givens. Universalism versus sectoralism is not a simple or compound dimension like the four basic dimensions of the human but a complex one.

However harmful the failure to do so, escaping well-worn but distorted grooves goes against the grain of ordinary people as strongly as does ambidextrousness. Difference is not typically overcome but negated. Stuck in sectoralism, most refuse existential balance. Even when willing, they encounter a kind of dyslexia in trying to see the whole. Their minds recoil from the complexity of universalism, and they clutch the nearest determinate position.

If the personal universal harmonizes one person's sectors, the collective universal does the same through its far-flung sectors, including those of the lower-level collectivities and persons of which it is composed. In the collective universal people sublate the various macro oppositions, adjusting socio-cultural forms and allocating resources in a balanced way. Understanding and identifying with every level up and down the hierarchy of the human in all its diversity, the collective universal harmonizes relations within and between its member collectivities and persons. Insofar as the human becomes oriented to the universal, its indefatigable working becomes holistic, and the solutions it accumulates bring harmonization.

As is the case with the other dimensions, universalism and sectoralism are intimately interrelated. How much so is apparent in the fact that only the intervention of the universal allows the sectors to get beyond their rudimentary expressions and reach their mature ones. What keeps the superid or superego from mistreating the id and ego or consensus or politics from mistreating community and association is intercession by the universal. The latter takes counsel from both sides and builds leadership in place of tyranny.

Movement toward the universal entails acquiring a new kind of reflexivity. Elementary self-consciousness and self-control are associated with purely sectoral reflexivity, such as that exercised in the superid or politics. Here one or more lower-level sectors are brought under self-consciousness and self-control, but such reflexivity pertains only to particular sectors under their purview separately, *not* to them as plural modules or sets of diverse functions within the whole. With universalism and its reflexivity, however, the human becomes self-conscious of its modularity per se and begins to feel the need for balance between sectors. For example, the universal may monitor time spent in various sectors and route the attention back and forth between them. In other words, where sectoral reflexivity entails self-awareness of one sector at a time, universal reflexivity entails self-awareness of and across multiple sectors simultaneously.[4]

Sometimes the rational universal's reflexivity is sparked by the dawning awareness of problems brought on by one-sidedness as people become aware of their own or their society's folly, and its source in sectoralism and imbalance, sometimes by the perception of the same in other persons or societies. Overwhelmingly, however, it arises with the help of direct and indirect exposure to philosophy. Whatever the source, becoming rationally self-conscious about sectoralism is a most important developmental step for persons and societies. Sectoralism is neither our only nor our better way of finding orientation amid pluralism and difference.

No particular degree of ontological differentiation is prerequisite to the formation of a personal or collective universal, only self-consciousness about inner opposition and sectoralism per se and feeling a need to overcome them. What sectors there are to harmonize, given the societies and classes involved, each with its distinct character, merely sets bounds to the kinds of harmonization possible and appropriate. There can be fairly simple personal universals harmonizing nothing more than id and ego, complex ones harmonizing two-tiered basic personalities, and very complex ones harmonizing three-tiered personalities. So too, there can be less complex archaic collective universals reaching over only priests and horticulturalists; and more complex agrarian ones encompassing aristocrats, priests, soldiers, merchants, artisans, peasants, and other social classes. In the far more complex contemporary world of densely developed higher reflexivity, a still higher overarching universal is required.

Taking the perspective of the universal gives rise to feeling the needs of the whole. Each sector has its particular desire for pleasure, gain, beauty, order, knowledge, etc., but what drives the universal is the complex need for the long-term well-being of the whole—that things go as well as possible overall and in the long term. Indeed a need in the profound sense is a want that enhances general well-being over the long run (see Maslow 1968, 159). Some wants are needs and some are not—people have true and false wants. Genuinely absorbing the inner plurality of the human, the difference within, allows people to feel from all sides and to desire what harmonizes the many opposed wants. Seeking to balance all motivation, the universal monitors the many sectors under its purview and adjusts their expectations and assessments of reality, decreasing unduly high expectations in some and increasing unduly low ones in others, both of which threaten well-being in their different ways. The gap between universal expectations and reality creates the moral tension driving the universal. To the extent to which the goals of the universal are realized, the results are the best possible ones for people.

Several distinguishable needs hierarchies accompany the respective forms of development, including that to higher levels of sectoral reflexivity and that from individualism to collectivism, but the most important is the one from sectoralism to universalism. Moving to the universal is the profound sense of moving up the needs hierarchy. Although important, development of higher levels of sectoral reflexivity must ultimately be secondary to development of the universal. Differentiation, in other words, is finally less important than integration. However, in the broadest view there are not really several separate needs hierarchies but a single many-dimensional needs surface accompanying the ramifying development of the human. People may make progress in any of several directions at once, although in what directions can only be determined by the universal. Properly coordinating our many sides toward consonance with the universal is the most difficult and rewarding challenge we face, for it is the master challenge optimizing the meeting of all other challenges.

The pinnacle of the states toward which the universal works, the emotion accompanying the well-being of the whole, is the rich and abiding sense that multifarious expectations are being well met. Since it comes from fulfilling the range of expectations across sectors, achieving well-being has everything to do with holistic workedness. Hence the Stoics' view that "[h]appiness in general means nothing more than the feeling of harmony with oneself" (Hegel 1995, 2:265). However, this is overwhelmingly subordinate background for those with the universal because they tend to be actively engaged and relatively undistracted from their work, for as Aristotle (1962, 283) says, "happiness is activity and the complete utilization of all our powers, our goodness, not conditionally but absolutely."

Beyond Method

Deliberate, methodical use of the dialectic and systematic, multiple position-taking significantly develop the rational universal, but with procedural employment of the dialectic, opposition by opposition, people are still awkwardly placing one foot in front of the other in the universal, as it were. While the universalism continues to be dialectical, and must if the human is to be gripped determinately, it goes on to develop considerably.

Toward the upper limit of the dialectic's use as a deliberate method, with a relatively complete ontology and a great deal of practice, all major polarities and the sectors formed of them are regularly overcome and held in mind approximately at once. The whole at this stage is presented by repeated coursings back and forth through all sectors in the conscious effort to view them simultaneously. The attention remains relatively confined, but the leveraging of a mature ontology enables us to draw a vast panorama before our gaze, sweeping across large portions of the whole. Such a robust universal is only possible with the development of apt concepts spanning the range of existential space and time and providing a large enhancement of our already prodigious pattern recognition.

The highest stages of the universal go beyond deliberate method to a fluent and free holism rooted in long experience of systematic contemplation or meditation. Even in its ordinary action our attention often spills over between sectors, for the modules are never fully walled off. As we move closer to the universal in contemplation supported by a mature ontology, what had been noise through the partitions becomes distinct sounds concerted in the whole. Just as perception flips spontaneously back and forth in viewing a Necker cube, so our minds come to perform when visualizing many perspectives at once. Sympathetically entering multiple worlds, profoundly absorbing their perspectives and needs until all have been entered repeatedly, these worlds leave their afterglows. When the many horizons of the human are brought into short-term memory simultaneously in contemplation, one sees across the ontological divides. The complex perspective which then arises is more than and superior to that of a superego, superid, superassociation, supercommunity, or any other sector—it is that of the vibrant, living universal.

As the rational universal becomes practiced to the point of mastery in a rare few, all heuristic aspects of it fall away, its implementation moves from the instrumental to the consummatory mode, and it becomes habitual and dominant in the character. The rational universal at the peak retains a rational philosophical language and logic but runs them with emotion dominant. Where the instrumental is inevitably rigid and somewhat arbitrary, the consummatory is the ultimate source of all great integrative insights. With the necessary ontological capital and background knowledge, one meditates upon the problems at hand, works intuitive insights into a rational medium and organization, and systematically builds a model of the world informed at every point by the consummatory (although, to be sure, the consummatory immersed in and serving the rational universal, not the flippant right brain of the id). Just as night vision comes to us when we pause in the dark, holistic vision comes to us when we distance ourselves from the world and reflect.

Even at modest levels of the universal, the consummatory and instrumental minds must always work together. For very complex problems—those beyond our ability to solve with pure rationality—as for example the choice of a spouse or vocation, the consummatory is the mode of choice. The purely rational mind is well suited to making small, repetitive, and above all determinate decisions, often quickly calculating excellent solutions, but by itself the rational mind is poorly suited to the most complex decisionmaking. For it, working independently, to measure up to the large problems facing us would require a degree of comprehensiveness and coherence of rational thought seldom if ever encountered in life. Yet for just such tasks intuition[5] is at its strongest. As rational understanding becomes more universal, intuition becomes more reliable.

At the ultimate stage of the universal's practice when no conscious rotation is any longer necessary and it has come effortlessly to dominate character, we eat, drink, sleep, and dream the universal. Distinguished scientists often report that their best ideas have come to them at odd, relaxed times. But when all of one's time is spent in leisurely contemplation, then all of his life comes to be filled with such ideas. And for every year this goes on they compound. When one who is broadly educated long immerses himself in contemplation, the consummatory mode perceives and thinks across the dimensions of being and into the whole. The intuitions generated by contemplation are grasped in inward, passive perception in which pattern recognition by the unconscious mind does the creative work. Such a universal can only come as the culmination of long study, experience, and contemplation, but something approaching it is available to educated and thoughtful people who give themselves time to reflect.

The Need for the Universal

That the need for the universal is paramount owes to the radical interconnectedness of all things human. Given our interactive modularity, significant change in any sector brings the need for countervailing adjustment throughout our beings. New location, knowledge, employment, partners, and associates are common sources of disruption in persons. New scale, values, missions, industries, members, and markets are in collectivities. Because the human is regularly acting upon countless important sectoral matters, it also always necessarily has even more offsetting adjustments to make—if never more so than when epochal transformation brings upheaval and structural change on several dimensions at once. All sectoral working and development are in and of themselves divergent with respect to the whole and contribute to disruption and unworkedness overall. Economic growth is a particularly salient source of ramifying disorder and incoherence. However beneficial overall, the rise and fall of technologies, particularly transportation and communication technologies, bring large and disparate negative side-effects.

Further demands on integration arise from the more differentiated existence conferred by each institution newly added to a developing personality or society. Mere ontological unfolding no more leads automatically to coherence and harmony than does the pell-mell growth of government agencies or business enterprises. The proliferation of functions represents divergent ontological development and renders the task of coordination between perspectives ever more complex. The perspective is always strange across new institutional divides; people have difficulty recognizing themselves or their own across them. Such divergent unfolding must be balanced by reintegration that can only come from the universal. For any particular circumstances there is an optimal amount of ontological differentiation.[6] Maximal furtherance of well-being requires a continual vast working from the perspective of the universal. Sectoral development is anything but automatically undesirable, but it must be accompanied by comprehensive attention to reverberating side-effects if it is not to be followed by unnecessary grief. At high levels of universalism, sectoral and holistic working are related contrapuntally.

Irrespective of the path, because it perceives, thinks, and acts from all perspectives and feels all needs, the universal is the key to smoothing the oscillations and reconciling the discord to which sectoralism is prone. Its working adjusts the diverse parts into progressively more developed and balanced wholes increasingly productive of well-being. As holistic working—Nietzsche's (see e.g., 1967, 129) "digestion"—accumulates solutions to universal problems, progressively greater harmony and increasing levels of well-being are made possible. The human flourishes only under universalism. When people take performance in any single sector—for example sexual gratification or income maximization—as their criterion, they are headed for tragedy, for decisions then systematically go wrong for the whole. Jung (1971, 80) gets at the problem when he decries the barbarism of one-sidedness and bad measure. Without the universal there can be neither coherence nor true harmony.

In all that pertains to the universal, however, there is a distinction between genuine and specious harmony. In genuine harmony the elements are worked to coherence. In specious harmony they may be rendered familiar or in other ways given the appearance of holistic workedness but without attaining a natural fit. Extreme British conservatives who extol virtually any tradition for its own sake can sometimes protect longstanding incoherence and refuse genuine coherence. Geertz's (1980) memorable portrayal of classical Balinese culture in *Negara* provides examples of working without true harmony and of the persistence of larger incongruities amid stunning refinement of detail. The common American pattern of taking as the real thing what is welladvertised or lobbied for—e.g., junk food or tariffs on broomcorn—is no less spurious. Whatever the source, the simulacrum of coherence without its substance in interconnectedness and proper balance between aspects yields false practices as familiar as a lame step and as unneeded as ill-fitting shoes.

For the human sciences, omitting universalism is above all empirically deficient. Such phenomena as philosophy, religion, morality, and statesmanship can only be understood by grasping universalism. People can neither address nor comprehend nor replicate the extensive and crucial harmony in traditional societies or the less-extensive but no less-crucial harmony in our own without grasping universalism. How can one understand the harmonization of high Gothic Europe in which diverse social classes shared significant meaning and showed considerable mutual appreciation; that of later Han China in which elaborate and refined patterns of respect governed the five Confucian relationships; or that of the *jajmani* system of traditional Hindu society in which small shares of what was produced were carefully meted out to those in many necessary occupations—without grasping universalism? How can one understand the profound thoughtfulness in much of the United Kingdom's handling of the postwar unraveling of its empire and in its continuing relations with its former colonies, or the peaceful formation and expansion of the European Community, or the overarching conciliation of the welfare state in industrial and global capitalist societies, or great parenting wherever it is found—without grasping universalism? Most of the many examples of mutual understanding and harmony in the world come not from coincidence but from working and overcoming with the universal. None of which is to say that there have not been significant aspects of conflict in each of these settings that also require understanding. However, we began to see in the last chapter how central the notion of the universal is even to understanding conflict.

Nor can human scientists comprehend philosophy and study it historically and causally without grasping the universalism at its core. Philosophy, as the detached, rational study of the whole, particularly in its universal aspects, is the home of the ideal rational universal. The center of philosophy is the universalistic ontological knowledge that Aristotle termed theoretical wisdom (*sophia*), which necessarily entails but is not restricted to basic conceptual work. Philosophy is an institution of the whole while all sectoral institutions, such as the economy or the arts among collective institutions or the id or pre-superego among personal ones, are institutions of the parts. As such, philosophy's existential location is distributed through all other places—its being is a complex interpenetration. Philosophy, together with the larger humanistic culture radiating from it, is the ultimate source of all developed manifestations of the rational universal in persons and collectivities. The less-developed examples of the universal in the intuitive good sense of many thoughtful people and the insightful flashes of especially receptive ones, are important but uninstitutionalized forms.

* * * *

To gain access to both poles of dimensions on one's own is to become multiply jointed or hinged in a way that can startle oneself and others. At first, having such may seem a dubious gift. Unlike so many whose character is relatively frozen in one lopsided posture or another, the person becomes double-jointed and then n-jointed with respect to life. Before he acquires the knowledge to become accustomed to the acrobatics of the human and find his balance, he is likely to seem and to be somewhat unstable. His horizons will lurch when others' do not; his mind will juxtapose when others' will not; his life will be dangerous when others' are not. As in the Chinese novel, *Journey to the West*, he pitches, yaws, and rolls in his simian playfulness in ways that would lose many overboard, but with luck his uncanniness and systematic exposure to philosophy will get him through. In time, as he comes to know himself, he who would dwell in the universal finds a capacious, many-leveled residence and a balanced life in which all of his faculties are fully engaged and equally at home—not the safest path to the universal, but the most direct and most sparkling.

But alas! As has been implicit all along, the universal is itself internally differentiated. What I have been describing is only the rational universal with its instrumental language. Of every bit as much importance is the universal conducted in nonrational language. A paen to philosophy brings us directly to religion and the other central institution of the whole.

Notes

1. See Gadamer's (1976, 19ff.) critique of Hegel's view of contradiction.
2. Its use as a language will be treated in Chapter 15.
3. Additional real-world examples applying the dialectic will be provided below and in Chapters 13 and 14, and ideal-world ones in Chapters 15 and 16.
4. One of the major difficulties of Hegel's philosophy is that it fails to distinguish clearly between the sectorally and the universally reflexive.
5. See Chapter 1.
6. However, holistic integration is not the opposite of ontological differentiation; not only increasing reflexivity but *any* ontological change requires such reintegration—as in a shift from community to association, from ideal to real dominance, or from one level of collectivity to another. Moreover, dedifferentiation requires reintegration as much as does differentiation.

Bibliography

Aristotle. 1941. "Topics." In *The Basic Works of Aristotle,* ed. R. McKeon. New York: Random House.
———. 1962. *Politics.* Harmondsworth, Middlesex: Penguin.
Forster, M. 1993. "Hegel's Dialectical Method." In *The Cambridge Companion to Hegel,* ed. F. Beiser. Cambridge: Cambridge University Press.
Gadamer, H. 1976. *Hegel's Dialectic: Five Hermeneutical Studies.* New Haven, CN: Yale University Press.
Geertz, C. 1980. *Negara: The Theatre State in Nineteenth-Century Bali.* Princeton, NJ: Princeton University Press.
Hegel, G. 1967a. *Hegel's Philosophy of Right.* London: Oxford University Press.
———. 1967b. *The Phenomenology of Mind.* New York: Harper and Row.
———. 1995. *Lectures on the History of Philosophy.* 3 vols. Lincoln and London: University of Nebraska Press.
Jung, C. 1971. *The Collected Works of C. G. Jung.* Vol. 6. *Psychological Types.* Princeton, NJ: Princeton University Press.
Maslow, A. 1968. *Toward a Psychology of Being.* 2nd ed. New York: D. Van Nostrand.
Nietzsche, F. 1967. *On the Genealogy of Morals.* New York: Random House.
Taylor, C. 1975. *Hegel.* Cambridge: Cambridge University Press.

10. Religion

Religion and the central role it has played in society and history can only be understood by grasping the universal. Societies and persons do actually develop universalism in religion, and the social and psychological impact of this is both profound and pervasive. Let us look carefully at the basic elements of religion and then at their interpretation.

The Ontology of Religion

The universal must always be carried out and its results communicated in either rational or nonrational language. Its conduct and expression in the first is philosophy; its conduct and expression in the second is religion. Philosophy and religion are institutions of the whole, unlike all others which are institutions of the parts. In philosophy one takes her place with the rational whole; in religion she takes her place with the poetic whole. Like philosophy, religion is not a simple or compound perspective but a complex master perspective that harmonizes all other perspectives. Like those of philosophy, religion's concerns are summary ones that encompass all other needs. Like that of philosophy, religion's ultimate aim is to unify and harmonize all aspects of persons and societies with themselves and each other, reconciling all differences. In its distinct manner each universal institution is oriented toward what best serves the long-term well-being of the whole.

Religion is based upon revelation featuring the universal in a figurative mode. The sources of universal symbolic content who lay down world images and impart charismatic force to the poetic universal are prophets. Prophecy provides beacons of revelatory insight into the essence of things. Religion builds upon the archetypes of sacred myth and scripture as philosophy builds upon ontology. "The sacred reveals absolute reality and at the same time makes orientation possible; hence it *founds the world*. . . ." (Eliade 1959, 30).

The whole is so vast and manydimensional that even the great religious revelations must be supplemented, interpreted, and analyzed by secondary literatures. These prominently include textual criticism of the sacred documents in the counterpart to literary criticism, and rational theology grounded in religious concepts. To the extent to which prophecy errs, omits, or blurs, theologians, exegetes, ecclesiastical authorities, and/or additional prophets must develop a tradition. Prophetic content has to be woven into a systematic fabric reaching over the entire manifold of existence for its full potential to be realized.

Moreover, in time, all manifestations of the poetic universal slowly become more remote as accumulated socio-cultural changes loosen their fit with prevailing conditions and diminish their charismatic appeal. A tradition must counter this entropy of slow recession with fresh interpretation and spiritual inspiration if it is to continue to flourish. Vigorous new religious interpretation and thought may extend the run of prophecy considerably, but in time entire traditions may become freighted with accruals and estranged from needs and render these means of developing them no longer sufficient. More fundamental renewals of tradition in the form of continuing revelation may also become necessary.

Renewal becomes more pressing when large-scale collisions occur between different traditions. Discordant elements then lie side by side, and people cry out for harmony. In such times of religious markets when adherents are exposed to great difference, those who are able must be open to what is universal in other traditions if they are to avoid serious disorder. To the extent they are receptive, the renewal and reconciliation of traditions may then proceed together, which results in a relatively rapid working of difference in light of fresh, continuing judgment of what best fits the whole.

We have two central modes of imparting meaning to history and thereby telling us how we got here and who we are. We look to rational inquiry for the philosophy of history and to religion for myth. While philosophy is too often remiss in its historical function—Hegel and Marx being the great exceptions—religion features it prominently. As Eliade (1959, 30) says, "the religious moment implies the cosmogonic moment." Revelation's historical dimension is myth. In both philosophy and religion narrative sets the stage for the universal and its relation to us. In myth the stage and *dramatis personae* are unveiled together. Sacred myth provides grand integrative stories of God, man, and the world.

Across all religions a personal God or impersonal One (or Heaven) symbolizes the universal in ourselves. In other words, God resides in ourselves, individually and collectively, in our universal modes. This is why God is also associated with the ultimate good. In Hegel's (1984, 1:385) words, "God is the absolutely universal in-and-for-itself. . . ." The divine spirit is present "essentially in his community. . . ." (Hegel 1984, 1:164). To be one with God is to be one with the whole, a person or collectivity in full unity and harmony.

Whether deity is taken impersonally or personally depends upon whether the transcendent being is considered abstractly or concretely, which effectively means rationally or nonrationally. Both philosophy and high criticism view God abstractly. The abstract deity, the *Logos*, lies behind the many concrete manifestations of God. "The 'Personal God' is . . . none other than the personification of the Essence" (Schuon 1984, 214n; see also 17). In that the universal ultimately makes possible all that we do and are, God may be viewed as the creator.[1]

As philosophy centers on a relationship with the rational universal, religion centers on a relationship with God (Hegel 1984, 1:448, 3:62; James 1958, 42; Temple 1960, 54). In that each of us is part of the whole and counts in the whole, it may be said that each of us matters to God, that He cares for us. When there are many gods or spiritual beings in a tradition, the whole is not yet coherently represented, and religion is not yet well developed. No pantheon of deities can as integrally or powerfully represent the universal as can one supreme God. Each of the plural gods in a polytheistic system gives ultimate representation only to a particular aspect of the whole, which leaves the world partially disjointed. When the narrower perspectives are integrated into a unitary whole, its representation is the one true God. When newly interacting plural traditions later juxtapose differing images and concepts of the one God, religion again has the task of reconciling the conflicting representations of deity in a fully universal form.

Promoting and supporting religion is the place of worship (whether that be a church, temple, mosque, synagogue, or other such venue). It represents the central vehicle of collective action by the poetic universal. The place of worship, which may have any degree or kind of organization, brings meaning to the faithful by conducting ritual, engaging in religious education, and ministering to its members. It may also carry out various other universal or sectoral activities, such as conducting basic education or dispensing welfare. The place of worship makes "a collective expression through a common way of being" (Taylor 2002, 25) and forms a community of the universal in a collective relationship with God.

Religious ritual (such as prayer) consists of meaningful dramaturgy vis-à-vis the figures of the founding myths evoking adherents' highest commitments. Religious ritual is dramatized myth as myth is narrated ritual.[2] Ritual provides collective experience in prescribed relationships with archetypal figures by rehearsing religious life and promoting religious community. Finite religion's concrete and poetic analog to meditation, ritual is inherently nonrational but only superstitious when taken in a naïve and magical way.

Turning from structural to motivational ontology, a religion's theodicy is its identification of what is ultimately problematic in personal and collective life and poses the central problem for the tradition's members (see Weber 1958, 271, 274ff., 358). What *is* ultimately problematic in the world is that people in their narrowness do not know and follow God and thereby fail to pursue the well-being of the whole. What *is* problematic "is whatever is opposed to God either by its nature or on the plane of its manifestation, or it is whatever *de facto* is harmful to man. . . ." (Schuon 1984, 80). That people do not pursue what will lead to their long-term well-being brings great misfortune upon them, in such forms as war, tyranny, crime, and despair.

Something converging upon this understanding is expressed poetically in the theodicies of the world's major religions. People are to be on guard against worshiping false gods or yielding to man's fallen nature or straying from ritual obligations or lapsing from a contemplative mode or remaining trapped in an endless cycle of rebirths. What is taken to be problematic depends upon the circumstances of the religious leaders and the faithful around whom the tradition has arisen, i.e., upon the spiritual needs of the group or groups to which it is addressed, as well as the inherited symbolic traditions upon which it draws. Each character type formed by a particular socio-cultural nexus and experience having its motivational possibilities, the universal works with what is available.

In the religions of Middle Eastern provenience, another, spurious notion of theodicy is often encountered among the naïve. Here the notion of a creator God is taken naïvely, and with burnished logic the deity is blamed for what is wrong in the world. But as the universal, God can only be the solution, not the problem. Since God does not literally bring us earthquakes, tidal waves, plagues, and other natural disasters, naïve doctrine with respect to creation and providence is terminally inconsistent in treating the problem of evil (construed broadly). As to the many unavoidable negative side-effects of good actions, Schuon (1982, 46) is right when he says that "God does not will evil as such, He wills it only inasmuch as it is a constitutive element of a good, therefore inasmuch as it is a good. . . . [E]vil is only evil by the cosmic accident of a privation of good, willed by God as an indirect element of a greater good." There are still casualties in a just war, and some still experience hardship under the most moral possible economic policy. But to the literalist who has yet acquired the capacity to intellectualize superficially about putative contradiction, there is obliviousness to poetic truth. As Whitehead (1926, 77) says, "[a]ll simplifications of religious dogma are shipwrecked upon the rock of the problem of evil."

Every religion then has one or more ethics, conformity with which is demanded of adherents. The ethics are ordinarily the means of overcoming the problematic (as specified in the theodicy) and attaining salvation. In their various ways the ethics represent ways of contributing to long-term well-being, given the circumstances holding for the peoples in question.[3]

A tradition's soteriology is its figurative representation of the better future, saving the person or society from its woes. It is the person's duty to overcome a certain problematic while following God's way. He is judged by his performance of this responsibility, and his salvation depends upon it. Broadly interpreted, personal salvation means living on, so to speak, in one's beneficial influence. To the extent which the nonrational universal is developed in a person, the profound emotional need accompanying it is for oneness with God. Without the same problem of mortality, the salvation of the collectivity may be framed more directly in terms of its well-being. In more popular religion the soteriology tells the faithful how they and what they hold dear will be rewarded if they follow a moral life. All religions have theodicy-soteriology pairings with problematic presents and salvific futures linked by ethical imperatives. The basic religious story spiritually motivates by binding together summary images of the woeful present and glorious future in exalted narrative that gives solemn direction to the human.

There is salvation, and there is life after death, and they are metaphoric. Eternal life is about well-being and fulfillment individually and collectively as part of a larger whole. How we are saved is by finding God via the route best articulating with our character, society, and circumstances, whether by meditation or doctrine, faith or works. Religions inspire members according to the leanings and needs of those around whom the tradition has grown up. The basic building blocks and architectures of religions are different, but each seeks to promote the well-being of the whole according to its light. The diversity of socio-cultural configurations and spiritual possibilities has both allowed and required the diversity of revelations. All of humanity is unlikely to have been able to respond to a single revelation. In its many-sidedness the universal transforms itself as possible according to the circumstances. Insofar as they are able to reach it, all religions present the same universal.

Religion and philosophy are also two different valid perspectives of the same universal, and while imperfect representations of either may clash with the other, there can be no ultimate incompatibility between them. To the extent they are fully developed and approach the universal, they converge. As the human sciences and the arts are ultimately complementary, so philosophy and religion are ultimately complementary. God is isomorphic with the philosopher's universal. What meets religious ethics meets philosophical ethics. The goal of religion is ultimately the same as the goal of philosophy, developing and disseminating universal understanding toward enhancement of the long-term well-being of the whole.

Universalist and Sectoralist Religion

The two major perspectives on religion, accordingly, are those of universalism and of sectoralism. In Leo Strauss's distinction these are respectively the sophisticated and naïve adherents of religion. The universal accord religion the comprehensive meaning it finally demands. The sectoral, unable to do that, give it a literal, doctrinal, and magical interpretation. (There are, of course, many who fall in between.) Universalist faith takes flexible guidance from religious tradition. Sectoralist faith attaches fixed imperatives to it. The universalist sense of the sacred is profound reverence. The sectoralist sense of the holy is sublimated magical charisma. Consulting with all of her moments in embracing the spiritual, the universalist has a fundamental inner harmony. Coercing herself in the resolution to have faith, the sectoralist has a fundamental inner disharmony. The one freely and openly participates in the religious universal while the other commands herself, becoming a "believer" (see Nietzsche 1974, 289). As Hegel (1984, 1:175) puts it, "[t]he determinate [in the sense of particularistic] concept of religion . . . is religion in its finitude . . . something one-sided constituted in opposition to other religions as one particular type set against another." The force the sectoralist directs against herself to achieve salvation may also be directed against others in fanaticism.

The relationship between universal and sectoral religion is dominated by an enigma. In religion, as in other areas, ordinary people can be disequilibrated by elite culture, for which reason there is need for care by elites in communicating with each other whenever the people have some awareness. Via the prudence necessitated by this enigma, universal versus sectoral religion becomes esoteric versus exoteric religion. If one makes an exoteric move, he lowers or camouflages his voice in order not to be heard or understood by the other. There is a complex and subtle language by which the naïve are led religiously.

Active poetic universalism in prophets and other leaders is the ultimate source, the gnosis behind religion. Particular religions are the concrete, immanent manifestations of the universal. In its generality universalist religion remains steady through the plural worlds in which it navigates. Oriented to the invariable, esoterism universalizes the dogmatic systems it encounters, apprehending both the transcendent and its immanent manifestations (Schuon 1981, 19, 37). Universalist religion, however, is too abstract to give much orientation or comfort to average people, for which reason it is predominantly confined to elites.

All of the major religious traditions offer subtle and important truths about the way things are and ought to be. Ideally, just as it should not be a question of which philosopher one would "believe in" and repudiate the rest, so it should not be a question of which revelation one would hold to and ignore the rest. Philosophy is bigger than any one philosopher, and religion is bigger than any one prophet. Universalist religion is receptive to and draws from all traditions. Each of the major prophets and traditions has authentic insight that helps us comprehend and align with the whole to attain salvation. Rising to the general faith behind all particular faiths, even the religions of the East and West are fundamentally complementary and not in conflict or only superficially so (Cobb 1982, 67–68). In Schuon's (1982, 137) words, "the undeniable presence of the transcendent truth, of the sacred and the supernatural, in religions other than that of our birth ought to lead us, not in the least to doubt the Absolute character proper to our religion, but simply to acknowledge the inherence of the Absolute in other doctrinal and sacramental symbols. . . ." as well. Religions seem fundamentally incompatible only to naïve believers.

In order to appeal to more than an enlightened few, however, there must be particular sectoral religions. As Hegel (1984, 3:188–89) says, "Religion . . . does not exist only for educated, conceptual thought, for philosophical consciousness. . . ." Since people are at different levels of understanding and interpretive facility, there is a good and wise reason why the great religions manage the relationship between sophisticated and naïve adherents by putting things as they do.

Some religions approach the universal better than others, as do some philosophies. As Cobb (1982, 116) says, particular religions "are more and less illuminating, adequate and accurate." No religious tradition is perfect. All have their strengths and weaknesses. All have failed to overcome or have only imperfectly overcome some oppositions. Moreover, some religion is false and immoral, such as the brand of Christianity at Jonestown or the fundamentalist Islam that preaches global jihad (in the aggressive sense). True religion is religion that accurately and fully represents the whole poetically and furthers its well-being. Those who are universal criticize religions as they criticize philosophies, albeit with more circumspection.

All of this poses a formidable problem for religion quite analogous to the problem competing philosophies raise for philosophy. For those seeking the fullest truth, the different religions must be reconciled and combined harmoniously within a larger whole. If part of the truth remains outside a tradition or is only imperfectly integrated within it, the tradition remains incomplete. Thus, for example, the Western notion of God and the Buddhist notion of emptiness are complementary and mutually enriching (see Cobb 1982, 114–15). The Christian strong self can be complemented with the Buddhist no self. Here, as elsewhere, oppositions can only be overcome with the universal.

However, the most taxing quandaries of religion arise because it must also reconcile the internal opposition between its simultaneous universalism and brittle particularism. At every step of religion's progression, the naïve declaim, inveigh, stumble, and wander with minimal comprehension. Religion is always at once high art and popular culture, in the way that Shakespeare played simultaneously to the galleries and the pit. Religion is—or at least, has been—more comprehensive even than philosophy precisely because it also reaches average people and, sublates this most demanding difference of class.

In sectoralist religion the universal is necessarily forced into fixed forms both ill suited to its infinite nature and clashing with the equally valid forms of others. Yet if teachings are not broadened as contact with new neighbors occurs, destructive conflict arises (see Voegelin 2000–2001, 4:96, 264). For this reason literalism can be dangerous in a setting of diversity and mixing. In the raw difficulties of interfaith encounters among the naïve, religion runs the real risk of doing more harm than good, although wise leadership, overarching political authority, and strong norms of tolerance can mitigate this concern. Different classes' needs and vulnerabilities must be balanced as religions develop.

Adaptation in a changing world brings confusion to literalist believers, who form the considerable majority even among religious leaders. The naïve must be kept on board and steadied while the formula is changed on them. This dilemma poses daunting problems for universalists. Simply adapting, as philosophers might, would leave too many of the dependent in the lurch. Voegelin (2002, 74) poignantly evokes the forlornness people feel when finite religious expressions dissolve, and nothing remains but sophisticated ones. If the naïve are to be aligned with the universal, it must be in concrete forms suited to their requirements. Because background change is constantly under way, however, the universal has to be forever in motion. Consequently a very large portion of religious energy must be expended on the task of slowly adjusting the sectoral forms and their adherents to emerging realities—much of it in patient ministering. For religious specialists to retain clear sight of the horizon from this posture is no small feat.

Adaptation also brings dangers for the sophisticated. In their embrace of diversity the temptation is corrosive gnosticism in which they one-sidedly elevate contemplation and derogate ordinary religious practice. Not only is contemplation not the only activity of religion, but day in and day out, it is not the most important one. Sophisticated faith avoids hubris and remains within the pale by simultaneously accepting the infinite poetic truth and its finite expression in everyday religion.

The work of religion is made still more difficult by its antagonists. God exists as a matter of fact—as surely as do atoms or buildings. But since the deniers of religion persistently miss the divine reality standing before them, I direct to them the following proof of the existence of God. Let the *dubidoso* take on the God of sophisticated religion instead of that of naïve religion.

I begin my proof of God's existence, one kindred to Hegel's, by asking the atheist denier precisely *what* it is he supposes not to exist. If the human exists, and it has plural aspects, and these may be harmonized into a balanced whole, and we have rational and nonrational ways of representing this balanced whole, and God is the latter way—then God exists. God *is* empirically real—as palpably real as we in our many sides and the world around us. To deny God—the universal as figuratively expressed, the One, the Absolute, and the Real—is to refuse the universal. Religion is a fundamental and vital aspect of our personal and collective being, and we are disabling one of our two central institutions if we disavow it—to our own impoverishment and others' loss. We all have religious needs because we all have consummatory sides with which we have the need to address and harmonize the human comprehensively. To deny God—the real atheism—is to deny our capacity for wholeness. Even self-proclaimed atheists have spiritual sides, though they refuse them. "[T]o deny divine, is to deny human personality. . . . [The agnostic] ignores or explains away the elements in man which point to God. . . ." (Illingworth 1899, 211). However few are able to raise themselves to directly apprehend the whole or probe its sources or assess its consequences, the universal is there, and it is real.

No philosopher who approached the universal could be an atheist in the true sense, for he already encounters God by means of reason. If one understands religion, she does subscribe to it. As Hegel (1984, 1:388–9) says, "I do not believe that a sky is above me; I see it. . . . [T]he absolute testimony to the content of a religion, is the witness of the spirit and not miracle or external, historical verification."

Although they are wrong, the atheists and their comical agnostic fellow travelers are not as wrong as they are obtuse. To attack naïve religionists' simple, particularistic representations of the universal is to engage in embarrassing and destructive one-upsmanship with children. To the ratiocinating doubters I say, "Wake up to the poetry, and develop your sense of the whole." Previous defenses of the existence of God have done mock jousting with these blustery knights of intellectuality. This one shames them. The point is not to try to win these intelligent but unsubtle skeptics to belief when they reject all basis for it, but to invite them to include emotionality and the universal in their lives—to develop themselves. For those who were worried, the good news is that there is a God, the bad news is that deity is not what they thought it was.

Only the narrow would have room in their lives for the human sciences or the arts alone but not for both since each speaks to us in its powerful and irreplaceable manner. In a similar way we all have both philosophical and religious needs by virtue of our human natures. We must develop both sides of the universal if we are to be more fully realized and balanced. If we were completely universal, we would at once and in perfect harmony think philosophically and religiously.

Yet, in Plato's (1961, 527e, 533d) words, "the eye of the soul" in ordinary people is incapable of relating directly to the universal. Not knowing the universal, they cannot be directly inspired by it. As Illingworth (1899, 120–21) puts it, "[a] man cannot understand a character with which his own has no accord." Their need is for myth that personalizes and dramatizes the conclusions of the universal (Schuon 1982, 155).

In most circumstances societies have depended profoundly upon religion for their well-being. They have done so through the spiritual needs of all social classes, but some more directly and immediately than others. Schuon (1982, 146; see also Hegel 1984, 1:131) turns ultimately to a pragmatic moral argument for religion: "the common man, who is not disciplined by social necessity and who, precisely, is only disciplined by religion and piety, degenerates in his behavior when he no longer has religion containing him and penetrating him. . . ." The inconveniences of sectoralist religion are borne by the universal in stoic solicitude for the well-being of the whole. Popular aspects of religion are the gymnastics through which society has had to go to enable average people to follow their best impulses and avoid their worst ones. More effectively than any logical proof, the Sophoclean stakes have humbled the proud and drawn protectors and adherents to fixed religion. Because a religion is ultimately engaged in the world, its highest test is how much it objectively contributes to the long-term well-being of the whole.

However, religion is necessary even to those with comprehensive philosophy if they are to reach their fullest development and understanding. For as Illingworth (1899, 196) says, "we find the desire for union with God to lie at the very basis of our being. . . ." That oneness is most perfectly attained in contemplative universalism, as found, for example, in the *Upanishads, Bhagavad Gita,* Rumi's verses, and Meister Eckhart. By raising oneself to the universal, one is not distant from religion but at the heart of it. No sacrifice of the intellect or embrace of the absurd need accompany religion.

Yet universal religion can never long forget itself in contemplative bliss or God's work because such religion forever appears threatening to those rigidly bound to the fixed forms it spawns and whose sectoralism puts them in constant danger of confusion, disorientation, and intolerance. When their sheltering can be the overriding concern, the universal may defer to the vulnerable and insulate them by withdrawing in its more active manifestations for a time. But countervailing concerns come to the fore in times of socio-cultural tumult and skepticism—that the literalists might rudely presume to have access to more than partial and conditional truth and act aggressively upon it, or that the universal might cede so much ground that potential leaders who need to understand should be misguided. In such matters, as in everything else, one must find the balance.

Through all of this, the universalist never loses sight of the central fact that sectoralist myth and ritual remain metaphorically true. Both universal and sectoral interpretations are preserved within the world religions in sublime dualist overcomings not yet approached by modern philosophy.

Notes

1. In Hegel's (1984, 1:323) idealism "creation" refers to God's *positing* of the world. In my usage it refers to the creative potential of the universal.
2. I owe this insight to Frank Bergon.
3. This will be elaborated upon in the next chapter.

Bibliography

Cobb, J. 1982. *Beyond Dialogue: Toward a Mutual Transformation of Christianity and Buddhism*. Philadelphia: Fortress Press.

Eliade, M. 1959. *The Sacred and the Profane*. New York: Harcourt, Brace and World.

Hegel, G. 1967. *Hegel's Philosophy of Right*. London: Oxford University Press.

———. 1984. *Lectures on the Philosophy of Religion*. 3 vols. Berkeley and Los Angeles: University of California Press.

Illingworth, J. 1899. *Personality, Human and Divine*. New York: Macmillan.

James, W. 1958. *Varieties of Religious Experience*. New York: New American Library.

Nietzsche, F. 1974. *The Gay Science*. New York: Vintage Books.

Plato. 1961. "Republic." In *The Collected Dialogues of Plato*, ed. E. Hamilton and H. Cairns. Princeton, NJ: Princeton University Press.

Schuon, F. 1981. *Esoterism as Principle and as Way*. Bedfont, Middlesex: Perennial Books.

———. 1982. *From the Divine to the Human*. Bloomington, IN: World Wisdom Books.

———. 1984. *Logic and Transcendence*. London: Perennial Books.

Strauss, L. 1983. *Studies in Platonic Political Philosophy*. Chicago: University of Chicago Press.

Taylor, C. 2002. *Varieties of Religion Today*. Cambridge, MA: Harvard University Press.

Temple, W. 1960. *Nature, Man and God*. New York: Macmillan.

Voegelin, E. 2000–2001. *The Collected Works of Eric Voegelin*. Volumes 14–18. *Order and History*. Columbia: University of Missouri Press.

———. 2002. *The Collected Works of Eric Voegelin*. Volume 6. *Anamnesis: On the Theory of History and Politics*. Columbia: University of Missouri Press.

Weber, M. 1958. *From Max Weber: Essays in Sociology*. New York: Oxford University Press.

Whitehead, A. 1926. *Religion in the Making*. New York: Macmillan.

11. *Ethics*

Introduction

Where the core of philosophy, which is ontology and particularly the ontology of the universal, is very ideal dominant, ethics, which looks at and guides active decisionmaking, though from a distance, goes as far as one can go within philosophy in the direction of the real. As the universal has rational and nonrational manifestations, so it has ideal and real manifestations. Aristotle in *Ethics* (book 6) captures the relationship between ontological and applied ethical knowledge in his distinction between theoretical wisdom (*sophia*) and practical wisdom (*phronesis*). In taking up ethics we note further internal differentiation in the universal, concerning ourselves with its real-world application.

The human sciences today have a particular need to engage the philosophy of ethics, for they misunderstand and frequently badly mistreat morality. How misguidedly the contemporary human sciences approach the ethical is suggested by the fact that across much of their territory it has become socially acceptable to study deviance but not to study morality. In their postmodernist negativism bad has largely become good and good bad in morality, although in psychology and political science, which are moderately less afflicted by skepticism than the other fields, it is still possible to study morality straightforwardly, as in the work of Kohlberg. Having substantially negated the ethical, the primary residual moral desiderata retained by most of the human sciences are a loose norm of tolerance and the minimalist one associated with the negation of all other moral forms.

I propose a philosophy of ethics that restores the balance and enables the human sciences again to address ethical phenomena in a constructive light—not to the exclusion of inquiry into the deviant but in addition to it. Ethics is not something one can omit as extraneous to the human sciences. If their practitioners do not know the nature of the ethical, they cannot observe it in the empirical phenomena they study. Having largely forgotten how to think about ethics and morality, the human sciences have a particular need for reorientation in this regard. Studying the good (and not as bad) reopens a large and important field for empirical inquiry by human scientists. A sophisticated practitioner of the human sciences need not neglect or negate ethics.

At the same time, an ethical philosophy informed by the human sciences is of special interest to the philosophy of ethics. As yet, philosophers have only hints of the crucial role that human science knowledge can, must, and will play at the core of their own enterprise. Universalism's philosophy of ethics is one that gives a prominent role to the human sciences, utilizing their resources to solve problems philosophers have long been unable to solve independently. While broadly Hegelian, what follows does not utilize Hegel's language of freedom, which is less helpful in ethical than in social philosophy.

****

I begin ethics with the assumption that well-being is the ultimate point of all moral desirability.[1] In Aristotle's (1961, b93) words, "it is leading to or following from well-being that all things are worthy of choice. . . ." As the only suitable way of determining what would contribute to this condition, the universal in its comprehensive, balanced self-consciousness and self-control is intimately associated with all ethics. Insofar as the universal reigns, morality does as well. Ethics in the basic, real-world sense is action putting the universal into practice, particularly but not exclusively at the level of the person. The ethically or morally good is what has the probability of optimally contributing to the long-term well-being of the whole. This goal is the ultimate criterion of all moral value and moral oughtness and is the aim of all action by the universal. All moral obligation is directly or indirectly tied to it. Nietzsche's (1966) question, "Of what use is morality?" is a great one and critical to ethics. What the moral does is contribute optimally to the full range of our true needs. Ethics acquires a crucial element of the empirical from the fact that in the largest view action is moral only to the extent to which it is based upon correct assessment of what is likely to make the greatest contribution to long-term well-being, considering all consequences direct and indirect.

Moral action, or would-be moral action, may be conducted more or less well, as in the giving of a well- versus a poorly chosen gift. Attempts at moral goodness may and frequently do go awry—because the understanding, factual knowledge, or sensitivity is not there or because the moral forms are out of step with circumstances, for example. Just as certain forms of corporate organization under certain business conditions are empirically likely to work out for the best, certain forms of morality in certain conditions are empirically likely to work out for the best. To the extent that the universal is successful in its efforts, the well-being of the human is maximized over time—all else equal. Of the actual outcome, however, we have no guarantees.

If the *M*oral or absolute morality is what contributes optimally to the long-term well-being of the whole, the "moral" is the set of particular norms, virtues, and other expectations proffered or in effect at a given time that lay claim to Morality. A great deal of "morality," tied to the superego or superid, is what someone or some group or person believes to be Morality; but Morality is often only moderately well approximated by "morality" and is sometimes detracted from by it. For something to be Moral and to be labeled moral are two different things. "Moralities," the concrete ethics of particular places and times, reflect the sectoral perspectives of particular social classes and introduce varying degrees of imbalance.

Within the basic sense of the ethical as what maximally contributes to the long-term well-being of the whole, it is necessary to distinguish between the ethical proper, i.e., the explicitly moral, the special contribution, direct or indirect, of the universal over and above any sectoral contribution—and the ethical in the broadest sense that includes the implicitly moral, what contributes to the whole via the pursuit of purely sectoral ends. The one is the proximate contribution of the universal, the other the contribution of the sectoral. The ethical proper works through the sectors but adjusts their forms and ends to the needs of the whole. However, the ethical in the broadest sense includes everything that contributes to the whole, even what is predominantly sectoral, such as earning money and engaging in play. Driving a taxicab for a fee is moral in the broadest sense. Because everything that is amoral in the strict sense without being harmful is also residually moral in the broadest sense, we do not morally disparage the amoral, i.e., nonmoral. Whatever satisfies any need, all else equal, is ipso facto moral in the largest sense.

Although the central focus of our care is the human itself, since it has possessions and an environment that are of great moment to it, the ethical also reaches over the artificial and natural worlds around us. To the extent to which one approaches the universal, she also stewards possessions and cares for the environment. Respect for the human and an abiding concern not to transgress hubris tell us as much.

It should be self-evident that the master good, which is the moral good, can come only through the overcoming and synthesis of all other goods. Why the universalist criterion of the moral good is the right one is because, as the long-term well being of the whole, it is the one with which we are best off overall and make the most progress. How could anyone disagree with pursuing the long-term well-being of the whole? Would they want only the short-term well-being of the whole? Would they want only the well-being of the part? Would they want a moral code that did not contribute to long-term well-being? I don't think so. I think they believe their particular approach does contribute to the long-term well-being of the whole. The very fact that people possess and argue for an ethical position suggests that they tacitly accept the criterion of the long-term well-being of the whole. As I see it, the only significant argument against this ethical criterion could be epistemological, that of radical relativism and skepticism, which I will address in Chapter 18.

****

Ethics in the basic sense is applied universalism; ethics in the philosophical sense is the conceptual study and systematic universalization of the same. Like the two main senses of the word "history," one sense of ethics is the real thing, and the other is the study of the same—a distinction necessary for making progress on the problems of ethics. However, this formulation is again an ideal type. In carrying out their systematic inquiries, ethical philosophers in practice have most often done little more than describe the most general content and/or form of their own communities or social classes' moralities and impute full universalism to them. Drawing from a distance upon real-world experience in particular kinds of societies, ethical philosophers have instructed people concerning how they should lead their lives and proposed programs for imprinting the universal that moralize action in the real world. Ethical philosophers have then appealed to their communities to adopt their understanding of how all human beings may best follow the universal. Philosophical ethics has been less removed from applied ethics and the real world than might appear.

From antiquity to the present there has been a tendency on the part of philosophers and the social classes they represent to affirm one pole of a basic dimension of the human as moral and negate the other as immoral. In doing so they have wrongly introduced sectoralism into philosophical ethics. One instance of this, made repeatedly by Plato and the German idealists (though not by Kant), has been to cling to collectivist forms and shun individualist ones, holding immersion in and mindfulness of the larger group to be inherently moral, irrespective of the circumstances or cost.[2] Other ethical philosophers have wrongly conflated community and association respectively with morality and immorality. To the contrary, in extremely associational relations, such as interaction with tolltakers at bridges, or ticket agents at movie theatres, the whole is frequently served by considering persons with whom we interact almost entirely as means, although even in these cases small and fleeting gestures of respect often still matter. Plato and others have also wrongly conflated the ideal and the real respectively with morality and immorality. Ethical development in a person or collectivity isn't fighting against individualism, instrumentalism, or the real world, it is overcoming each dimension and finding the balance with respect to it.

Traditionally, ethical philosophy has been restricted largely to personal ethics, having considered primarily the moral imperatives on persons, not those on collectivities, and it has correspondingly underexplored obligations to and via collectivities. Like persons, however, collectivities are morally good to the extent to which they act to further the long-term well-being of the whole of which they are parts. Even national societies must discharge obligations to the larger community of nations—even while they also have significant obligations to their members. Of what would benefit the whole, a great deal lies at the macrolevel, pertaining to what economic, political, communal, and cultural forms and resource allocations would be most beneficial. In the practical universalism of collectivities the good—in the form of building and accumulating solutions to problems—is worked into social institutions and moralizes them. Corporations are moralized as respect for their obligations as collective members of society is diffused through their cultures. Government agencies are moralized as dedication to civil service becomes more widespread in them. Educational institutions are moralized as commitment to standards of research, teaching, and extracurricular experience rises in them. Good economies, regimes, families, schools, and persons all further the well-being of the whole. Collective morality stands over and against personal morality and cannot be reduced to it. Macroethics is directed to the collective or social policies we ought to pursue as societies to further the well-being of the whole, policies that have their separate claim to moral validity and must be balanced against the claims of personal morality. A major part of our moral responsibility must consist of staying informed about and active in collectivities, transcending the biases of interests and emotions.

Political philosophy has generally been taken to parallel ethics, but ethics and political philosophy are not commensurate since political philosophy addresses only one institution of society, namely politics, and ignores all other institutions. Political philosophy in the usual restricted sense, as in Aristotle's *Politics,* tells primarily what regime structure and rules are best, saying next to nothing about the economic, communal, or cultural policies we ought to pursue. Social philosophy, broadly construed to include all such concerns, including political ones—or political philosophy in this comprehensive sense—is the true macroanalog to ethics. The macroparallel to the question of how a person should lead her life is how a people should lead its collective life or how society should conduct itself. This said, I set aside macroethics as outside the scope of this work.

What Is the Relevant Whole?

If ethics revolves around the self-consciousness and self-control of the universal, a basic problem of ethics[3] is what is the morally relevant whole, who are the "we" whose long-term well-being is at issue? In near unanimity great books, religious prophets, noble leaders, and good citizens entreat us to become part of something larger than ourselves, but they differ markedly with respect to how much larger than ourselves—over how great a geographical or social reach—we should be identifying and maximizing well-being. Who belongs to society as a whole? Who is our neighbor? Who is our brother? To be human, as Heidegger understands, is to care, but care for whom, for what, if we are to be moral? With whom we are to be concerned morally is the problem of moral reach.

The standard by which moral reference is apportioned should be set by our ethical criterion. Taking the reach to be fully universal for this one issue, we determine which ethical reference would itself contribute maximally to the long-term well-being of the whole. In practice the relevant whole varies by issue as our resources vary. Insofar as we are able to make a difference in a certain area of life, we are obligated to direct our resources to the long-term well-being of the appropriate whole. If we do not have the resources of knowledge, wealth, or time to affect others beneficially, they cannot practicably be considered part of our moral reference. Just as a firm cannot enter every market, a moral agent cannot meliorate every adverse condition. The greater our power vis-à-vis certain others, the greater the moral import of our relationship with them. Orienting oneself at impracticable distance from resources and real relations errs in an ineffectual idealist direction. Investing unduly remote others with moral concern can only be a wasteful exercise. On the other hand, failing to orient oneself practically far out lags behind resources and real relations, erring in a realist direction. This range of obligations to ourselves and our families, friends, neighbors, associates, communities, and regions—on out to the world—presents competing needs that require harmonization. In order to maximize the well-being of the comprehensive whole we must find the balance across the entire range with reference to which we have moral obligations and weigh needs against our means. Any degree of otherwise presumptively moral identification with higher groups that is out of balance becomes less than Moral at the point at which it becomes so. One of the most formidable problems of ethics is the result.

The effective whole whose balanced well-being forms the criterion of ethics is not just the top layer of the dome—it is the synthesis of all the layers. One portion of the corresponding problem is the controversy in ethics between those, especially German philosophers, who say that the good is a collective attribute only derivatively applying to persons, and those who think it only inheres in persons, especially Anglo-American philosophers. The truth lies at once in both, for this opposition must be overcome, as must those through all of the intermediate levels up to society as a whole. In the Third Reich there was an extreme imbalance in which a national interest was defined grotesquely but also in utter mutual exclusiveness with other levels, to the ruin of so much. Morality can never be exclusively focused on a particular level, as in aggrandizement of the state, or in the "amoral familism" of mid-twentieth century Calabria (see Banfield). Each level has to be assigned its due. By that I don't mean that a person or group may not specialize morally in contributing to a small, manageable set of levels and groups from the whole range—indeed in a complex society we all must do so to some extent. What I mean is that while doing so, the whole ascending range of the human must be kept in mind and respected simultaneously. For example, if someone satisfactorily meets obligations to herself, her family, and all overarching layers, it may be perfectly moral that she devote most of her remaining energy and resources to the betterment of her neighborhood or city because of special knowledge and feasibility. On the other hand, crystallized, hard, exclusive commitment on any level to the inordinate expense of other levels with which it forms an interlacing hierarchical community—as in the above cases of Nazi statism and Calabrian familism—is a problem, one of which Plato was far from free.

Serving the whole very prominently includes serving one's family and oneself, which is therefore presumptively moral, all else equal. Our personal well-being is part of the whole and part of the criterion of the moral. And as Luther, Mandeville, and Smith all understood, in many respects we know best and are best placed to take care of and satisfy the needs of ourselves and those close to us. Morality is not a one-way service by the member of the larger group. It is also a service of the person and small group by themselves and by the larger group. We count morally, too! However, our devotion to ourselves and those near and dear must be in proportion with everything else.

Nevertheless, there is a higher-level self which, in identification with the good, will move lower-level selves through great sacrifice when necessary—even as we send the best-placed regiment toward battle or sell a losing subsidiary to save the company. How this expenditure is determined is by considering the long-term well-being of the whole. On such occasions self-concern on the part of higher-level collectivities and their members will be accompanied by sacrifice of lower-level ones. Under certain circumstances, particularly in individualist settings, it can be helpful to conceptualize this process as a matter of altruism; while in others, particularly in collectivist ones there is not really an other involved. When we are strongly identified with and emotionally attached to people, our generosity with respect to them is automatic and natural, as it is to our children. To be human is to pursue *our* well-being, but who *we* are may be distinct individuals or it may be members of families, cities, or countries. The more profoundly one is a part of something larger, the more he acts gladly rather than merely dutifully on its behalf. Even though what is morally good is not necessarily what we like, want, and need as individuals; insofar as we identify with the larger group, what we like, want, and need comes into alignment with the needs of the larger whole of which we are a part. The sentiment accompanying this posture is perfectly expressed in Deuteronomy (4:40): "that it may go well with thee, and with thy children after thee, and that thou mayest prolong thy days upon the earth."[4] It is not that in caring we take pleasure in others' pleasure—although in such a condition we do—it is that others' needs become our own (Maslow 1954, 251). When sacrifice is warranted, what is sacrificed (literally that which makes holy or does good) is always dear to us, its needs are carefully considered, and we grieve for it. Sacrifice is the yielding to the whole by the part that is central to all morality.

The breadth of the morally relevant whole and of the appropriate moral reference has changed many times in history, though in balance it has moved from narrower to broader wholes. The reach of the whole is especially altered by changes in political community and by economic growth and decline. Under today's conditions, unlike those of the twelfth century, the reference for major collective moral decisions can often be the world as a whole. Morality must change to reflect the changing reach of influence, as it must change to reflect movement from community to association or from nonreflexivity to reflexivity. What transpires within different societies, insofar as it is self-contained and they are separate, need not concern others. However, insofar as its consequences spill over to affect others in ways that are controllable, the ethically relevant whole changes, and they must alter their reference, identification, and ways. No inherent mutual exclusiveness exists between the needs of the levels, yet because different resources, consequences, and circumstances call forth very different moral profiles, there is major potential for disharmony between them that requires assiduous working.

If identification across an optimal range of the human contributes to the greatest possible well-being, the problem is not usually too broad an identification, although some exceptionally misty-eyed and ineffectual Buddhists, Christians, and humanists have fallen victim to it. Moreover, there have been historical situations in which a shrinking frame of reference was necessary. Given the final collapse of Rome and the slow jelling of feudalism in the sixth and seventh centuries, for many purposes it was important that Western Europeans again get used to identifying more restrictively. However, immorality from inappropriate identification predominantly takes the form of undue narrowness of identification—one's self, family, class, people, or country to the detriment of others. Because how broadly one perceives, thinks, feels, and identifies determines the range over which the human may act morally, moral action ordinarily has as a top priority the creation of understandings and sentiments that link the local to the cosmopolitan and the part to the whole so that people may come to see and feel their commonality with others. Reconciling Antigone's obligations to the state with those to her family, holistic working enhances breadth and enables people to contribute to the whole in harmony. But restrictive identification is not necessarily immoral—to the contrary, it is moral to the extent to which it does not at the same time have countervailing side-effects for others who also matter.

In most cases and certainly today, little contributes more to well-being than growing identification spanning broader community. Persons and aggregates with narrow frames of reference all too often pose problems for themselves and those around them. A person stuck in her individual frame of reference might steal from her neighbors or fail to participate in an important community project while attempting to do right by herself. Or she might mistreat her children or carelessly damage public property. Collectivities with unduly restrictive frames of reference pose analogous problems. Radical Spanish Basques who have sought to be moral in their misguided fashion have disrespected the larger references of Spain, Europe, and the world. On behalf of narrow and distorted references Serbian nationalists have slaughtered Kosovars, and self-righteous Muslim fanatics have attacked innocent Egyptian Copts. All of these actions, contravening the whole, represent the opposite of Morality.

The ultimate emotional basis for morality is then the higher-level desire for the well-being of the family, tribe, community, or society and its members. The relationship that holds between persons when they come to acknowledge the larger community spanning them is that of brotherhood or neighborhood. In caring for the whole one cares for those of whom it is composed, and therefore his brother and neighbor. In keeping with this, Chu Hsi speaks "of love (the principle of aggregation in the universal) as the motive force of all things" (Needham 1978, 1:244).

As we want to identify with as much of the human as we are able in the present, we want to identify with as much of it as we are able into the future. All else equal, having a longer and fuller time horizon is always more moral. Again there are practical limits, however. The more universal our knowledge, the more distant our time horizon can be, the less universal, the less distant. The further our considerations reach into the future, the less certain they can be, and conversely—for which reason our desire to benefit all future times must be balanced against the constraints of limited knowledge. As we often best benefit the whole by taking good care of ourselves and our families, so we often best benefit all times by conducting ourselves well on the more proximate issues at hand while accumulating reservoirs of knowledge and resources that will enable us and our successors to cope flexibly with whatever might arise. This indefinite optimal future point of reference is what I understand by taking the long-term perspective.

Direct and Indirect Ethics

There are two most basic kinds of ethics, direct and indirect. Direct ethics is autonomous action employing the universal on behalf of the good. Indirect ethics is heteronomous action without direct engagement of the universal but in adherence to its surrogate moral forms. With an indirect ethics the universal comes to be stamped in character as people are inculcated in concrete moral virtues and rules, bringing action into conformity with the good. Indirect ethics are constructed by those whose moral action is direct. To the extent to which the resulting moral forms are valid, they consist of the best routines for people to follow, considering all consequences of their actions. Direct moralities create and use new moral forms; indirect ones act with established moral forms. Moral goodness is alignment with the universal, irrespective of whether that comes from direct possession of the universal or from its indirect imprint on the superego, superid, or other sector. There being no Morality without the universal; if one does not possess her own, she must have its sectoral imprint. (Although it is convenient to use ideal types, what we actually have is a continuum from direct to indirect ethics.)

Yet nothing but something's probable empirical connection with the well-being of the whole confers Morality. The morally right or virtuous can be so only vis-à-vis social circumstances that render it contributory to the long-term well-being of the whole, i.e., Moral. Ultimately no concrete form is inherently moral. What is alleged to be such is something moral authorities have declared to be inherently moral in order to encourage conformity with it. Even when rules or virtues have proven themselves in many circumstances to have been necessary to avoid great harm, and people from many traditions hold them sacred, their ultimate claim to being ethical is that they have been found empirically linked with the good—for circumstances comparable to those in which the results have been obtained. This said, there are indeed many cherished rules and virtues experience has taught the most perspicacious of many societies to follow in almost all circumstances. However, even these would be supersedable by direct universalists should adherence to them in unusual circumstances threaten overriding harm to the whole. All moral authority and all moral law and virtue are ultimately grounded solely in the moral good and have no standing outside of it.

The extent to which one should lead her life with direct or indirect morality depends upon her resources. One must know her potential and her limits. Erring up or down is moral error: it is not Moral for one who is out of her depth to attempt the path of direct morality, and it is not Moral for one whose potential is universal to subordinate herself to flawed indirect morality where she could do better on her own. One acts well morally and as part of ethical society when she follows her own or others' universals, whichever is better aligned with the whole. Thoughtful people tend to use a balanced combination of both, striving for the best direct ethics while harmonizing with a considerable structure of indirect ethics. The two are ordinarily complementary and mutually enhancing.

Such complex matrices of considerations are difficult for ethical philosophers rigidly rooted in indirect ethics such as Kant. Aristotle with his comparatively fluid balance between direct and indirect ethics would find them less difficult. They are relatively easily accommodated by Bentham and Mill whose flexible structure readily allows the addition of subsidiary indirect ethics.

The World of Direct Ethics

When engaging in direct moral action, people overcome all sectoralism and take the viewpoint of the whole. The active moral agent autonomously finds his way by independently surveying the ramifications of his conduct, determining what moral routines maximally contribute to the well-being of the whole and then acting upon them. Caring universally, he balances and harmonizes up and down the hierarchy of the human from the most overarching collectivity to the person, even as he balances among sectors at each level. Although he consults them and is seldom far from them, the universalist does not necessarily follow all of the rules and virtues. To the extent to which universalist leaders exercise power on their behalf, collectivities may also act with direct morality. No subtler or more demanding task exists than the conduct of direct ethics and the exercise of practical wisdom.

An early and most memorable, if atypically rational, example of direct ethics is found in the depiction of the dominant Athenian moral character in the fifth century BCE by Thucydides. As he describes it, projecting to no small degree, the privileged young Athenians of the time paid great attention to how to contribute to their city's betterment. While educating themselves to the greatest possible extent, they constantly thought about what their unique contribution to the city-state might be. When they found it, they then threw themselves with all their energy and resources into carrying it out. Their emphasis was upon not merely caring for the city-state, for which they felt deeply, but doing so supremely well. In this ethic our purpose in life, our calling in the largest sense, is making the greatest contribution we might to society. For those who love the good—and direct ethics is accompanied by love of the good, as Socrates and Plato express it—Thucydides' approach is doubly beneficial. Pursuing it is at once the best possible way of contributing to the whole and the best possible way of making their own lives fulfilling. The Thucydidean ethic perfectly anticipated the highest expression of Jesus' message of loving and serving God and one's neighbor.

On the tactical level, in his autonomous action on behalf of the good, the practitioner of direct ethics engages in the constant application of universalism. His applied dialectics finds the many-dimensional moral balance overcoming oppositions in particular circumstances. Although they largely frame their ethical philosophies in a different context I will describe shortly, this could be taken as a generalizing from Aristotle and Confucius to all kinds of moral situations and forms. Those two philosophers are at one in their emphasis on the importance of finding the mean or balance in life. However, both emphasize how very difficult it is to find the proper balance, the great majority instead listing toward one extreme or the other.

Despite the great good of which it is capable, the world of direct ethics is a venturesome one fraught with risk. The ancient Greek direct ethic of development hedged its risks by taking a more cautious corollary in the norm against hubris. In a many-sided world, practitioners of direct ethics must guard against overconfidence and drifting away from the balance through the constant checking of what they have been doing and how they have been doing it. Hubris should be avoided and all contentment tinged with some anxiety in the knowledge that perfect balance is never attainable and hazards abound in life.

Being in the world of direct ethics, however, is not entirely of one's choosing. Turbulent times confront us with a bewildering variety of conflicting moralities. In cosmopolitan crossroads we encounter wide-open moral marketplaces in which one trades or goes out of business. In complex, dynamic times, to the variety of indirect ethics is inevitably added the further moral pluralism presented by direct ethics.

Few reach the point at which they possess well-developed universals and are able consistently to form wise original ethical judgments. If the world had to depend on every person's independently finding his ethical way, it would be in dire straits, for on our own we are morally vulnerable. A central problem for ethics has been how to formulate and distribute wisdom coming from the active universal for use by those less able to carry out independent moral action, and then to motivate compliance with the received forms once inculcated.

Types of Indirect Ethics

With indirect ethics, the types of ethics predominantly in popular use, someone's or some group's direct, original determination of the good leads to construction of relatively fixed moral forms designed to realize the good indirectly. One engages in moral action in conformity with its moral routines on the basis of the faith placed in that person or group. Indirect ethics relies on moral authority to link the ethically dependent to the ethically independent. If they are to best realize their moral potential and lead ethical lives, ordinary people and especiallly the young must be guided overwhelmingly by moral forms made determinate for them.

Social classes necessarily stamp their leanings on all indirect ethics. People of different sorts must be moralized in different ways, depending upon their characters, which vary by time, place, and circumstances. The major kinds of indirect morality represent universalizations of the different major kinds of personalities and are framed according to the sector dominant in their character. Those in whom a certain sector is weak, however, may also have the corresponding kind of morality subordinately or to a lesser degree. Yet it is not only the demand side that matters, for indirect ethics are also marked by the classes supplying their concrete forms. Indirect ethics approach the world from one particular sectoral perspective or another because, absent the active universal, one can act Morally only via different kinds of fixed morality.

Each sector of the human may be divided into an amoral (i.e., nonmoral) and a moral subsector, according to the degree to which it has been infused with ethics and particularly with indirect ethics. Thus there are laws and moral laws, norms and moral norms, art and moral art. The dynamic task of holistic working is to universalize each sector of society and the psyche and bring its forms into harmony with the needs of the whole. The economy, family, politics, and culture all need to be worked into patterns as conducive as possible to the well-being of the whole. New perspectives tend to be at first amoral, but with time and working they are moralized.

Even the id may be moralized, after a fashion, through development in it of sensitivity to the moral expectations of others. An id-based morality centers upon whether the id's action exceeds, meets, or fails to live up to a group's ways, and feelings of honor or shame arise in the person. Someone with a moral id comes to act in such a manner that the moral way is followed and the whole benefited out of desire for acceptance and/or fear of rejection by fellows. Among the id dominant, those with more resources in traditional societies had the greater possibility of pursuing lives of honor. The love of glory pristinely conveyed in the warrior ethic of the *Iliad* exemplifies this beautifully. The ordinary rank of the id dominant in very communal settings like agrarian villages, without the possibility of acquiring skills in leadership or warfare, primarily have the possibility of avoiding shame. But even they can display a resplendent supererogation in their generous sharing of what little they have, even with strangers. Id-dominant moralities are collectivist, group-bound, and rooted in strong community. They focus on moral ways and make use of the powerful mechanism of social approval and disapproval. Group-bound morality is based upon the spontaneous moral emotions of everyone involved: the swelling of the honorable and shrinking of the shameful, together with the spontaneous moral approval or disapproval of their fellows. A shame morality is quintessentially that of traditional peasants. Id-based ethics is front and center only in simple societies, but it lives on as an important supplement to other forms of morality in more developed ones.

A moral ego, to the degree one may be said to exist, involves rational calculation of what is in the interests of the person, or, to the extent to which the ego is a collectivist one, of the group. The ego-dominant moral agent may be drawn by benefits to herself or the collectivity, or she may be deterred by threats to herself, as in fear of the Lord or of the law. A simple variant of this involves rational deduction from magical assumptions, as often occurs in the Greek tragedies. The social ego may be deterred by harmful consequences to the collectivity as in fear of weakening one's family or ritual pollution of the clan or city. All deterrence represents an ego-based ethics in this most strained application of the concept. It is an ego-dominant ethic which Weber (1978, 470) disparages by saying that insofar as the religion of ancient Persian peasants was ethical at all, it was based upon quid pro quos with priests and deity.

Deriving from external rather than internal sources, id- and ego-based forms of morality are personally nonreflexive. While they were central in earlier societies and are still of importance today, most would concur with Weber in seeing all such ethics as only the most tenuous possible morality. The id- and ego-dominant have a chronic, characteristic problem of lack of self-control. Only external pressure has any hope of bringing order to their lives.

The moral superego, with which we begin taking up the reflexive ethical forms philosophers have traditionally accepted as moral, is most often of the rule-bound type that accepts and enforces the moral law received on authority. This rule-bound superego includes Heidegger's (1962, 335–41) everyday conscience. As it is moralized, the superego's discipline comes to be channeled by rules or principles directed to the well-being of the whole. The rationally couched do's and don'ts regarding action of which the rules consist are verbally formulated and may be verbally taught. What the rules command is the right. However, the moral superego may also take an individualist ad hoc form in which it ratiocinates independently to determine what moral policies would be beneficial to the group (or sometimes to the person) and pursues its own independent course. In superego morality the primary motivation for following the rules is one of duty, and the person's self-concept becomes linked with morality. A sense of moral self-respect is the moral superego's positive emotion and moral guilt its negative emotion. The best can be brought out in superego-dominant people via moral rules. A rule-bound superego ethics is quintessentially the morality of the bourgeois.

The moral form accompanying the superid is that of the virtues, moral patterns in the style of life that make up the nonrational parallel to the moral rules.[5] Such virtues as courage, honesty, justice, and temperance, when consistently modeled to young people, establish a framework within which a flowing and beautiful ethical life may be conducted. As it is moralized, the sensitivity achieved by the superid is directed toward respect and care for others and for the community. Since the virtues are primarily framed in images rather than words, and since superid morality links a person's self-image with morality, one may also guide the moral superid with such imageries of nobility as those in the Homeric or Arthurian legends or the lives of the saints. It is also possible to some extent to communicate such a morality by abstract and rational philosophical discourse. But the preponderant force of a superid morality must lie in a particular way of life that has charisma and is modeled to others for direct apprehension and imitation. Moral self-esteem is the superid's analog to the superego's moral self-respect; moral self-disgust is its analog to the latter's moral guilt. A virtue ethics is quintessentially the morality of the upper classes of agrarian societies and particularly those significantly urbanized. The best can be brought out in superid-dominant people with virtue ethics. When rule-based and virtue-based ethics come into contact, adjustment between the two is required, but one or the other will tend to dominate, subordinating the substance and tone of the other.

When the superid is amoral, one has the self-indulgent aestheticism of a stylish rake, such as that of Beau Brummel of two centuries ago or of the playful "valley girls" of Southern California circa 1980—morally neutral life styles both. Whether a superid is moral or amoral, one is pulled toward it by the beauty or charisma of its form. In the case of the moral superid this is fixed by reference to the whole.

What qualifies the superid's content as moral is the same as what ultimately qualifies the superego's as moral, that it accord with the long-term well-being of the whole. The moral rules and the moral virtues are the dominant forms in which people receive imperatives from moral authorities, whose precepts or modeling are directed to us with an explicit or implicit claim that they encapsulate Morality. Accordingly, the primary established forms of the good are the right and the virtuous. The two central kinds of indirect morality by which, once socialized, a person may remain independent of all social pressures and act morally despite prolonged subsequent exposure to disruption and turbulence are those of the superego and superid.[6]

The dominant class characters of the different concrete moralities of the world vary markedly. They manifest a larger consistency, however, in that each represents what a moral person would lean toward in similar circumstances—expressing care for the whole in the different but complementary ways appropriate to particular conditions. The id's feelings of honor or shame before others, the superego's self-respect or guilt before the conscience, and the superid's pride or self-disgust before the moral sensibility are different valid moral modes of relating to the whole. Either individuals or members may also be oriented to the morally good, but they too must be so in different ways. Although most people are predominantly under the influence of one or another type in accordance with their characters, all benefit from the simultaneous development in them of the different basic forms of morality. Thus Greek aristocrats in whom a moral style of life was dominant sometimes supplemented the virtues with subordinate moral rules while the bourgeois in whom the moral rules were dominant frequently developed ancillary life styles of virtue. Both have also been complemented by group-bound honor and shame moralities. The inherent compatibility of the basic ethical forms is compellingly suggested by the force of a Christian style of life in outstanding religious schools, which augments the traditionally dominant moral rules.[7]

While following a concrete morality such as the moral rules may be entirely ethical, it is only one aspect of and does not exhaust morality. Each kind of ethic works as best it can toward the good, but only from the perspective in which it is based. Morality is approached as particular moral forms undergo holistic working, but no one determinate morality or set of the same can ever cover the range of what is morally good. Only the universal can do that. Those who sought to be perfectly and fully moral would have to live up to all of the basic forms of morality simultaneously in a continuously updated full-spectrum balance, something that would be impossible without direct ethics.

The forms of immorality follow the forms of imbalance. These may be categorized by the orientation and motivation via which they represent departure from the universal beginning with frame of reference up and down the hierarchy of the human. Much immorality comes from imbalance in juggling competing loyalties, claims, and needs from overly narrow identification. Much immorality is personal or subgroup selfishness or weakness that brings wider harm. All too often action is morally responsible vis-à-vis one level or entity and its needs but seriously derelict with respect to one or more others. This disparity is especially likely in an unworked society with considerable vertical disharmony. Whether it is employees cheating employers, hoods mugging theatregoers, bigots attacking religious dissenters, or nations elbowing trading partners, immorality very often comes down to personal and collective actors rejecting larger groups of which they are a part. They take themselves to be caring for themselves or their own while bringing harm to others. They may have their honor among thieves, embezzlers, fanatics, or freeloaders, but they do harm to the larger whole of which they are a part. A lot of immorality reduces to such narrowness of reach in one form or another. Over and over again those seemingly moral at one level—among their peers, sectaries, or countrymen—turn out to be immoral at a higher one.

Much immorality also involves weakness of self-control allowing norms to be violated or vice engaged in. Moral intentions are disregarded in the midst of riots by the id or coups by the ego. This is equivalent to saying that the wish lacks strength or that the would-be governing sector lacks power with respect to what it would rule. The instrumental version of the problem entails weakness of the will or akrasia. Here there is temporal errancy or lack of future orientation. The worst case is that of the profligates who are utterly present-oriented. The consummatory version of the problem entails inability to hold to the virtues.[8] Those whose self-control is deficient do not intend ill for the whole but nevertheless bring it about.

The moral superego and moral superid provide the two different main avenues for overcoming weakness of self-control and rising above the crude external moralities of the id and ego, for which reason morality proper begins with them. This perspective also notes the possibility of unduly severe self-control by either the superego or superid. Raw, unrefined early-bourgeois superegos or severe, cultlike, archaic superids can bring major problems of their own. When self-control works together in balance with the unreflexive sectors, there is neither weakness nor undue harshness of self-control. These forms of immorality are the pursuit of what would be good were all else equal when all else is not equal. The immoral typically bring harm to larger needs accidentally.

Some immorality also arises from inadequate knowledge of and thus flawed performance with the moral rules or virtues. Here the person may have the proper reference and requisite self-control but utilize an unbalanced moral form or a balanced one in an unbalanced way, such that when it is implemented harm is wrought. Any of the indirect moralities may be deficiently constructed, learned, or applied, as may direct morality.

What is ethically amiss in the world is not mainly a matter of good versus evil, for evil, as I see it, is action bringing harm to the whole in self-conscious, profound negation of the good. This negation may be indirect, as when the right or virtuous comes to be despised for what it is. Self-conscious polarization against the whole as such, either explicitly or implicitly through its surrogates—something very different from experience-borne chariness or skepticism about imperfect claimants to the universal—is comparatively rare. In other words this worst form of immorality is characterized by dedication to the morally bad, unrighteous, vicious, and/or shameful. Evil is a hardened, self-conscious immorality.

****

A comprehensive sociology of ethics is a prerequisite to a comprehensive philosophy of ethics, for accompanying and rooted in each major kind of morality is a kind of ethical philosophy (see MacIntyre 1984, 23). The two great ethical philosophies that are based predominantly in the moralities of particular sectors, those of the superego and superid respectively, are Kantian and Aristotelian ethics. Kant describes and praises the moral superego following its rules; Aristotle describes and praises the moral superid following its virtues. Kantian ethics primarily reflects a morally developed bourgeois society and particularly its middle class; Aristotelian ethics primarily reflects a morally developed agrarian society and particularly its aristocracy. The two ethical philosophies address different indirect ethical forms with each effectively saying, "My society's and class's moral type is the best." Each ethical philosopher draws upon the mode with which he is most familiar. Each theorizes and sublimates from the morality of the dominant social group immediately around him, which is his own social class.

At the same time, these two major sectorally based ethical philosophies disparage each other. Aristotle has contempt for the disciplined man, the "enkrasiac," and thinks of him as one form of bad man, who of himself would fall into vice. Stern inner rule is necessary to neutralize his vicious character and keep him from actually doing the bad things toward which he tends. In Aristotle's view moral self-control by the superego is grim, brutal, and ignoble. Kant (1956, 87), however, is completely in league with the disciplined man while dismissing the noble follower of the virtues, saying that "[t]he mind is disposed to nothing but blatant moral fanaticism and exaggerated self-conceit by exhortation to actions as noble, sublime and magnanimous." Kant (1956, 159n) is extremely cautious about heroism, supererogation, and actions displaying "a great, unselfish, and sympathetic disposition and humanity." He sees any elevation of the soul as but fleeting and ephemeral ebullition. He (1956, 78 and 155–68) views moral self-control by the superid as dependent upon unreliable emotion. To him, the moral law displaces all "impulses of sensibility."

Kant's and Aristotle's ethics are particularistic in complementary ways. They pose an opposition that universalism overcomes by demonstrating that each is worthy in its sphere and can take the lead under suitable conditions. As Nietzsche first observed, most of the problems of conflicting ethical philosophies are due to different perspectives stemming from experience with different social classes and class characters. Aristotelian and Kantian ethical philosophies, primarily representing different indirect ethical forms, are appropriately different ways of reconciling people with the whole, given their circumstances. Each is correct but only part of the story. This synthesizes the ethics of rules and the ethics of virtues.

Reconciling Direct and Indirect Ethics

Universalism divides the world into those who are direct universalists, those who are indirect universalists, and those who are neither. The "indirects" are predominantly sectoralist but allow the imprint of universalism to meliorate their particularism. The "nons" remain incorrigibly sectoralist and immoral. The upper and upper-middle classes of the most developed countries of the world make substantial use of the active universal and direct ethics and independently take positions in the moral marketplace. The lower-middle and respectable working classes, who are somewhat dependent and partially sheltered under local moral monopolies, rely primarily upon indirect forms. The underclass, without reflexivity and absent the coherent external pressures of traditional society, has neither direct nor indirect ethics. However, many if not most in such societies to some degree combine the forms, leading their lives partly in the moral markets and partly sheltered from them.[9]

The opposition between those in whom the universal can be relatively direct and those in whom it can be only indirect may create major difficulties for those of both camps. Active universalism, while comforting to directs, is threatening to indirects. Fixed ethical forms are wise counsel and default routines for the directs, but they are permanent security for the indirects. The indirect befriends an existential panic—"I am weightless; what can I do?"—that she has difficulty admitting to herself or sharing with others. She cannot linger in this place. At the core of her being lies an existential rout in which she flees responsibility and cedes all to moral authority. Active universalism is scary to her. The direct, however, is the lingerer. In proximity to universal knowledge and caring, fixed ethical injunctions and models can be constricting, and the direct universal can be liberating. At a distance from universal knowledge and caring, the direct universal can inspire moral confusion while the established forms represent stability and salvation. Consequently, for all its goodness, direct ethics can also stress and dishearten, as Kant well understands. Concern with the side-effects of actions ramifying across this divide again brings up the need for some discrete separation between the esoteric and exoteric.

With the direct universal to some extent sequestered or veiled, authoritative dissemination and enforcement of an unquestioned indirect ethic may encourage popular morality. Under traditional conditions of a fairly full moral monopoly, this was for the most part both necessary and feasible on a large scale, although different civilizations and classes had very different ways of approaching it. Under postmodernist conditions of a thoroughgoing moral marketplace, things are much more complicated. On the one hand, the morally dependent may find limited sanctuary in partial local monopolies, if not as many as need protection and not as securely as they need it. On the other hand, today there is a much larger downside to conspiring silently with the inevitable oversimplifications, rigidities, and excesses of monist indirect moralists. They can be at armed loggerheads with other variants of their own sectoralism and all too often would cauterize the active universal and ban any holistic working subsequent to that by their own set of long-departed universalists. Not only must the forms of indirect ethics be harmonized with each other, but they must be harmonized with direct ethics and the moral good.

Accordingly, even though he might have ceded much to a leader or tradition asserting moral authority, one who is following his or its rules or virtues must always say at least tacitly, "It is good that I follow these rules [or virtues]"—and he is morally accountable for that judgment. The Nuremberg trials remind us that all action, irrespective of the authority upon which it is based, must be subject to comprehensive review against universal moral judgment. The low-level worker in Stalin's N.K.V.D. or Hitler's extermination program who selflessly dedicated himself to doing exemplary work for an enterprise with immoral overall purpose was acting immorally. The one who sabotaged or betrayed acted morally. In most cases of today's jihadists taking death to the infidel, there is again the allegedly inherently moral that is profoundly immoral. In turbulent times, if they are to lead a moral life, the vulnerable must at least call forth the inner resources to make a wise leap of faith among the many beckoning possibilities.

Moreover, even in ordinary circumstances the human condition is such that some ongoing independent moral judgment cannot be escaped and particularly today. While the great practical ethics from the past are largely valid, they are often susceptible to widely varying interpretation and application and therefore can be very difficult to apply in complex settings where several different forms may apply at once. Even eminently wise ethical laws must be used appropriately, for there too we have oppositions—between strict and loose interpretation and between severe and lax application. Applying any general moral injunction to a particular case requires the wisdom of the universal, if considerably less so than practicing direct ethics. People underestimate the role of direct ethics in determining how to interpret and apply moral law and virtue. As we and our endeavors become complex, veritable internal juridical systems and critical establishments become necessary to order the many principles and virtues regularly in play.

A ticklish problem concerning the status of moral authority therefore arises: Moral authorities do have real authority, but it is always limited. Within our community or group, to the extent to which we cannot be morally independent, our moral tradition holds; its notion of the right and virtuous must be taken as authoritative. Under such circumstances, we are morally obligated to follow tradition. That is for the best over the long run, and moral authorities' declarations and modeling must be taken as right and virtuous by the appropriate moral publics—but only up to a point. If we cannot find our ethical way independently, we can never shirk the default responsibility of finding and acceding to valid moral authority that does know the way. So long as that foundational choice remains valid and in force, and effective moral rules, virtues, and ways are in place, there is the great advantage that one no longer fully needs the active universal to lead a moral life. Even then, however, we may never abandon our higher scrutiny of moral authority. In the modern world all of this is accentuated, and the extension of moral authority is more tenuous, much like the authority of political officeholders in a democratic society. In a complex society there can be no deep, abiding moral security but only shallow, tentative moral security.

Exercising wise moral leadership bridging the moral classes under such circumstances is a most demanding and estimable enterprise. Moral leaders must minister and convey assurance authentically and with feeling and do so while withholding a large measure of reserve and wisdom. However fervently they pursue their concrete ethic and inspire their flocks to enthusiasm on its behalf, they themselves must be able to withdraw regularly into the active universal to shape, trim, and contextualize the forms. Moral leaders must also forever maintain the respect for the dangers of hubris not to push the forms so far, so inflexibly, or in such a manner as to do more harm than good. This includes harm to other forms of morality and to bearers of the living universal. There is a fine line between getting the most out of followers and stepping into intolerant extremism. Across this line lies immorality, often enough carried out in the abused name of morality—the moral physician's caution regarding iatrogenic disease.

The comparable concern on the other side, with its own need to avoid hubris and respect certain moving and situationally determined lines, is that direct ethics not overly shake those practicing indirect ethics, for whom it is either mysterious or disquieting. There are always negative externalities from disregarding established forms of morality, centering on the disturbance of the less by the more universal. Those practicing direct ethics must be particularly mindful of the need for a sense of legitimacy by indirect ethical systems, which is important for the acceptance and the passing on of a moral culture (cf. Williams 1985, 44). Adjustment by the universal that might be warranted on all other grounds may still be unwise because of such costs.

Under conditions of radical social and cultural mixing, the turbulence may reach such lengths that almost no fixed moralities are able to cope adequately with the myriad situational complexities and contradictions encountered in life. Under such conditions automatically following established moral laws or virtues all too often misguides even the best intentioned. The at-risk moral dependent must often be left to his own uncertain light for knowing when to conform to and how to interpret which determinate rules and virtues. If he errs and places faith in moral forms that do not fit the unseen good, his life is going to be less than a Moral one and have the potential for many casualties. In tumultuous times and places there may not even be the necessary period of stability during immature years for rule- or virtue-bound ethics to take proper hold in children and young people. Yet even then, for most people most of the time, the drawbacks to moral freelancing are no doubt still more perilous than attempting to follow tradition. In these circumstances, only the highest moral development—a strong general attachment to the moral good and possession of the wherewithal to make one's moral way irrespective of conditions—is truly up to the task of guiding ethical decisions. Where the balance lies depends upon the complexity of the times and the resources of the moral agent, together with the condition of the available forms and those who minister with them. The greater a society's freedom, the necessarily greater its admixture of direct ethics in selecting, interpreting, and implementing indirect ethics. Where homogeneity and stasis reign, established forms can be much more relied upon.

An optimal surface exists for each of us on the continuous manifold between direct and indirect ethics, one that depends upon the issues and circumstances. We should act directly with the universal to a certain warranted degree on certain questions. Elsewhere, across a good part of the spectrum, we should act in conformity with extant moral forms, ceding authority to others over what we think and do. We can cede authority only to the extent to which doing so would itself be moral. If we know what will maximize the long-term well-being of the whole (counting the costs of setting aside established forms), and it is different from the right or virtuous as currently promulgated, then we ought to pursue the good directly. If we don't, or don't as well as those who assembled the current moral forms, then, all else equal, we ought to follow the rules and/or virtues.

Finding the balance between direct and indirect ethics entails weighing many benefits and costs. Major costs of direct ethics include those of acquiring the necessary knowledge and engaging in the requisite contemplation to make direct moral decisions well. On the other hand, a major cost of indirect ethics is that the moral agent is unable to take into account anywhere near as many circumstances as she could with direct ethics, thereby getting many things wrong. Moreover, indirect ethics are unavoidably rigid and partial, leaving their carriers susceptible to needless moral conflict. In dynamic circumstances a major problem with following the established moral forms is that since the nature and needs of the whole are always changing, what is Ethical is always changing: rules that were once actually right become wrong, and forms that were once actually virtuous become vicious (as pride did through the long centuries of antiquity and as hypocrisy has at various times).

A particular set of moral ways, laws, or virtues may or may not be a valuable inheritance, depending upon conditions. At its best, an indirect ethics is a wise and rich inheritance channeling people with the universal. At its worst, it is a rigid apparatus forcing people into disfigured potential and squandered resources. Morality is very difficult to get right, and many "moralities" have missed the mark and done momentous harm.

In the lives of thoughtful people with considerable capacity to intuit the good, yet without being moral luminaries, combining the ethics of the good, right, and virtuous is a daily requirement. They use their independent moral capacity on certain major issues but seldom on ordinary ones, for it is often too cumbersome to use on every moral decision. Saving their highest moral powers for important issues or where contradictions arise, they fall back on moral rules and manners for much of what they do. The more developed a society and person, the greater the freedom and scope for direct ethics. Living universalism, in ethics as in religion, must be outspoken in some conditions and reticent in others but always present.

Recall the actions of Lord Nelson in boldly forcing the Battle of Cape St. Vincent. Did he act Morally in disregarding orders, breaking the law, and peeling toward the Spanish fleet? I hold that he did, even considering the harmful effects of his spectacular insubordination—however few similarly disobedient others have done so in comparable circumstances. The beneficial consequences of his great deed far outweighed the harmful ones. Yet one had better be careful in following the path of Nelson. The vast majority of people the vast majority of the time, whatever their determinate morality, would be wise to accept that certain things are wrong or vicious and hold firmly to their moral superegos and superids. Yet today—far more often than most would like or are fully prepared for—each of us is in the position of Nelson.

* * * *

The situation in ethical philosophy again runs parallel to that in the real world of morality. Some ethical philosophies take the perspective of direct ethics and some that of indirect ethics. Those that take the position of direct ethics bring the universal into the open and effectively accept that different moral forms are appropriate to different social and psychological situations. Those that take the position of indirect ethics veil the universal and endorse a single indirect ethical form as the exclusive way—whatever the type to which it is linked. The one is dualist or pluralist, and the other is monist.

Aristotle emphasizes indirect ethics, but he seamlessly interweaves it with a large component of direct ethics. In his exemplary harmonization of the two, Aristotle directly brings in the universal, most often by asking us to find the mean in applying virtues that are largely but not entirely habitual. He says, however, that on occasion we may have to employ the universal in a fuller way, using the theoretical wisdom (*sophia*) and practical wisdom (*phronesis*) that he describes as the master virtues. Although it draws on theoretical wisdom and direct ethics in Aristotle consists of exercising practical wisdom and knowing the ethical way to act in any situation. This practical wisdom is a kind of holistic prudence, which perfectly reflects the consequentialist nature of ethics.[10]

The most well-known ethical philosophy that predominantly features direct ethics is utilitarianism of which universalism in ethics is a version. With utilitarianism one autonomously determines the impact of potential actions and policies upon general well-being and seeks to contribute directly to the moral good. Like this ethics, much previous utilitarianism is dualist, subsuming rule-bound ethics through the extension of rule utilitarianism by means of the principle that people should follow those moral rules that would contribute to general well-being. Utilitarianism could also easily be broadened to incorporate virtue ethics and/or group-bound ethics in a similar fashion by enjoining that people follow the moral virtues of the superid and/or the moral ways of the social id that would contribute to general well-being. Thus the structure of a subsidiary rule-, virtue-, and way-utilitarianism under the larger umbrella of utilitarian direct ethics. Utilitarianism also has the major advantage that it is better adapted to framing macroethical problems than any indirect ethics. As Mill's utilitarianism does with its criterion of the "interest of the whole," universalism requires that its proponent be "strictly impartial as a disinterested and benevolent spectator" (Mill 1957, 22).[11]

Kant's ethics, to the contrary, is decidedly monist and indirect. At the center of his ethics is the Categorical Imperative.[12] Kant (1985, 6) holds that, to be ethical, action must conform to and be engaged in for the sake of moral law. Emphasizing moral law and duty, he argues that all ethics should be restricted to a single indirect form, that of rules or deontology.

The key to interpreting Kant's ethics lies in a too-little discussed passage appearing early in the *Foundations of the Metaphysics of Morals* (1985, 21) where the philosopher worries that intellectuals' knowledge is not very reliable. Hence, it is wise "in moral matters to acquiesce in the common rational judgment" of the people or at most to refine and clarify that judgment to some degree. To Kant (1956, 38) "what duty is, is plain of itself to everyone, but what is to bring true, lasting advantage to our whole existence is veiled in impenetrable obscurity, and much prudence is required to adapt the practical rule based upon it even tolerably to the ends of life by making suitable exceptions to it." Most are not able independently to determine and follow what is in the best general interest. Adhering to the moral law, however, is something people can do, so long as that law is kept simple enough that "even the commonest and most unpracticed understanding without any worldly prudence" should be able to grasp it (1956, 38). Of an empirical, utilitarian ethics Kant (1956, 36 [emphasis added]) says, "were the voice of reason with respect to the will not so distinct, so irrepressible, and so clearly audible to even the commonest man, *it would drive morality to ruin*." The implication is that we must therefore propagate an atmosphere of apodictic certainty for the vulnerable and dangerous masses.

Pessimist and authoritarian that he was, Kant fretted about the dire consequences for civilization were the people ever to become disillusioned. Where British utilitarians keep everything open in an atmosphere of optimism and democratic trust, Kant's ethical philosophy aims at keeping the moral market closed around bourgeois forms tempered to militaristic hardness. With its restriction of ethics to rules, emphasis on obedience, and insistence on certainty, precisely this welding of the severely authoritarian and bourgeois was the Hohenzollern way—at once goose-stepping and Calvinist. The other labels do not point to the essential difference, which is that Kant is ethically conservative and Bentham and Mill are ethically liberal.

What precisely could Kant mean by asserting that the Categorical Imperative requiring that everything we do be capable of extrapolation to universal law, *holds* but also that we cannot speak openly because the naïve can too easily be misled? As Rorty (1989, 34) astutely notes, there is far more to Kant's ethics than ordinarily meets the eye. Kant implies that to some degree he possesses an esoteric philosophy, that his public ethical doctrine is partly exoteric fare and illocutionary rather than locutionary. He comes close to admitting as much in a letter to Moses Mendelssohn, in which he says, "Although I am absolutely convinced of many things that I shall never have the courage to say, I shall never say anything that I do not believe" (quoted in Cassirer 1981, 79). A significant portion of what Kant is telling us is not what he holds philosophically but what he thinks necessary to minister spiritually to German and European society. While denying that it does so, Kant's ethical philosophy to some degree puts into practice the dualism I defend for certain circumstances. Kant worries about the less reliable and less knowledgeable. If those needing principles were ever to seek their own happiness in life, they wouldn't know enough to be certain, to have definite principles to act upon (1985, 36). This paternalistic judgment echoed the larger moral consensus in martial, late-agrarian Prussia.

Not surprisingly, Kant is palpably conflicted with regard to the issues of cultural tutelage and unfreedom that are central to his monist undertaking. At the end of *Foundations,* he directs some mild, schoolmasterly aggression back against the authoritarian leaders with whom he has just finished conspiring, while extolling the Enlightenment he has just finished betraying. Kant concludes the book with the hope of a slow shift to greater freedom and autonomous use of reason. For "[m]en work themselves gradually out of barbarity if only intentional artifices are not made to hold them in it" (1985, 91)—precisely. In the late twentieth century, after having experienced long, agonizing decades with the same authoritarian forces, Leo Strauss (1983, see e.g., 168) was understandably even more timid and chary of the *popolo*, daring no more frankness than had the dour Koenigsberger. Trepidation about opening direct ethics to the light of day is at the heart of Kant's ethics as it is of Strauss's. Kant, like all sophisticated proponents of inherentist indirect ethics, is substantially dissembling.

To some degree, pursuing a covert dualism is what a universalist would do in a hierarchical setting, but one may still ask whether, given his circumstances, Kant found the proper balance. I would argue that he did not. Considering what we know about the last two centuries, neither Prussia nor the world was benefited by being so extensively and coercively protected from markets, economic, political, communal, or, here, cultural. No, Prussia's main problem was a sinister combination of militarism, authoritarianism, and restriction of all markets—those individualistic forms which alone held the potential for countering that country's building proto-fascism. Substantially on the wrong side of history, Kant's ethics of discipline went too far in cooperating with this ruinous constellation. I direct Kant's Enlightenment motto back to him: *Sapere aude!*

The opposition between consequentialism and inherentism in moral philosophy reflects the broader enigma of relations between the universal and sectoral and the sophisticated and naïve in all complex societies. In order to develop and contribute to the fullest, the more able require an open culture, which, however, can be destabilizing to the less able. This enigma is at the heart of Kant's as it is of every other ethics. Indeed ethics has the same central problem religion does: How open are we going to be, and with what consequences? Once again the answer is that we must overcome the opposition and find the balance, which will vary according to conditions. Instinctively recoiling from dualism is not an option or at least not an aware and honest one. All "inherentism" is limited by and grounded within consequentialism. Ultimately, moral acts are such because of and only because of their long-term overall consequences. Most hallowed norms and virtues coincide fairly well with the universal, but they also frequently carry distortions from the circumstances of their origins. For this reason the ultimate criterion of moral goodness in ethics cannot be escaped. Kant-like ethics must be created, operated, and adjusted by Mill-like ones. Kant-like ethical philosophy is always incomplete. How did the inherentist rules come to be framed in a particular way? How did they get to us step-by-step through all of the various forms in the ethnographic and historical records? Under what circumstances and by whom are they to be changed in the future? A pure inherentism is untenable. Effectively the choice is between acknowledged and unacknowledged dualism. The enigma of social classes and their different needs vis-à-vis the universal is overcome only by some degree of dualism or pluralism, as in rule- and virtue-utilitarianisms under a larger act-utilitarianism. This synthesizes direct and indirect ethics.

If Kant's situation entailed some need of veiling the universal, though not as much as he practiced, is ours in the same need of ethical exoterica and indirect ethics? I don't think so. In an open society it does not befit moral philosophy that it secret the ultimate authority for what it says behind the authoritarian and obfuscatory. Like Bentham and Mill, I make direct ethics my public doctrine. Like them, I trust that all but a few of those for whom it would not be appropriate would have neither the interest nor the ability to penetrate it. Much more even than Bentham and Mill, we live now in an open society that both cultivates and makes significant demands on the common sense of broad segments of the population. Today we have the widespread popular skepticism Kant feared and because of which he demurred and dissembled. At the same time, with the masses no longer reading—yoked not to plows or looms but to the internet, headphones, television, and videos—we can again speak our minds more easily in print. Today the greater fear than that exposure to the universal may shock and confuse is that it be lost altogether in rampant skepticism and negativism.

More than two centuries after Kant, amid culture wars with the nihilist likes of Foucault and Derrida, I don't see how those who love the good can tiptoe about treating their ethics in a noble conspiracy of silence. Embattled by radically particularist and virulently skeptical forces, philosophy can no longer nod conspiratorially to those who already basically get it. The need for authentic and powerful philosophical ethics is now acute. Bombarded by far more upsetting things than the truth, many able and well-intentioned people today are pained and disrupted by the cacophony. Meanwhile, large numbers of people have accumulated reservoirs of good sense and toughmindedness from centuries of experience in the very cultural markets Kant labored to deny them. Unable to distinguish between the Righteous and the merely "righteous," unable to deal with moral rules that are blunted or broken, Kantian ethics is helpless in the midst of the contemporary world's extreme socio-cultural difference and faltering authority.

More puzzling than Kant are his postmodernist epigones who, in their misapprehension that this is or ever could be a monist world, attempt to make of him the straightforward deontologist he never was. The central philosophical topic has always been how to balance direct and indirect ethics within a larger whole. Under what circumstances would reliance on what kind of moral authority be warranted? Who does best with what mix of direct and indirect ethics under what developmental and historical circumstances?

These are the transparent and worthy questions raised by the clarification of ethics.

In his own way, Hegel (see 1967, 75–104), like Kant, attacks and veils direct ethics, expressing concern about the dangers of "subjectivity" and caprice—at least in any but times of heroes in less developed societies. Even more than his predecessor, however, Hegel was under the watchful eye of Prussian authorities (see Pinkard 2000). The moral situation of the times was also very different then from ours today. For both reasons, we do better to work with the spirit than the letter of Hegel's ethics.

****

My ethical philosophy demonstrates all major forms of morality to be but variants of one, giving the different ethical forms their due within a comprehensive yet determinate universalism. At the same time, as ethos and ethics are again joined, this universalism incorporates the major ethical philosophies deriving from the respective moral forms within a single comprehensive and reformulated utilitarianism. Placing special emphasis on the importance of historical knowledge, its criterion is maximal contribution to the long-term well-being of the whole. There are ways of organizing and conducting our activities that empirically do contribute better to the well-being and progress of humankind than others, and these ways define the Moral. It is of the utmost importance that human scientists as well as philosophers understand this.

Notes

1. Just as we must have fundamental locutionary assumptions, we must have fundamental illocutionary ones. "Oughts" are a different realm from "*is*es" and deserve respect in their own right.
2. See Popper (1962, 1:101ff.) concerning Plato and Chapter 13 concerning Hegel. See Chapter 6, fn. 6, and the discussion of individualism and collectivism in Chapter 9 as to how this can be problematic. I do not say that these philosophers are not universalistic, only that they would be more so if they acknowledged a larger place for some individualistic phenomena under certain circumstances.
3. One can restate any substantive approach as one of pursuing problems, including ethics and religion, without changing it substantively.
4. Scriptural references are to the King James Version of the Bible.
5. This differs modestly from Aristotle's view of virtues as settled dispositions to act, moral habits acquired in the course of a proper upbringing that lead the person to wish to act well or nobly and to do so habitually. In my view, it is more helpful to say that they become settled dispositions to act when they become ingrained and habitual, although they are already virtues while being learned.

Insofar as the virtues are present, they lie in the superid. As they become habitual, they become more fluent and more deeply rooted but remain there. The virtuous being the parallel to the right, it would be awkward in a similar way to define moral rules as securely established moral norms.

6. If moral rules, virtues and ways are distinct conceptually, distinguishing between them in practice is not always easy. For example, the virtue of courage may be stated in commandment-like form as "Be courageous!" The Commandment, "Honor thy father and thy mother," is a rule enjoining a moral way. The virtues of prudence and temperance are sometimes construed to endorse reliance on the superego, moral and amoral.

7. A moral SSE has not yet developed, somewhat as, prior to Luther, a moral superego had relatively little developed. Moral forms develop only after the amoral ones do.

8. By defining the virtues as settled dispositions, Aristotle makes it difficult to analyze cases of weakness of the virtues, but they too are important.

9. I am aware that my use of ideal types regularly makes it difficult to remember that in reality the phenomena about which I speak are continua from little to much universalism.

10. Although Aristotle describes theoretical and practical wisdom as virtues, albeit special ones, ontologically they are not virtues in my sense of moral patterns in the style of life but perspectives of the human, namely the ideal and real sides of the universal.

11. Nevertheless, serious objections may be raised to much past utilitarian thinking. It has suffered from ontological poverty and a narrow, bourgeois notion of a highly individualistic, rational human nature on the one hand and its lack of an adequate philosophy of human science and associated expectation of being able to calculate a moral course on the other. Most variants of utilitarianism have also been cavalier with the moral law and insufficiently careful regarding the destabilizing implications of their tacit antinomianism. The weaknesses of previous utilitarianism have given it an air of flippant ad hocery and scientism that has driven many away. Providing a powerful means of framing and conducting that philosophy, universalism's approach to ethics is essentially to ground, broaden, recast, and refine utilitarianism.

12. The Categorical Imperative has three versions: The first is "Act only according to that maxim by which you can at the same time will that it should become a universal law" (1985, 39). The second is "Act so that you treat humanity, whether in your own person or in that of another, always as an end and never as a means only" (1985, 47). The third is that the will should be determined solely by universal moral law (1985, 49; 1956, 75). Kant (1985, 54) maintains that the three are equivalent.

Bibliography

Aristotle. 1953. *Ethics*. Harmondsworth, Middlesex. Penguin.

———. 1961. *Aristotle's Protrepticus: An Attempt at Reconstruction*. Goeteborg: Institute of Classical Studies.

———. 1962. *Politics*. Harmondsworth, Middlesex: Penguin.

Banfield, E. 1967. *The Moral Basis of a Backward Society.* New York: Free Press.

Cassirer, E. 1981. *Kant's Life and Thought.* New Haven, CN: Yale University Press.

Hegel, G. 1967. *Hegel's Philosophy of Right.* London: Oxford University Press.

Heidegger, M. 1962. *Being and Time.* New York: Harper and Row.

Kant, I. 1956. *Critique of Practical Reason.* Indianapolis, IN: Bobbs-Merrill.

———. 1985. *Foundations of the Metaphysics of Morals.* New York: Macmillan.

MacIntyre. 1984. *After Virtue.* 2nd ed. Notre Dame, IN: University of Notre Dame Press.

Maslow, A. 1954. *Motivation and Personality.* New York: Harper and Row.

Mill, J. 1957. *Utilitarianism.* Indianapolis, IN: Bobbs-Merrill.

Needham, R. 1978. *The Shorter Science and Civilization in China.* 2 vols. Cambridge: Cambridge University Press.

Nietzsche, F. 1966. *Beyond Good and Evil.* New York: Random House.

Pinkard, T. 2000. *Hegel: A Biography.* Cambridge: Cambridge University Press.

Popper, K. 1962. *The Open Society and Its Enemies.* 2 vols. New York: Harper and Row.

Rorty, R. 1989. *Contingency, Irony and Solidarity.* Cambridge: Cambridge University Press.

Strauss, L. 1983. *Studies in Platonic Political Philosophy.* Chicago: University of Chicago Press.

Thucydides. 1998. *The Peloponnesian War.* Indianapolis, IN: Hackett Publishing.

Weber, M. 1978. *Economy and Society.* 2 vols. Berkeley and Los Angeles: University of California Press.

Williams, B. 1985. *Ethics and the Limits of Philosophy.* Cambridge, MA: Harvard University Press.

12. Individualism and Collectivism in the Universal

Having focused on two dimensions as they internally differentiate the universal—the instrumental and consummatory in the opposition between philosophy and religion, and the ideal and real in that between ontology and ethics—we must now consider the opposition between individualism and collectivism in the universal. Universalism sometimes appears in individualist forms and sometimes in collectivist forms. At the microlevel, universalism may be borne by leaders, monks, or moralists whose characters are predominantly individualist and solitary or collectivist and communal. John Calvin and Abraham Lincoln were "individuals" while many in Aristotle's lyceum or the Renaissance academies were "members." Prophets are typically individuals while great leaders and diplomats are usually members.

At the macrolevel, individualist and collectivist expressions of the universal take the form of markets and hierarchies respectively. Since the state, church, or moral consensus enveloping the universal may be strong or weak, the universal may be relatively free and open to new expressions or constrained and closed to them. The universal may manifest itself in diverse practitioners with different approaches or within collective entities monopolizing universalism. Today expressions of the universal are disparate and take the form of markets. Contemporary philosophy is supported by no substantial organized entity. Contemporary religion is often borne by churches, temples, mosques, or synagogues, but in most parts of the world these are fragmented into numerous competing entities. Moral leadership is extremely scattered and disparate today. In other times and places each of these kinds of universalism has been unified. Philosophy formed unified establishments in its periods of dominance in China and Korea. Religion has frequently been monopolized, as it largely was in Medieval Europe or under the Abbasid caliphate. There have also been moral monopolies in traditional societies all over the world. The extent to which bearers of the universal form an open market or a hierarchy has major implications for societies. That a universalistic establishment had significant political and social influence in the United States during the industrial period (see Baltzell 1966), but no such entity has been present in the postmodernist era, is a most important historical fact about our country.

In universal markets holistic working takes place, and various imperfect manifestations of the universal thrown together by development and mixing are critiqued, modified, and selected while they are slowly reconciled. As was apparent from our treatments of religion and ethics, the universal may engender disruptions of its own that confuse and disorient some in the course of its development however invaluable this might be overall. There were those dispirited by the development of universal philosophy in classical Greece and those disheartened by the spread of Christianity in ancient Rome, for example. Like other forms of working, holistic working should therefore proceed at the proper rate. Schumpeter's analysis of the destruction, rigors, and hardship of economic markets holds for universal as it does for all other markets. As dissonant expressions of the universal are worked toward harmony and authentic closure is approached, the various forms of universalism converge. Aquinas's medieval synthesis of Greco-Roman philosophy and Christianity and Chu Hsi's Neo-Confucian synthesis of Confucianism and Taoism are examples of such convergence.

How wide open the markets in the universal are allowed to become determines how fast the universal develops. Liberalism and conservatism in the universal are central to its development as they are to sectoral development. The analysis of individualism and collectivism therefore yields a dynamics of universalism just as it does of sectoralism. Although the universal smoothes sectoral cycles, it is subject to its own oscillations between a liberal expansionary phase in which universalism is opened up and a conservative contractionary phase in which it is consolidated. The one boldly engages in horizontal integration, incorporating disparate elements, while the other engages in a more routine vertical integration, digesting what it has. When liberalism or conservatism vis-à-vis the universal predominates, those participating in it are under the predominant influence respectively of hope or fear in their universalism. The liberal phase generates variations of philosophy, religion, and morality analogous to the confusion of styles in the arts. The conservative phase moves toward unity in the forms of universalism analogous to the reign of a distinct style in the arts. Philosophy, religion, and morality tend to develop rapidly in times of chaos and mixing and slowly in times of hierarchy and homogeneity.

The internal development of universalism may be most rapid during the expansionary phase, but the negative side-effects of its development are also most pronounced then. Accordingly, the strength of adherence to religion and morality tends to vary inversely with their openness and rate of development. Thus, for example, the more people move into the moral marketplace, the more ethical mistakes they tend to make. As Nietzsche understood, the more venturesome and entrepreneurial our lives the greater the moral risks. Moral mistakes may stem from bad character or from good but enterprising character tripped up in difficult markets—just as economic bankruptcy may mean bad character or the noble but necessarily uncertain effort to start a business. Some of the problem results from people's inappropriate exposure to sophisticated religion or direct morality. Even though mistakes bring harm to the whole, the bold in all arenas pick up the pieces, mull them over, and again move into the markets. This process occurs at varying degrees of proximity to the universal.

Either market or hierarchy may be the appropriate form of the universal, depending upon circumstances. There are times when more freedom in the universal is warranted and times when less freedom is warranted. Inflexibly attached to the expansionary phase, moral liberals like John Dewey seek wide open moral growth, with little attention to consolidation. Inflexibly attached to the contractionary phase, moral conservatives like Michael Oakeshott shun growth and emphasize integration above all. Both are one-sided, for each orientation has its place. Once the universal genuinely works through to closure, less need for openness exists, and a consensus arises to that effect, although this outcome should not be forced prematurely. We therefore do not automatically condemn the hierarchies of the past. As in the sectors, so in the universal: neither individualism nor collectivism is right for all times.

Nevertheless, all else equal, as Hegel overly emphasizes, collective expressions of the universal are higher than individual ones. While recognizing appropriate contexts for either, Hegel repeatedly extols the collectivist universal in the form of the church, state, and ethical life (*Sittlichkeit*), while frequently taking issue with individualist manifestations of the universal (see e.g., 1967, 108 and 1956, 267, 450). Part of Hegel's position in this regard stemmed from a warranted response to the different needs of the times, part from the authoritarian power and influence bearing on him in Berlin, and part from his insufficient development of a higher universal.

Bibliography

Baltzell, E. 1966. *The Protestant Establishment: Aristocracy and Caste in America.* New York: Vintage.

Hegel, G. 1956. *The Philosophy of History.* New York: Dover Publications.

———. 1967. *Hegel's Philosophy of Right.* London: Oxford University Press.

13. Balancing the Balancing Mechanism

At a certain point the universal becomes sufficiently developed that it begins to become conscious of itself as universal. This is no mere quasisectoral self-consciousness but higher self-consciousness of the universal by the universal itself. The universal then becomes internally differentiated between a first-level universal that performs all of the tasks we have so far attributed to the universal but is *not* reflexive vis-à-vis its own universalism, and a second-level universal that *is* reflexive vis-à-vis its universalism. In time, the higher universal may then begin to empower itself via higher self-control. The universal's higher self-consciousness looks over all sectors and aspects of the first-level universal's differentiation and relations and harmonizes across them. In modulating itself from the standpoint of a higher universalism, the universal applies to itself its central wisdom of always finding the balance. This constitutes doubly reflexive universalism.

The higher universal has a number of oppositions within the universal to overcome, beginning with that between the consummatory and instrumental as they pertain internally to the universal, particularly in the opposition between religion and philosophy. These greatest of human cultural achievements both have the capacity to overcome all oppositions and are equally oriented to the long-term well-being of the whole. Nevertheless, the two have different modes of representation and different perspectives that may come into conflict. At the ideal level, the higher universal translates between their languages and reveals to each the wisdom accumulated by the other. At the real level, decisions must be made about the relative prominence of philosophy and religion under varying circumstances. Real-world frictions between them must be overcome and the two enabled to work together. Western philosophy and religion are replete with the universal's own quasisectoralism in their substantial incomprehension of and resistance to each other. One thinks of Russell's dismissal of religion or Schuon's of secular humanism.

Another central need of the higher universal is to balance between the ideal and real universal, ontology and ethics, as well as theoretical and practical wisdom, which may also sometimes come into conflict. One example of such reconciliation would be the critique of Western philosophy since the demise of the ancient schools for having had no significant real-world presence, no developed analog to the church, not even in ethics and political philosophy. Modern Western philosophy should learn from religion that, when possible, it ought to place a balanced emphasis on adapting itself to the needs of wider segments of the population. Like religion, developed philosophy is a blueprint for civilization. Confucianism offers a model of philosophy that has applied itself successfully by providing political wisdom and social ethics that have contributed immensely to China's comparative stability and well-being. Particularly when religion is limited in its ability to provide universalistic guidance, this task should not be overlooked. Opposition between individualist and collectivist forms of the universal must also be overcome by the higher universal. How bold the universal should be and how fast it should be allowed to develop are questions that can only be resolved in the higher universal.

However, the crucial need also remains to balance the universal with what it controls. This task of self-control of the universal by the universal includes reconciling the first-level universal with everything below it, which is to say, balancing that universal's needs qua universal against all sectoral needs. Sufficient activity and experience in the first-level universal may lead to higher universal self-consciousness and the need that the first-level universal itself be balanced vis-à-vis its parts under a higher universal. Not only are positions on each of the basic dimensions altered by major changes on any of them, but they are altered by changes in sectoralism versus universalism, and conversely. The universal, too, must be regularly adjusted as the human changes and develops.

A number of difficult questions about the universal yield to this insight. How much contemplation would it be wise for us to engage in? How much liberal arts education do we need? How much should we invest in knowing ourselves? How fully should we commit ourselves to philosophy? How much holistic working by the rational universal is itself optimal? Who needs how much rational universalism? Such questions raised by all employment of the rational universal are answered by the higher universal that balances universalism and sectoralism under a doubly reflexive universalism.

Comparable questions arise in religion. To what lengths should we go in bringing God into our lives? How strongly ought we to support religion? How much spiritual education is too much or too little? When do we put aside religion and take up other matters? Again, only an active higher universalism can balance religion within the larger whole of which it too is a part.

The injunction to balance the balancing mechanism applies with special urgency to exoteric religion because of its more applied mission, popular audience, and greater proclivity to authoritarianism. The dangerous personal enthusiasms and wild policy perspectives too often associated with such religion badly need adjustment by a higher universalism. Yet through their leap of faith the adherents of naïve religion have already jettisoned most of the very universalism with which they might balance their very retreat from balancing. Those of simple faith are always at risk of excess, for which reason wise leadership and norms of tolerance and moderation are particularly essential curbs to fervor.

Such questions are just as central to ethics. How much is too much or too little ethical deliberation before acting? How far is it ethical to push the ethical? How strictly should we enforce the moral law? How should we balance direct and indirect ethics? Much of what serves the long-term well-being of the whole is basic activity of the ego and association or the id and community, namely the mundane building of infrastructure and private wealth or simple activities with family and friends. Neglecting such activities for the moral proper can often be less Moral than pursuing them, because it contributes less to long-term well-being. In the terse commandment of Jesus, "Render unto Caesar the things which be Caesar's, and render unto God the things which be God's" (Luke 20:25), both clauses are moral ones. Comparable commandments could be framed for the claims of business, family, and friends. It is often Moral to put aside or trim down morality proper and operate more freely on the basis of interest or emotion. Neither the best person nor the best society is all morality proper, and only a higher morality that balances between the moral and amoral can tell us where to draw the line.

We do not sacrifice everything to morality proper—that would be self-contradictory—we sacrifice for the good of the whole, which includes our own well-being. If some are sacrificing themselves heroically, that may be laudable; if too many are sacrificing too much for too long, something is likely to be seriously wrong. Suicidally imprudent "morality" is not Morality at all. It overemphasizes the first-level universal or its surrogate products, neglects the value of the part in the whole, and therefore misses the real substance of morality. The good and wise very frequently do not act on their narrowly moral impulses (cf. Chu Hsi 1990, 188).

Yet examining the universal's special reflexivity reveals that it can never be complete. By its very nature the human always leaves the loose end of needing to balance its highest perspective within a whole that is perpetually just beyond its reach. Any new level of universalism may harmonize everything but itself. Because that crucial need remains inherently open, trying to wrap up things once and for all is forever like trying to pick ourselves up by the seats of our pants. Even as people approach closely to the whole, another is forming above it, ad infinitum.

The consequence of this inability fully to grasp the universal and infinite is that people can never perceive, think, or act with absolute finality or apodeictic certainty. We cannot pursue anything with reckless abandon, even our best approximation of the universal. We must always take very seriously the dangers of hubris and prudently remain receptive to Background intuition concerning excess. However stunning and inspirational a new philosophy, religion, or morality, there always remains the question of how to balance this new representation of the universal against that which it is about. The human's inherent openness is a major reason why the truly universal will always act with caution. There can be no fanaticism, not even in applying or following the universal. Such fanaticism clings to that last closure the wise know to be provisional and incomplete.

Universalism reaches its Olympian summit in the injunction to balance all modes of universalism against each other and itself against all other concerns. The highest self-awareness and self-control of the universal fine-tune all other manifestations of the universal, making possible a wise and balanced application of universalism throughout. Here philosophy and religion, naïve and sophisticated religion, and ideal and real universalism all find the balance and pull together in harmony. Under the guidance of the highest universal people do not go to excess with any of the levels or forms of universalism. The nimblest of universals is always ready to jump to still higher levels and vigilantly monitor its own tendencies to excess. The highest universal is the ultimate extension of Aristotle and Confucius's entreaties that we seek the mean in all things and the refusal of Plato's consummate extremism.

＊＊＊＊

Higher universalism is one of Hegel's two capstone notions. By higher universalism in the relevant sense, he means an exclusively collective as opposed to an individual form of higher universalism.[1] The notion of higher universalism, developed primarily in his political philosophy, is evident, for example, in his view of the monarch as the universal and absolute authority over society, including over other expressions of the universal (see Hegel 1967). It is also apparent in his view of the church as overcoming the opposition between God and man, and therewith between sophisticated and naïve religion. Hegel's (1984) philosophy of religion, like Pannenberg's theology, is organized around an interpretation of the Trinity: the Son, representing man, is the lower, sectoral mode of deity; the Father, representing God, is the midlevel "subjective" universal; and the Holy Spirit, representing the church, is the higher universal that reconciles the Father and Son. Similarly, Hegel sees "ethical life" or the social order as overcoming the opposition between customary ways and individualist "subjective" morality, which is to say, direct ethics. Hegel's overriding concern is reconciling individual and society—and especially individualist and collectivist manifestations of the universal—but virtually always in favor of collectivist ones.

Lacking in Hegel is full development of the higher universal with which a self-sufficient, doubly reflexive collective or personal universal might be able to monitor itself. For this reason he is therefore unable to address who is to rule the rulers, guide the church, or monitor "ethical life." In addition to considering the higher universal as it exists within such overarching collectivities, we also need to be able to consider the higher universal as it exists internally within concentrated entities such as the monarchy or the person. As an important supplement to other sources of their optimal performance, established authority and developed persons need to oversee their own universalism. Even the church, state, and ethical life require a higher universal to guide and moderate them.

Like consummatory and instrumental and ideal and real forms of the universal, both individualist and collectivist forms of the universal require monitoring by the higher universal. Missing in Hegel is a higher universal that might balance between collective and individual expressions of the universal. Hegel's state or church does not harmonize between itself as a collective form of universalism and dispersed individual or subjective universalisms; it only sublates various forms of these. Without a fully developed higher universal to balance his first-level universal, Hegel tipped his support disproportionately to collectivist manifestations of the universal, slighting individualist ones. That his notion of the higher universal was incomplete is responsible for some of the authoritarianism in Hegel's political philosophy. To Hegel, the only circumstances appropriate for subjective universalism are early times of heroes and prophets, but he is not entirely forthcoming in this conclusion. Like Kant, Hegel is less than fully reliable on matters of authority, due to his social circumstances. Albeit most disappointingly in Hegel, the whole line of German philosophy tended to lack a higher moderation, something Spinoza and many British philosophers, however philosophically flat they may have been in certain other respects, admirably did not.

Want of a fully articulated higher universal also in part lies behind problems associated with Hegel's other capstone notion, the rather too abstract and metaphorical concept of the world-spirit, with which he attempts to draw world history into a single collective being (see e.g., Hegel 1975, 55, 74; 1956, 341). One *could* fruitfully theorize about a world-spirit but only in a different sense, as a tangible global collectivity, not as a quasimythological entity. Such a collectivity hardly existed in the nineteenth century, although with the rapid growth of globalism since World War II, it has become a significant, if still nascent, reality. Hegel lapsed concerning the world-spirit, but he did not about church and state—there he simply reached the limits of his development and his ruler's tolerance and displayed one-sidedness. We take Hegel's thinking a step further when we fully lay out the higher universal.

****

The entire ontological apparatus of Part I is ramified again in Part II in the universal's internal manysidedness. Although I have presented them in a different way and in a different order, all of the dimensions of the human appear again in the internal mutiplexity of the universal. Each of the fundamental oppositions internally differentiating the universal has been noted and sublated by thinkers in the past: the opposition between philosophy and religion has been reconciled by the perspicacious of many traditions; that between the ideal and the real in the universal has been beautifully overcome by Aristotle; that between individualist and collectivist expressions of the universal has been harmonized by a few, including Aristotle; and that between the first-level universal and higher universal has been partially sublated by Hegel. What has never been surmounted before is the compound complex universal determinately described by the nexus of these dimensions.

Note

1. He sometimes also speaks of higher universalism merely to indicate a more developed universalism in general.

Bibliography

Chu Hsi. 1990. *Learning to Be a Sage*. Berkeley and Los Angeles: University of California Press.

Hegel, G. 1956. *The Philosophy of History*. New York: Dover Publications.

———. 1967. *Hegel's Philosophy of Right*. London: Oxford University Press.

———. 1975. *Lectures on the Philosophy of World History: Introduction*. Cambridge: Cambridge University Press.

———. 1984. *Lectures on the Philosophy of Religion*. 3 vols. Berkeley and Los Angeles: University of California Press.

14. Harmony and Conflict

The standoff between harmonist and conflict theory has been the great, continuing theoretical opposition in the human sciences. Social and psychological thinkers tend to assume either harmony or conflict to be the normal state of affairs for the human. Parsons exemplifies the one and Marx the other. The respective positions have been taught primarily as opposing theories, and that they are. They rest, however, upon opposing philosophies. Previous harmonism in its naïveté or abstractness has tended to play down or ignore conflict. This chapter sketches a conflict theory grounded not in conflictualism but in harmonism, yet one that is neither naïve nor abstract.[1]

The first central determinant of conflict is the negational perception of essential difference. This brings a sense of mutual exclusiveness. When persons or collectivities first encounter the other or what seems utterly different, a radical tear opens in their fabric, rending long familiar worlds. As a result, when under rude conditions or early development, the mixing juxtaposes contrasting leanings, aggression and conflict easily occur. The poorly developed id relishes the low pleasure of expressive aggression against those who are different. The poorly developed ego gains base satisfaction in taking wantonly from others, looting and pillaging in the manner of Attila or Tamarlane. Poorly developed cultures and societies turn against perceived essential difference of identity, interests, beliefs, or practices.

Aggression arising from the perception of this difference is the most primitive form of action, and one that very often does more harm than good. Where force and violence reign, all that people could better do with their time and all that they have accumulated are put aside as precautions are taken to stave off catastrophe. Serious conflict is so destructive and so much to be avoided that in many respects the first and most basic collective and personal task is maintaining security, something upon which the fruitfulness of every other endeavor rests. Dealing with the rudimentary negation entailed by conflict is the holistic working that has primacy. In any but the simplest and most homogeneous humanity it is also the first area that universalism must work through to closure.

The second central determinant of conflict is the relative strength or weakness of the universal as opposed to the sectoral. The greater the development and resources of the universal, the greater the ability to overcome conflict. Decisive for conflict resolution is not the relative power of the parties to it but the relative power of the universal as opposed to the sectoral in and over them. All of the various forms of holistic working by which oppositions are overcome require resources of many kinds. Only to the extent that the universal is empowered is it able to resolve conflict.

Engagement of the universal is the only ultimate solution to conflict, for it is the universal that reconciles difference by slowly removing the inclination to conflict, even though many sorts of actual difference remain. Difference of a certain magnitude might be sufficient to provoke conflict when people are sectoralist but not when they are universalist. Difference is not the problem—unworked difference is. Conflict always reflects the failure of at least one party to rise to the universal. Why difference of identity or interests, of the ideal or real, or of individualism or collectivism *seems* essential is because of inability or unwillingness to rise above it. While barring destructive action resulting from the perception of essential difference, the universal builds understanding and acceptance of difference even as it harmonizes actual difference. As the universal does its work, difference is put in perspective, becoming familiar variation on the theme of human and societal nature.

Insofar as the holistic working of community is carried out, people come to see each other as socially or culturally different in only inessential ways, and a sense of larger community and increased fellow feeling arise. As people and collectivities come to perceive diversity as benign, they cooperate more easily and begin accumulating solutions to their common problems, further reconciling difference and harmonizing relations. Where holistic working is not carried out, the perception of essential difference persists, and a vicious circle of friction, animosity, and division takes place.

Insofar as the holistic working of association is carried out, people are taken from the perception that interests are essentially incompatible to the perception that they are essentially compatible. Belief in essential difference of interests is just as unwarranted as belief in essential difference of identity, for people's personal and collective interests, as properly understood, *are* essentially in harmony with those of others. Yet because of the challenge of understanding true long-term interests, the narrow and sectoralist all too often err by considering others' interests to be essentially at odds with their own. In competition's regulated contests between claimants, it is often quite difficult for people to see through the scramble to the larger harmony of interests that unites them. Perceiving differences of interest to be essential misses the larger interest people share as players in a competitive game with overriding aggregate benefits. Indeed, the costs of conflict are frequently so high that even people's narrowest interests are served by overcoming it. The greater the development of the universal, the greater the recognition that peaceful, properly regulated competition, in its place, is overwhelmingly salutary.

Perception of essential difference entailing fundamental negation is always ultimately a philosophical and religious error reflecting lack of self-knowledge. As follows from our analyses in earlier chapters, there are no ultimate differences between human beings. People draw essential lines between themselves and others or between one inner sector and another only when and where their insight, empathy, and ability to reconcile come to an end. As possible, others must be included within the moral whole, even as both they and we are adjusting to the dynamic, enlarging, and developing unity that includes all.

Holistic working takes place at the ideal level as broadened cultural understanding allows a larger sameness to be seen in difference. The more universal the understanding, the more all-encompassing the vision and less easily the human is drawn into conflict.

Holistic working at the real level consists first of building higher-level, more encompassing community and association that establish and enforce norms and policies to suppress the worst lower-level conflict, tangibly facilitating harmonious order. In this preliminary form the universal is often present to some degree from the onset together with early sectoral institutions. At all stages of development the real universal also institutes policies and adjusts and harmonizes social practices that more routine frictions might be minimized. In time, some homogenization tends to occur as rough edges are smoothed and more comfortable and useful forms are introduced, but many sorts of difference persist that are reconciled and still others arise. As unnecessarily offending ways and harmful practices are modified, the recognition of a common humanity and shared interests is made less difficult. Holistic working similarly overcomes the inner alienations of persons, promoting inner perception, understanding, trust, and balance that we might rise above psychic conflict and become whole and fulfilled. As the universal is approached, ideal oppositions are brought under overarching structures of meaning and real oppositions under overarching structures of action.

None of this is to say that there cannot be a sharp but provisional perception of difference by the universal itself against aggressors. That entails the drawing of necessary lines between reasonable, peace-loving people who work through their differences and the unreasonable, violence-prone hoodlums of the world who seek to force their will upon others. Although when one understands all peoples and traditions, she no longer considers anyone essentially alien, she will treat the incorrigible provisionally as such while defending against and defeating them. The conditional acknowledgment of difference and wielding of blame by the universal are a profound, stoic commitment to protecting the whole in the course of slowly inducing the recalcitrant or their offspring to bring out better in themselves. Provisional marginalization occurs until such a time as the miscreants desist and reform or are displaced by others constructively inclined. When, how, and to what extent the universal itself draws lines and engages in conflict is determined by our ethical criterion, what contributes optimally to the long-term well-being of the whole.

* * * *

When spurious difference divides, it is often not simply that universalism has not been reached but that it has been contravened. All sectoral resistance by the parts against the whole is the opposite of the open and flexible receptivity demanded by the universal and a source of conflict. Obstinate traditionalism and fundamentalist religion form perfect wedges between peoples, thwart holistic working, move toward caste, and sow the seeds of conflict. The refusal of holistic working is the ultimate source of much war, revolution, and terrorism, as well as of turmoil in communities, families, and personalities. Unwillingness to work holistically takes a number of forms, prominently including hubris, defensiveness, and conflictualism.

Hubris is a major barrier to the universal. In its worship of what one is in all his particularism, hubris entails the obdurate refusal to look freshly at reality and search for the true and good with an open mind. Hubris is the profoundly destructive denial of people's need to raise themselves to the universal by those who are already arbitrarily and absolutely certain. Its consummate idolatry occurs when one is so sure he is right that he clings haughtily to a set of concrete forms, new or old, and exempts himself from further examination and working of them. Arrogantly refusing the truth, holding up extravagant fantasies or rationalistic designs, hubris is a major source of conflict when seemingly essential difference puts humans at odds with each other.

A second great barrier to working and promoter of conflict is the collective and personal defense mechanisms, the negative and equally destructive analog to hubris. The defenses with varying degrees of consciousness wall off the mind from all that is alien and threatening or upsetting. Inherently dangerous for society and the person, the defenses gratuitously refuse the developed and universal. Especially in situations of complexity and turbulence, reality can be frightening and disruptive for a less-developed society or mind in which the ability to think is rudimentary or basic emotional needs have been frustrated. In response to distressful images and impulses that lurk about, those succumbing to the defenses compulsively repeat the secure past and evade the dreaded present and future.

Crying for internal and external tariff walls via the defenses is a drastic and counterproductive means of responding to disturbance. Selectively and temporarily we may allow the traumatized their respite, yet, however understandable, the defenses block the real solution to problems, which can only be development in light of the whole. Trapped in sectoralism, conflict, and stagnation, unworked defensives clash as easily with themselves as with others. Defensiveness is pronounced in the thinking of Michael Oakeshott (1974, 170–71), to whom every "change is a threat to identity . . . an emblem of extinction," for which reason the endangered self has to be protected "against the hostile forces of change."

With development of the universal one or one's group or nation can learn to face the unfaceable. As we come to know and understand our many parts and their needs through experience in the social and cultural markets or in meditation or therapy, we slowly overcome our injuries, dispel our fears, and dismantle our defenses. We cease blaming others and overcome our outer conflicts, and we cease blaming ourselves and overcome our inner conflicts. In place of the abundant raw sensitivities of the unworked we come to terms with ourselves and others. The defenses are primarily the fearful, counterproductive resistance of the unworked, authoritarian, and conflicted to their own growth. The defenses are not a necessary part of life, and as we become whole and balanced, need for them steadily evaporates. Free and open external and internal conversation brings reconciliation and authentic belief and practice.

As hubris brazenly proclaims itself perfect, the defenses fearfully clutch the familiar. The two are respectively the manic and depressive forms of the same willful flight from reality. Hubris manifests itself in the proud recklessness of princes, revolutionaries, and fanatics; the defenses appear in the base timorousness of the lowly. The one is cavalier with the truth; the other is cowed by it. The one is mesmerized with its own arbitrary way; the other is terrified of any other way. In either case the mind disengages from reality, development is forestalled, and conflict is exacerbated.

All utopias violate the norm against hubris. Far overreaching the world, they seek to impose vain and fanciful ideologies. All fundamentalisms, be they Judaic, Christian, Muslim, Hindu, or even British, risk sinning via both hubris and defensiveness. Privileging the past, they oppose looking at the whole and freshly determining what is good and right. Holding fast to formulas devised in another era under conditions very different from our own, they stubbornly oppose all living universalism. Over and against such throwbacks is a respectful but critical esteem for the luminaries of the past in conjunction with an open but careful search for truth in the present. Hubris and the defenses come together in vicious tyrants' cynical manipulation of the confused—the peremptory and sheltered joined in collective flights from reality. The pyrrhic comfort of the one is to indulge its narcissistic revelry, and that of the other is to perpetuate its vacant apprehension. The result of both is the exchanging of harmony and development for conflict and stasis.

Another important source of conflict is conflictualism, along with the associated socio-cultural matrix, which often includes conflict theory. Conflictualism, frequently arising from prolonged experience of conflict, is the tendency to broadly embrace and justify conflict. Denying the possibility of peaceful reconciliation and commending aggression on principle, Marxism and many other forms of conflictualism promote the perception of essential group differences and/or conflicts of interest. Imputing the worst to adversaries and privileging the worst in itself, conflictualism also hardens and justifies hubris and the defenses. To give primacy to conflict is to elevate negativism, heighten division, resist the universal, and foster conflict. Conflictualism often means well but is badly misguided.

Harmonism, to the contrary, is the systematic promotion and justification of reconciliation. In its deep-seated sense that all difference can be reconciled and all conflict resolved, harmonism says both/and where conflictualism says either/or. Unfortunately, far too much harmonism is grounded in nothing more substantial than indeterminate abstraction. Hence the naïve harmonism that fails sufficiently to address conflict, in theory or in reality. Naïve harmonism is found wherever idealists blithely ignore or fail to deal with conflict, giving free rein to international aggression and domestic crime. Where naïve harmonism overemphasizes the whole, conflictualism overemphasizes the parts. Where naïve harmonism underemphasizes power, conflictualism overemphasizes it. The opposition between naïve harmonism and conflictualism is one more opposition to be overcome by the universal, along with that between the corresponding emotions of tenderness and toughness. The wise and balanced harmonism of the universal squarely faces difference, effectively restrains conflict, and works to overcome its sources. Self-consciously aware of the nature of conflict and the process of its resolution, as the universal overcomes conflict, it also slowly overcomes conflictualism, largely through the establishment and maintenance of peace.

Knowing human nature, the universal's sophisticated harmonism is not pacifist. It draws firm lines against predatory and barbarous action—between civilized human beings and those who would tyrannize, murder, and maim. Malevolent thugs will always be with us, and they must be forcibly deterred, confined, or destroyed. Reconciling naïve harmonism and conflictualism, universalism's sophisticated harmonism works toward authentic harmony as circumstances allow while carefully protecting against aggression. As the wise and tolerant universal engages in even intense and prolonged conflict, it attempts to broaden and develop the narrow and limited. Whether they acknowledge it or not, the particularistic too are part of the whole.

To the extent which people cannot or will not overcome their differences, they require a regulatory regime and enforced tolerance. For this reason, the first item on the agenda of the universal is always to establish or shore up a monopoly in the use of force. In the earliest societies, prior to the appearance of association, this monopoly could only be achieved with sovereign community. However, in all societies from the archaic on, it has been effected primarily by sovereign association, the state, which institutes a regulatory regime ensuring peace. While ordinary association is purely sectoral, the state spans the range from person to society and, with respect to this one dimension, is universal and reaches closure. (In other respects, in and of itself it remains sectoral.) The first substantial holistic working entailed by the brute integration of the state (or, in the earliest societies, of sovereign community) suppresses the most egregious negative-sum activities and the most disruptive conflicts to establish the minimum framework of order. If the sovereign association (or protection industry) is to become universally worked in other respects, it will develop hand in hand with sovereign community. Whether differences of identity and interest lead to conflict depends importantly upon the degree of development of these overarching institutions that play central roles in the balance of power between the whole and the parts.

Concurrently with its many-sided campaigns of defense, the universal earnestly ponders and addresses all causes of the violence it counters, seeking to redress any wrongs to which in part this might be responding, even though the perpetrators' action will ordinarily constitute a far greater wrong. As the threat is overcome, the universal encourages those who have aggressed and been defeated to reform themselves and rejoin the larger community— insofar as that does not undermine necessary punishment for the seriously culpable. The universal's reasonableness greatly diminishes conflict but can never end it completely. Where sectoralist narrowness and rigidity push the world toward ruin, universalist breadth and flexibility move to the trouble spots and deploy themselves to overcome oppositions and reduce tensions.

Yet where universalism is less than perfectly developed, restrained conflict may also serve a purpose, for conflict itself can constitute a crude form of holistic working. Restrained aggression may at least force the near deaf to listen. Examples of salutary conflict may include an emotional argument between husband and wife to clear the air or vigorous social protest to jar a political system from complacency. But conflict outside the bounds of integrative institutions leaves so much wreckage that we strive mightily to overcome it.

Of the forms of conflict, that over differing manifestations of the universal, whether religious or moral, is the most tragic. Although development will eventually overcome them, rude and intolerant interpretations and ethics create growth basins capable of forestalling development for long periods of time. In their dim light the narrow are wedded to the finite vessel and oblivious to its infinite content. In their obtuseness they lash out immorally on behalf of their hollow exoterica and putative moralities. When the religiously or ethically sectoral attack the religiously and ethically universal, it is the poor in spirit striking out against the rich in spirit and the morally dead rising up against the morally living.

Nothing is more important than whether people are building together or tearing down. The settled tendency either to resolve differences peacefully or to force them aggressively is a major pivot of personal and collective life. The cessation of mutual antagonism and achievement of reconciliation between groups are necessary for everything else in society, for which reason they are at the heart of ethics. Jesus and Buddha are at one in highlighting the messages of forgiveness and love. No more fulfilling life could await us than that of becoming part of the living universal—in whatever capacity we are called to contribute—working difference, overcoming conflict, and helping move communities and the world toward true harmony. Where sectoralism leads to nihilism, conflict, and ruin, universalism leads to meaning, reconciliation, and well-being. That the human is open-ended and we can only imperfectly realize the universal matters not the least, for advancing as we are best able toward our fullest potential is the worthiest possible aim.

As universalism tirelessly spreads the word of the broader unity we share and overcomes difference, resistance by hubris, defensiveness, and conflictualism eventually dissipates. As universalism slowly becomes established, its balanced dance between perspectives becomes habitual and the human becomes shimmering being in harmony. As it becomes better worked and more of its goals are realized, the human is nourished and enabled to pursue its unending quest on higher and higher levels. My view of the world is an optimistic one.

****

Because kinds of reconciliation necessarily imply kinds of conflict in their insufficiency, harmonist theory is ipso facto at the same time conflict theory, at least tacitly. However, harmonist theory must be developed if this is to be made determinate. When harmonism is determinately developed—and it is here—each of the major propositions of conflict theory may be found in a larger theory of harmony, thus overcoming the opposition between harmonist and conflict theory.

However, if as I have argued, grasping the universal is central to understanding harmony and conflict, and if harmony and conflict are the central phenomena of the human sciences, then not only must the concept of the universal itself be brought into the theory and research of the human sciences, but it must be central to them. In order for the universal to be incorporated at all satisfactorily into the human sciences, we are going to need a very different philosophy of human science from the regnant one, and we are going to need significant enhancement of the most suitable existing alternative to it. This does not go unopposed.

Paradoxically, to lay down universalist and harmonist foundations for the human sciences, under today's unusual circumstances, is to complete one's preparations for battle. For as we turn toward the epistemics resting upon these understandings, we encounter the two forces in philosophy and the human sciences most responsible for the chaos our foundations are meant to overcome. The first of the two unlikely co-combatants are the fundamentalist adherents of a strict scientific method imported from the natural sciences, one that has an important continuing role to play in the human sciences, but one that must move over and cede an equally prominent role to a very different kind of science. The second are the anarchist skeptics and radical relativists who oppose any notion of reliable knowledge in the human sciences and above all any with respect to the universal. So far both have been reticent, but they fire an initial salvo when we approach the epistemic. "That is all well and good," they say, "but of what use could it be? How could we ever reliably know such things about the human and especially the universal things about it?" I reply to their query in Part III.

Note

1. See also the treatment of conflict in Chapter 8.

Bibliography

Oakeshott, M. 1974. *Rationalism in Politics.* London: Methuen.

Part III. The Epistemics of the Human Sciences

15. *Dialectical Historicism*

Hegel's Dialectical Idealism

The most developed dialectical thought in existence, that of Hegel, is a tool allowing us to overcome and move through the fundamental oppositions of the human. The first and more fundamental use of the dialectic, in the overcoming of oppositions, we have already explored at length. Its second use, as a language, follows upon the first. Once we have overcome numerous oppositions, we need to keep track of the relationships between the various poles or nodes and between these and the whole. This is preeminently an intellectual task, but a very high-level one that yields the overall structure of scholarly work. The human phenomena it addresses must be both ideal and real.

In Hegel's radical idealism, however, the dialectical movement, such as it is, occurs primarily in ideas. Hegel (1975, 66) tells us that "forms of thought must be studied in their essential nature and complete development. . . ." But he also tells us that the gist of human phenomena lies in thought. To Hegel, the dialectic is a way of conceptualizing the progressive development of thought, and the great dialectical moves of history take place in collective thought. If Hegel encounters difficulty by treating the dialectic too mechanically, he seriously impairs his system by taking the world of ideas to be the primary one. Hegel's one-sided focus on the ideal reflects the bent of a German late-agrarian aristocratism in which cultural specialists were at once extolled and barred from power—a constellation that was also related to the romanticism of the times. Yet neither Hegel's dialectic nor his universalism has any necessary connection with idealism.

Marx's Dialectical Materialism

Drawing upon Feuerbach among others, Marx negates Hegel's one-sided idealism. To Marx, precisely the opposite holds: the real is emphasized and the ideal is not. Where the subject for Hegel is spirit, that for Marx is man. Marx terms his departure from Hegel "materialist," and while it is that, it is much more saliently realist. Marx (1963, 216; see also 200) views Hegel's idealism as only an alienation from the philosopher's "*being*, i.e., from his natural and human life," its "self-objectification." In Marx the dialectical moves take place not in the ideal but in the real institutions of society. Hegel wants to develop universal consciousness as he understands it; Marx wants to develop universal society as he portrays it (cf. Taylor 1975, 120). For Hegel reconciliation comes from recognition and awareness, and for Marx—such as it is—it comes from real structural transformation (Taylor 1975, 550).

Little noted today, where Hegel overcomes oppositions and reaches the whole on a number of dimensions, Marx does so on no more than one or two. Marx rightly negates Hegel's idealism but wrongly negates his holism as well, effectively undoing a series of reconciliations and slipping back developmentally. Marx doesn't see man or society as consciousness; both to him are objectivities. Marx's later discarding of the notion of personal development was one more instance of his general antiholism. Without holism there can be no true dialectic, and Marx's is an incomplete dialectic. In Marx, other than his comprehensive historical perspective and perhaps his anomalous mythical and idealist withering away of the state in the indefinite future, there are no reconciliations but only successive negations. This is why Hardimon (1994, 139) is right to emphasize the importance of Hegel's affirmation versus Marx's denial of "the proposition that the modern social world is a home." Marx's radical conflictualism is intimately associated with his antiholism.

Owing to his idealism and logism, Hegel could not easily talk about causation in the real world. Frequently all he could do is describe an abstract sequence of progressively higher conceptual forms and posit an unexplained tendency toward ever-greater development. Switching to realism, Marx's ability to explain was far greater. However, he too posited a background development, only his was economic rather than cultural. As Hegel's one-sided idealism limited his understanding of society, Marx's one-sided realism limited his understanding of culture. Marx is largely back to sectoralism, only now in a self-conscious and hardened form. However, there was another important, if mostly tacit, negation of Hegel, that posed by historicism.

Historicism

Hegel's rigors, idealism, and abstractness were such that application of his universalism to concrete historical phenomena was problematic despite his salubrious turn to history. The movement of historical scholarship in nineteenth-century Germany known as historicism, in many respects the first modern social science outside of economics—despite receiving early impetus from Hegel—also grew up largely in a spirit of rejection of his philosophy. Historicism essentially brought together the view that one can only understand human phenomena historically with the perspective of cultural relativism. Under the influence of scientism and German discipline, historicism was pragmatic and aphilosophical while attempting to be objective and value-free. With exemplary standards of scholarship, historians like Ranke, Meinecke, and Mommsen researched empirical historical questions large and small while seeking the innumerable factors behind particular socio-cultural forms and events. They depicted and analyzed myriads of historical patterns, such as those in family structures, economic adaptations, and religious practices from Africa, central Asia, ancient Mesopotamia, and many other exotic regions. The cumulative outcome was an astonishing library that yielded the first comprehensive, empirically and critically grounded record of world history, one self-consciously pragmatic and atheoretical, and partly in negation of Hegelian idealism. Although Hegel was himself a historicist (see Beiser 1993) in that he encouraged the use of socio-cultural context in the explanation of human phenomena and to a limited degree practiced the same, a rift opened because Hegel's metaphysics was far more salient than his historicism.

Dialectical Historicism

To turn Hegel upside down is to pose the antithesis to Hegel's thesis. In many respects the Hegel-Marx opposition represents the central theoretical fissure in the human sciences. With his more balanced view than either, Weber might have been able to overcome the opposition had he not been so resistant to philosophy. For more than a century and a half—until now—there has been no synthesis of Hegel and Marx. Nor, for as long, has there been a synthesis of Hegel and historicism in the human sciences. Philosophers have returned to their ahistorical self-privileging while historians have remained stubbornly aphilosophical. But dialecticians do not stop with negations—they overcome oppositions. Dialectical historicism, joining the dialectic to the ontology of this work, provides the two missing syntheses and restores a third.

Hegelian idealism one-sidedly emphasizes thought and slights the real, while Marxian realism one-sidedly emphasizes action and slights the ideal. The dialectical historicist synthesis of the ideal and real brings both into full relief, restoring their respective omissions.[1] It grants the autonomous contributions of the ideal and cultural and also those of the real and social, providing a richer theoretical matrix than either. Dialectical historicism at the same time resolves the holist-negationist opposition between Hegel and Marx. It does so in the earlier portions of this work by deriving holism anew and demonstrating the contradictions and incoherence of negationist anti-holism. Simultaneously, dialectical historicism overcomes the opposition between Hegel and the historicists. Although retaining more from Hegel than they were aware (see Beiser 1993), later historicists rejected Hegel's philosophy in exasperation, unable to bridge the large gap between their concrete empirical concerns and his abstract idealist universalism. Dialectical historicism remains steadfastly Hegelian philosophically while greatly developing and modernizing the historicism that Hegel drew largely from Montesquieu and Herder. By encompassing both the real and ideal and by fully engaging dimensions that were recessive in Hegel, dialectical historicism directs a Hegelian dialectic and universalism to the substantive concerns of historians, anthropologists, psychologists, and other human scientists. Dialectical historicism will demonstrate that history as a whole is far more than the endless, unfathomable chain of disparate events and forms averred by radical historicists. It will confirm Hegel's understanding that "historical relativism has as its beginning and end 'absolute knowledge.' . . ." (Löwith 1964, xvi). Dialectical historicism shares his comprehension that absolute knowledge and relativism are perfectly reconcilable.

The core task of dialectical historicism is, with respect to whatever fundamental dimension should be involved, to note the varying degrees to which actual positions, oppositions, and overcomings are presented in human phenomena. Its language enables us to visualize relations of aspects and parts to the whole and facilitates our getting around in the whole. With dialectical historicism one pans through the changing historical circumstances of collectivities and persons and watches the many-dimensional patterns within and between stages in relation to the whole. Thus the dialectical history of economies centers on the changing forms of economic systems, that of politics on the changing forms of political regimes, and so on, through the various social and cultural institutions. In our second major use of the dialectic (the first again being the overcoming of oppositions) the dialectic becomes a language allowing the determinate description of relations vis-à-vis the whole. Hegel uses the dialectic in this way among others, but his periodization is unworkable, and he too seldom follows through with causal analysis. Marx most often uses the dialectic this way, his periodization is far better, and his explanation is abundant and strong. Yet, his dialectic itself is frequently distorted in ways I have mentioned. Use of the dialectic as a language is derivative of the primary use because once historical and personal development are overcome and one grasps their fundamental stages, it becomes a relatively straightforward matter to talk about their configurations and the degrees of sublation these manifest. The perspective of dialectical historicism is the overarching view of collective and personal history as essentially a sequence of shifts on the basic dimensions of the human with varying degrees of polarity.

Dialectical historicism is at once Hegelian and Marxist. It retains a vibrant sense of the whole from Hegel while it draws from Marx an insistence that real historical events be studied causally and that the economic be accorded a prominent place in history. It draws from both that we should study the entire sweep of history. At the same time dialectical historicism subscribes to the historicist credo that all human phenomena be examined and their empirical differences accounted for by their settings. Yet dialectical historicism is of practical use to historical and developmental scholars.

Utilizing dialectical historicism, the central goal of the social sciences must be to construct a comprehensive comparative historical sociology of the world. Placing special emphasis on civilizational and subcivilizational blocks, this study should describe and explain the major structures and processes across all institutions for each major era of history—that is to say, especially foraging, horticultural village, archaic, agrarian, early capitalist, industrial capitalist or modernist, and global capitalist or postmodernist periods.[2] Different societies may be at different stages of development at the same time. For many purposes, the agrarian stage must also be divided into early, middle, and late substages. Late agrarian society on most of the Continent paralleled and was in competition with early capitalist society from 1500 until approximately 1885. However, when these stages and substages last long enough, additional multifaceted transformations occur and more epochs need to be distinguished to reflect the phases of the moral cycle. Thus, for both the early capitalist and late agrarian societies of Europe after 1500 a contractionary Reformation era was followed by an expansionary Enlightenment and contractionary nineteenth century. This is an important part of what lay behind the series of socio-cultural metamorphoses that so occupied Foucault's attention, for example. Parallel to and in competition with industrial capitalist society, militant and conflictualist neoagrarian society also arose. Sometimes, as for example for fully understanding Islamic civilization, it is also necessary to bring in a parallel herding society that can vary developmentally from approximately the level of horticultural village to that of early agrarian society (see Lenski, 1970). However, these demarcations are but conventional labels for the distinctive many-sided configurations of institutions and character associated with the dominance of particular historical classes. Institutional structures are pivotal because they channel so much perception, thought, and action.

The central task of psychology should then be history on the scale of the single lifetime. Here again stages of dialectical reorganization take place as development is undergone. The stages of personal development are quite analogous to those of social development—ontogeny recapitulates phylogeny. Once early childhood development is undergone and an id becomes dominant, subsequent development entails consolidation of the ego, super-ego, superid, and various additional sectors, ideal and real, individualist and collectivist. Although different sectors may be developing simultaneously, the key steps of psychological development are those to dominance by one sector or another. Child and youth development centers on a series of stages in sectoralism; adult development centers on a series of stages in universalism. Adult development is largely terra incognita to psychology today because it can only be fruitfully studied with the universal—one more major reason why the universal has to be front and center in the human sciences. The process is many-dimensional, substantially nonlinear, and may proceed in different ways, to different degrees, and at different tempos in different people and societies.

What the human sciences most need, and the central building to be constructed upon these foundations, is Weber-like comparative historical analysis and Piaget-like developmental study across all institutions of society and the psyche—with their periodizations grounded. Both would describe and explain the patterns at each stage and the developmental processes between them. Such a social science would emphasize the genesis and consequences of dominance by a certain character type in society, and such a psychology would emphasize the genesis and consequences of dominance by a certain character type in the person. These historical and developmental thrusts interact in many ways, as in the sociology of generations and the history and anthropology of socialization practices.

Dialectical historicism sees socio-cultural and psychological development as series of stages separated by many-dimensional rotations of ontological frameworks. While under ordinary conditions the structural changes tend to be cumulatively developmental, every shift need not be. Particularly when the human is damaged, as by conflict or aging, development may regress. Irrespective of their direction, the dialectical shifts and the formations regnant between them have to be explained. By itself, however, dialectical historicism does not explain. How we explain is with a phenomenology with which it works hand in hand. Alone among approaches to the human sciences, dialectical historicism joined to an explanatory phenomenology embraces the full complexity of the human and follows it through every permutation.

Notes

1.　Hegel did not use the language of thesis, antithesis, and synthesis, which came from Fichte and Marx. I do only rarely, primarily because it tends to exaggerate the degree of self-consciousness of human opposition, often with unwarranted

conflictualist overtones. In this case, directed to Marx, the usual reservation would not apply.
2. See Lenski (1966, 1970) along with Weber (1978) for the rationales of periodizations approaching this one. The stages identified in Hegel's general philosophy of history, however, are relatively ad hoc and unusable.

Bibliography

Beiser, F. 1993. "Hegel's Historicism." In *The Cambridge Companion to Hegel,* ed. F. Beiser. Cambridge: Cambridge University Press.
Hardimon, M. 1994. *Hegel's Social Philosophy: The Project of Reconciliation.* Cambridge: Cambridge University Press.
Hegel, G. 1975. *Hegel's Logic.* Oxford: Oxford University Press.
Lenski, G. 1966. *Power and Privilege.* New York: McGraw-Hill.
———. 1970. *Human Societies.* New York: McGraw-hill.
Löwith, K. 1964. *From Hegel to Nietzsche: The Revolution in Nineteenth-Century Thought.* New York: Holt, Rinehart and Winston.
Marx, K. 1963. *Early Writings,* ed. T. Bottomore. New York: McGraw-Hill.
Taylor, C. 1975. *Hegel.* Cambridge: Cambridge University Press.
Weber, M. 1978. *Economy and Society.* 2 vols. Berkeley and Los Angeles: University of California Press.

16. *Phenomenology and Method in the Human Sciences*

Human science may be approached productively in either an interdisciplinary or a disciplinary manner. The robust means by which we conduct an interdisciplinary human science is with phenomenology, by which I understand the study of consciousness and particularly its applied study in the human sciences rather than its foundational study in philosophy. The phenomenological method in the human sciences is to enter minds as a way of determining why people perceive, think, and act as they do. This method is so important to the human sciences because it and it alone promises to provide the comprehensive, coherent, and powerful description and explanation of the human experience that hitherto has been substantially missing.

Exemplars of Phenomenology

Although he was anticipated by Herder, Hegel may be considered the founder and first great exemplar of the phenomenological method. Approaching the human from the inside, Hegel profoundly grasped fundamental features of the mind at the basis of personal and historical develop ment. Hegel's (applied) phenomenology, whether directed at whole civilizations or at philosophy, religion, and the arts, was dialectical and made reference to stages within the overall course of history. It explicated thought by means of the socio-cultural context from which it arises (see Forster 1998, 464ff.).[1] It also powerfully explored the forms of the universal evident in world history. Unfortunately Hegel's phenomenology was largely restricted to inquiry into the cultural and slighted the social. Moreover, however suggestively Hegel grasped the overall course and meaning of history, his idealism hampered his ability to treat human events causally. Insufficient use of the consummatory-instrumental and individualism-collectivism dimensions together with a somewhat arbitrary, Christian-centered periodization further weakened his phenomenology.

Setting aside his sinister conflictualism, Nietzsche, the second exemplar of phenomenology, was a master at reading character and intuiting the experiential context of human forms. Although Nietzsche's ontology was little developed and highly unbalanced, his disclosure of the unconscious mind, and his holistic probing of phenomena, such as what lay behind the Eleatics' self-conception, Luther's theology, Kant's philosophy, Wagner's music, and radical politics, provides an extraordinary and enduring model of phenomenology. Nietzsche's insight into the bourgeois psyche in particular lies at the foundations of Freudian psychology and is indispensable for all who would comprehend the mind. Nietzsche's way of reading character and his understanding that socio-cultural patterns arise from the experience-derived mentalities of concrete social classes proved no less foundational for Weber.

The third and crucial social scientific exemplar of phenomenology was Max Weber, the greatest historian and social thinker of the twentieth century, who viewed mentalities as central to history. Weber studied civilizations by systematically focusing on character, explaining perception, thinking, action, and the resulting socio-cultural patterns by reference to the affinities of the dominant classes behind them. In his view, particular experience-based classes have shared tendencies to perceive, think, and act in ways reflecting their enduring characters. We understand human patterns when we understand the characteristic, ideal-typical leanings of the social class bearing them, and these leanings are uncovered primarily through immersion in historical materials. Weber, however, somewhat misperceived what he was doing in practicing phenomenology, and did so in a characteristically German-idealist way. He grasped that it was meaning he was getting at but took that to be the special preserve of culture or the ideal. Subjectivity, however, is no more ideal than real or cultural than social. Even though Weber somewhat overemphasized the ideal in his work, he progressively converged on studying the whole subjectivities of types of persons and collectivities. What he termed *verstehen* or interpretive sociology was brilliant phenomenology and remains of lasting value as such.

The fourth and crucial psychological exemplar was Piaget. In a prolific career Piaget introduced a holistic and phenomenological approach to studying personal development and indelibly conveyed the centrality of stages and dialecticality in human development. However, he concentrated on the acquisition of abilities rather than character and followed development only through childhood and youth.

The tendency the four thinkers loosely share is a holistic yet ultimately empirical way of analyzing human beings and societies. How we ought to conduct phenomenology and build the human sciences, I maintain, is by harmonizing and developing from the best of Hegel, Nietzsche, Weber, and Piaget, and especially the architectonic understanding of the first, the incisive character readings of the second, the masterly comparative historical sociology of the third, and the compelling dialecticality of the fourth.

The four exemplars are supported by two gifted proponents of phenomenology. Husserl, under the influence of Frege, devoted enormous energy to exploring the ontology of consciousness and laying down a program for phenomenology. Appropriately enough Husserl emphasized *intentionality*, the aboutness of everything human, but in his somewhat cumbersome, quasidisciplinary fashion he was unable to sufficiently ground phenomenology. His phenomenology got major parts of the foundations and method right but lacked the required framework of dimensions, absent which his programmatic insights for the conduct of phenomenology are of some but limited value.

In Schutz, Husserl was fortunate to find an indefatigable clarifier and amplifier. Also rendering Max Weber his full due, Schutz gave the best existing methodological treatment of the phenomenological approach in his *Phenomenology of the Social World*. But Schutz was unable to go significantly beyond Husserl in grounding phenomenology or providing it a framework, without which he could make explicit the method Weber had employed but could not improve upon it or much help others do so. For the undeniable ability it has marshaled and its considerable substantive fruition in philosophy, the movement Husserl spawned has had a somewhat disappointing legacy in the human sciences and precisely on account of its failure to clarify and emphasize the dimensions of the human.

The Hegel-Nietzsche-Weber-Piaget substantive and Husserl-Schutz methodological lines of phenomenology have remained lamentably separate, but the far greater concern is that until now only limited foundations and framework have existed with which to conduct phenomenology. With great intuitive force the substantive giants of phenomenology made their way on their own, but without a developed dimensionalization of existential space, they have been extremely hard acts to follow. However, with the needed foundations and framework now in place, let us take up the nature and conduct of phenomenological analysis.

The Nature of Phenomenology

The purview of phenomenology is the whole world of human consciousness. Phenomenology, as properly understood, seeks to grasp its subject in its entirety and at once, studying the entire mentality of each significant personal and collective actor in an event, of an era, or behind a structure. That is what makes it holistic. Most striking about us is that so many representational and motivational things are going on simultaneously, that our worlds are inherently so many-sided. Phenomenology pursues interior, three hundred sixty-degree views of the human.

People and societies are not one- or two-dimensional *objects* to phenomenology but many-dimensional *subjects*. An objective view becomes at once holistic and subjective as it becomes complete and a full view of the world from a particular existential location. As Nagel (1986, 26) says, objectivity "is just one way of understanding reality. . . ." Subjectivity is as inherent to the nature of representation as objectivity, for in representation there is what is represented and what holds representation—the object and subject. When the objective is dominant, the characteristics of objects or what is object-like come to the fore. When the subjective is dominant, those of subjects do. It is indeed possible that we have subjective views of others just as we have them of ourselves, although rarely with such vividness or richness of detail.

The meaning that phenomenology pursues is correspondingly holistic and subjective. In Schutz's (1967, 133 [emphasis deleted]) words, "[t]o know the subjective meaning of the product means that we are able to run over in our minds in simultaneity or quasi-simultaneity the polythetic Acts which constituted the experience of the producer." As Voegelin (2002, 78) puts it, for consciousness to be illuminated is for it to be "made experience-able from within." What something means holistically may be captured by depicting where it stands vis-à-vis the dimensions of the human.

In everyday life human beings constantly jump between objective and subjective and external and internal perspectives. We objectivize our own action, subjectivize that of others, and viceversa.[2] When we objectivize human phenomena, we narrow and compartmentalize them. Sometimes we do this for instrumental purposes of control and sometimes for consummatory ones of enjoyment or relaxation. So too, when we subjectivize in the human sciences in the way I am suggesting, we look at the human holistically, and when we objectivize it we look at it partially. The one perspective gives orientation and the other rigor. Having both at our command is vital.

Needless to say, in their usual employment by objectivist heuristic or hard science sorts, the concepts of objectivity and subjectivity take on different meaning, the former suggesting rational and disciplined and the latter emotional and undisciplined thinking. Equating subjectivity with partiality, objectivity is held up as scientific and rigorous while subjectivity is disparaged as unscientific and self-indulgent. This perspective overstates the value of the objective and understates the value of the subjective in the human sciences. Phenomenologists understand that objectivity in its narrowness and artificiality requires every bit as much caution as subjectivity. Not all objective views are helpful in the human sciences, only rigorous and empirically valid ones. But not all subjective views are helpful either, only broad, determinate, systematic, and empirically valid ones.

However, the human may be approached both determinately and in anything like its full richness only in a temporal context. As Heidegger convincingly establishes, temporality is inherent in the nature of the human. History is not an aspect of the human experience—it *is* the human experience—for which reason there is an absolute centrality of history in the human sciences. Persons and societies are treated in light of their entire histories and situations by phenomenology, as is the case with psychoanalysis, which is kindred to phenomenology. Much sectoral study in the human sciences also has a prominent historical dimension, though not a comprehensive one. Only its holism fundamentally distinguishes phenomenological from disciplinary inquiry— the two are equally theoretical and practical, social scientific and psychological, and descriptive and explanatory.

Prediction, control, and applicability to the world arise in both the phenomenological and disciplinary approaches, even though disciplinary human science may be more conducive to low-level, routine application to the everyday world of policy than holistic phenomenological human science. Yet the complexity of the human is such that the holistic weighing of action can never be far away if policy disasters are to be avoided. As the situation becomes more complex, the role of judgment on the basis of universal understanding becomes ever more crucial. While phenomenology allows predictions based upon its broad comprehension, they are more often general than specific. Phenomenology, in its holism, bears vitally on the major questions of society and our lives; it contributes broad knowledge essential to wisdom that should be called upon in all important matters pertaining to the human.

Phenomenology may be conducted at either the macro- or microlevel. At the macrolevel, it carries out comparative historical analysis of collective perception, thought, and action in which socio-cultural patterns are related to their broadest circumstances. At the microlevel, it probes the forms of perception, thought, motivation, and action of persons. Macro- and microphenomenologies can proceed fruitfully only with constant reference to each other. The character of society at once provides and reflects standard experience that shapes the persons of whom it is composed. Inseparable from the phenomenological analysis of whole dynamic societies is that of whole dynamic personalities, particularly as manifested in the changing forms of their institutions.

Phenomenology pursues both description and explanation just as the disciplinary human sciences do, for description is to perception as explanation is to thought. Husserlian and Wittgensteinian phenomenologists have tied themselves in absurd knots by effectively restricting their work to description. What has lain behind this constriction has been the one-sided idealism and conceptualism endemic to philosophy. Having had little contact with the real and empirical, professional philosophers have had little experience with explanation. In their different ways connotative and denotative, ideal and real, personal and collective, general and particular human phenomena must all be both described and explained.

Phenomenological description relies upon interpretative placement in a many-dimensional context approaching the whole, as in the interpretation of Moghul India as predominantly agrarian or Benjamin Franklin's writings as bourgeois. Phenomenology hermeneutically reads Japan's trade initiatives or Israel's settlement policies, France's style or the Nuer's religiosity. It interprets the characters of Saladin or de Gaulle, of ancient Mesopotamian priests or contemporary corporate executives. The broad forms of societies and lives require interpretation. Phenomenological interpretation is a perceiving of something to be what it is, a taking of it to instance a pattern in the context of the whole or significant portions of the whole. With phenomenology one reads human forms—configurations of perception, thought, motivation, and action—by perceiving that something lies where it does in existential space. To Wittgenstein (1953, 187), a "description is a representation of a distribution in a space," but describing affinities in complex human settings draws upon a many-sided perception in existential space across the ontological divides of the human. This is something qualitatively different from and richer than the simple sectoral perception of natural or human phenomena. Conducting phenomenology requires acute interpretation in which one notes the signs of different kinds of character and finds patterns in the most diverse social and cultural phenomena. In order to fathom the intended and unintended meaning in human forms the human sciences must engage in a high bandwidth perception, a rich fleshing out of meaning that Geertz (1973, ch. 1) terms "thick description." Just as we easily interpret a speech by Orrin Hatch to reflect a certain degree of liberalism versus conservatism, we interpret a child to be more emotional than rational or a political system to exhibit a certain degree of constitutionalism. By contrast, Nietzsche (1974, 335) aptly refers to disciplinary science as poor in meaning. Where there is comprehensive meaning, there must be comprehensive perception and description to match. The task of interpretation's seeing-as prominently includes a kind of *explication de texte* or criticism—only of all our forms, not merely the aesthetic ones. Since meaning extends far beyond explicit symbols, anything human may be looked at symbolically, i.e., as presentational, placing salience on its meaning.[3] If description is not gotten right, no explanation building upon it can be of value.[4]

Phenomenological explanation, as I recommend that it be understood, focuses on character—a holistic, summary concept referring to kinds of personalities and societies. On the one hand, phenomenology explains by pursuing the experiential sources of given ways of perceiving, thinking, and acting, together with their motivational accompaniments, particularly as crystallized in character. It studies how experience brings people to become who they are—for all that we do leaves residues, shaping us. On the other hand, phenomenology pursues the affinities between that character, or who people are, and the patterned ways of perceiving, thinking, and acting to which those of a certain personality tend because of their nature. Phenomenological explanation in its mature employment centrally includes explanation of the causes and consequences of character, for the central aspects of what we do are linked with the basic dimensions of the human as crystallized in character. Thus, social classes, above all, are made up of those bearing a particular character stamped on them by common experience. The central phenomenological analysis that does these things is the phenomenology of leanings.

The Phenomenology of Leanings

Owing to and as part of their character, people have certain fundamental leanings, as I refer to them, or *habitus* as Bourdieu (see e.g., 2000, 138–63; 1988 147–51; 1984, 223) does, which are often quite unconscious. A leaning is something natural for people to perceive, think, do, or manifest, given who they are, and they do not feel comfortable in life until the world around them fits their leanings. Without being fully aware of so doing, humans constantly strive to have their fundamental leanings prevail. They incessantly pull and build to bring the world into conformity with who they are, and, when successful, they bond with the worlds so created. The phenomenology of leanings explains why people and collectivities lean in certain directions and therefore why they perceive, think, and act as they do, considering their entire experience, characters, and situations (cf. Weber 1949, 72). Because one cannot understand the characters of persons or societies without grasping the dimensions of the human, one cannot do phenomenology with anything like its full potential without the foundations I have laid down in the previous chapters. Once one knows a person's or collectivity's leanings, one understands the central part of why they have the patterns of perception, thought, motivation, and action they do (cf. Hegel, 1975, 138). Phenomenology gets to the genotype behind the phenotype. That largely taken-for-granted genotype pertains to character, reflecting, among others, Aristotle and Hegel's view that we can only truly understand something by understanding its character. Possessing the ontology of the human is the key to performing effective phenomenological analysis and understanding the human.

The notion of a leaning is a crisper and more powerful way of getting at what Weber often speaks of as affinities or elective affinities (see e.g., 1958, 284–85, 324–25; 1978, 1180). When persons or classes share a certain leaning, Weber sometimes refers to an affinity that exists between them. Or when a person or class that leaned toward one form would also be expected to lean toward another because of the intimate connections between these forms, he also sometimes says that there is an elective affinity between the two. When persons or collectivities lean toward perceiving, thinking, or acting in a certain way because of their characters, we may speak of them as having an affinity to that pattern and to each other, but we do better to speak primarily of leanings. Study of the formation and consequences of leanings is central to phenomenological human science.

The phenomenological method makes use of ideal types, the particular combinations of polar positions associated with the characters of persons or collectivities. Ideal types reflect particular Rubik's Cube alignments of dimensional poles. That is why they are so central to phenomenology. Concrete entities seldom perfectly conform to ideal types, but they do approximate to them. Although phenomenologists can make powerful use of ideal types to analyze causal relations in the human sciences, they must always remember that reality is usually continuous rather than dichotomous (see Weber 1949, 43–45, 90ff.). Only when one proceeds with the full set of ideal types and does so dialectically may she conduct phenomenology as it should be conducted and get at the whole with respect to the human.

Until now, however, a key lacuna has substantially barred the application of phenomenology to matters involving the universal and has contributed massively to the disarray in the human sciences. Without a viable ontology of the universal, scholars cannot even say what philosophy, religion, morality, and statesmanship are, much less study them as social and psychological phenomena in a productive and balanced way. As a result, there is remarkably little history of philosophy today comparable to the subtle and powerful studies abundantly found in economic and political history or the history of literature. The study of morality fares even worse. Sociology, anthropology, and history are such bastions of doubt today that their practitioners frequently deny that morality exists, with the paradoxical result that it is often socially acceptable in them to teach a course or write a book about deviance but not one about morality. If we are to study the central phenomena of philosophy, religion, morality, and statesmanship productively, we are going to have to know what they are. However, the answer can come only from philosophy.

A most important part of what phenomenology must carry out in the future that has been glaringly neglected hitherto by the human sciences is studying the universal sectors of persons and collectivities.[5] For example, complementing Hegel's own treatment of it, we may explain the universalism of fifth-century BCE Athenian art as partly due to the proximity of that society to midpoints in long-term historical movements from community to association, ideal to real, and collectivism to individualism, facilitating the overcoming of these oppositions. We may also partly do so by reference to the unusually large leisure classes made possible by the relatively widespread ownership of olive orchards. These factors, along with many others, also arguably contributed to the rise of Greek philosophy. These are corroborable historical explanations which, irrespective of their empirical validity, have no bearing on the actual universalism and merit of that art or philosophy.

Where an ordinary phenomenology of leanings in effect probes the characteristic one-sidedness of people and collectivities, the phenomenology of the universal probes the overcoming of one-sidedness in the universal. Just as we need to describe and explain sectoralism and its effects, we need to describe and explain universalism and its effects. The universal being made up of sets within sets of wholes, the phenomenology studying this must follow its full complexity. Since the human can be only imperfectly universal, there is continuing need to describe and explain the residual sectoralism in particular approximations of the universal. In his most outstanding work, *Order and History,* Voegelin interprets and explains societies' fundamental conceptions of order and traces the effects of these on their religion, morality, and well-being. Universalism in philosophy, religion, morality, art, human science, and statesmanship empirically exists and requires scientific study as do sectoral phenomena. The universal as such is not determined, but its manifestation in the human is variable and determined.

Reaching across the whole, phenomenology gives a far broader, richer, and deeper description and explanation than any sectoral analysis. Think of the equally distinguished interpretation in Durkheim's *Elementary Forms of Religious Life* or Geertz's *Negara*. And think of the explanation of life change in a great, many-dimensional biography, such as Morris's *The Rise of Theodore Roosevelt* in its treatment of the hero's departure for the Dakotas following his early achievements in the New York legislature and his early personal losses—or of an epochal social change like the demise of Rome in a great, many-dimensional history like Gibbon's *Decline and Fall of the Roman Empire*. What we seek is the subtlest historical interpretation accompanied by the most powerful historical explanation.

The Phenomenology of Power

Although many have wrongly seen phenomenology to be incompatible with power analysis, the phenomenology of leanings must always go hand in hand with a phenomenology of power (and influence) that lays out how the leanings from certain experiences get to be realized while those from other experiences do not. Irrespective of what they might naturally lean toward, actors have a wide range of abilities to get what they want as well as to unintentionally influence things, and these abilities everywhere affect social, cultural, and personal life. A phenomenology of power (and influence) describes and explains the resources people and collectivities amass and wield, along with their consequences. It lays out how persons and collectivities acquire the ability to act upon their inclinations and what they do with that ability. The phenomenology of leanings explicates the proclivities, the phenomenology of power (and influence) their amplifications. The phenomenology of leanings addresses consciousness; the phenomenology of power addresses resources and their effects.

Concerned with the broadest meaning of power phenomena, phenomenological power analysis interprets and explains how resources are acquired and used. The phenomenology of power looks subjectively at the processes of power and influence. When phenomenology employs power analysis, it does so in a holistic context, interpreting and explaining the nuanced ways in which power is accumulated and exercised by collectivities and people and to what effects. Like the phenomenology of leanings, that of power emphasizes class and character. It might be concerned, for example, with the power and influence exercised via ritual correctness by the Brahmins in ancient India or that exercised through advertising in the contemporary world. Either a phenomenology of leanings or a phenomenology of power tends to be dominant, according to how ideal or real dominant the thinker. Whatever one's natural leaning, he must strive to balance the two.

The phenomenologies of leanings and of power are often combined as demand- and supply-side analyses. Demand-side analysis examines the direct experience of actors, the leanings flowing from it and the resulting forms or patterns. Supply-side analysis specifically examines cultural specialists such as priests or artists, tracing the ways in which their experience, character, and leanings are indirectly or vicariously transmitted to others. Since power and influence have to do with intended and unintended effects, whether ideal or real, it is clear that supply-side analysis is but a special case of a combined phenomenology of leanings and of power. As is apparent in Weber's work, there is little difference between analysis of the influence of the Chinese Mandarins, who were intellectuals, and analysis of that of the early warrior chieftains of Islam, who were not. Whoever is exercising power over or influencing others must be analyzed in the same twofold way, with respect to leanings and power/influence. The two basic phenomenologies may be seen in part as a response to Rubinstein's call in *Culture, Structure and Agency* for a dialectical overcoming of the theoretical opposition between explanation focusing on mental characteristics and that focusing on power.

Distinguishing in theory between autonomous leanings and heteronomous power and influence may be easy, but doing so in practice can be difficult. While natural leanings stemming from direct experience are always important, they can be countered by power and influence from others that may sometimes be profound, as when fundamental assumptions are internalized from others. When the charisma, public relations, or sheer weight of a person, class, or collectivity is so strong that its deeper forms come to be absorbed and taken for granted by recipients, the latter's forms often track closely with those of the powerful others with whose very existential coordinates they have become imbued, against their own leanings. The cultural power that really counts is ontological power. Among vicarious leanings a most important subset is made up of those with respect to the universal. Since natural leanings vis-à-vis the universal tend to be weak and only manifest themselves over generations, on the scale of an individual lifetime these natural leanings are dwarfed by tendencies toward the universal learned from others, particularly via religious traditions. Where natural leanings are prominent in the explanation of sectoral phenomena, exposure to traditions is prominent in the explanation of universal phenomena. The displacement of natural by vicarious leanings is an important and subtle phenomenon not to be overlooked by phenomenology. Just as an art historian reads the distinctive personal style in unsigned drawings in order to attribute them to a Michelangelo, a phenomenologist interprets the traces of leanings in perception, thought, and action in order to attribute them to the experience of particular persons, classes, and collectivities.

A third kind of analysis not to be overlooked, although most will want to use it sparingly, is the phenomenology of satisfaction. The phenomenology of leanings gets at the core disposition of the human. The phenomenology of power analyzes its relationship to the extrinsic bottom line registering the instrumental efficacy of its possessions. The phenomenology of satisfaction analyzes the intrinsic emotional bottom line having to do with the emotional value of its possessions. As needed, every phenomenological analysis of leanings and power may be joined by an analysis of the accompanying emotional consequences of action and forms. People's leanings and resources bring them differing emotional outcomes. Durkheim's *Suicide* is a great early work of this genre. The phenomenology of satisfaction is crucial to personal therapy.

The universal doesn't just identify with all times but understands all times, and does so phenomenologically. Engaging in continuous comprehensive judgment of the meanings of human phenomena, phenomenology brings the universal to bear on the many-sided nature of the human. In carrying out the holistic phenomenological inquiry that promises a much fuller comprehension of the human, many things must be balanced, including leanings and power, interpretation and explanation, person and society. All of the major events and institutional forms in history are explainable with the phenomenological approach. History as a whole becomes transparent under its gaze, as does the present.[6]

Disciplinary Human Science

By contrast, positivist, disciplinary social science and psychology have been most productive precisely when they have used simplifying assumptions to block off dimensions and compartmentalize inquiry by stringently holding constant the complexities of societal and human nature while setting aside human dialecticality. To achieve objectivity and focused, sectoral understanding, disciplinary inquiry formalizes concepts and purges broad meaning (see Mannheim 1936, 24), making it possible to analyze rigorously and establish lawlike regularities. Utilizing a model-building approach, it explores the extreme case of how decisionmakers act under conditions of pure rationality and scarcity in individual economic decisions or collective political ones. Or it confines its attention to the nonrational and cooperative or some other combination, but there must always be some such reduction. When a narrow set of orienting assumptions is made—the most central being to one pole or node of fundamental dimensions—all relationships become explicit and logically manipulable. This restriction provides deliberately blinkered practitioners with powerful local exactness. Neoclassical economic theory is the monument of this approach, but it also has been employed promisingly in psychology, political science, and elsewhere.

Holding our many-sidedness constant, the disciplinary human sciences with their mechanical models and *ceteris paribus* clauses are sometimes able to predict exactly. When supplied with suitable parameters, the numerous smaller-scale empirical theories auxiliary to larger and more abstract theories can be made to mechanically forecast. Especially in economics, this forecasting can be of great value. However, sectoral, heuristic prediction tends to work best where the concern is with the long-term unintended consequences of human action that are relatively inconsequential to the actors, as in large econometric models following the aggregate distant side-effects of countless small-scale economic decisions. Because humans are dialectical beings, we can predict tolerably well with rigid methods only in those areas of our action about which we are unconscious, unconcerned, or powerless. Humans sometimes allow trends to run for a long time without noticing or interceding. Once conditions change, though, all else is no longer equal. When we note and become concerned with such trends, we may at any point unexpectedly reverse course and intervene to obliterate them. For this reason predictions in the human sciences are frequently of limited value, and even economic trends are widely known to be exceedingly unruly.

Over and over again it is human complexity that invalidates otherwise perfectly good predictions about human beings. A boy is told that all of the men in his family become alcoholic, and he negates the pattern by becoming the first in memory to abstain. When proceeding partially and sectorally, our understandings, predictions, and actions always remain vulnerable to blind-siding. Economics, despite its extraordinary power, is forever limited by assumptions that fail to capture the complexity of the world. Very few economists can be particularly effective in the financial markets or make particularly useful predictions for large corporations—for which reason they are frequently ridiculed by portfolio managers and executives. All of this reflects the abject limits of the one- or few-dimensional in the face of the many-dimensional, of the finite in the face of the infinite. For its narrow purposes, positivist sectoralism can be quite powerful, but it is always vulnerable to a many-dimensional human nature that regularly makes sport of ceteris paribus clauses.

How do they know that all else is equal enough that their ratiocinations can have actual import? How do they know that consumers or political actors in certain circumstances really approach perfect rationality? Ultimately, unreflexive objectivity is based on the same intuition as phenomenology, for its assumptions are no less intuitive than the phenomenologist's judgment. Yet to the extent to which the various simplifying assumptions of model building are philosophically grounded in the same larger truth as that of phenomenology, their efforts can be very productive. Finding such coincidences, however, can only result from broad learning and contemplation. If unreflexive objectivism denies all subjectivism, it annuls its own foundations. For such reasons Heidegger holds that all empiricists are unacknowledged intuitionists. Bourgeois disciplinary science with its narrow assumptions is finally not so different from bourgeois ethics, religion, or law. The overarching strategy is always to lay down the framework by fiat—to posit moral rules, take the Bible as unquestioned word of God, hold up the constitution as rigidly fixed, or presuppose scientific assumptions—providing themselves an artificial zone of stability. As Nietzsche (1974, 288 [emphasis deleted]) says, there is an "impetuous demand for certainty" on the part of many that "discharges itself . . . in a scientific-positivistic form" as it does in religion. On each of these fronts the bolder and more ambitious approach is that of continuous judgment with thoughtful holism.

Nevertheless, in its way model building in the human sciences has been grounded and successful. Indeed, a most pressing need is for the approach to be extended on a large scale into nonrational phenomena. I don't mean Gary Becker-like forays with rational choice models, although they too have been valuable along the continuum between the rational and nonrational since many important rational phenomena occur in the midst of the nonrational and since accelerating movement from community to association has interjected much of the rational into the putatively nonrational. I mean rigorous scientific exploration of the nonrational as such, more systematically working out the nature of informal social relations and consensus. A need also exists for model building to be applied to cultural phenomena. However, inquiry on the basis of previously little explored combinations of assumptions has been slow to develop. We cannot expect all such study to be as well developed as economics, but model building in the human sciences needs to be more aggregatively comprehensive and balanced, reaching into all of the areas to which it might be applied.

If previous comprehensive work in the human sciences, though relatively ungrounded, has found some guidance in a few inspired works, and the major traditions of model building in disciplinary human science have obtained a certain grounding, ad hoc empiricism, representing the majority of work in the human sciences, has been more vulnerable. Acutely ungrounded and often without applicable touchstones, ad hoc empiricism has built a great deal of work on shifting sands. On the narrower and less reflexive end of its spectrum I have in mind study on such miscellaneous topics as scientific discovery, socio-economic mobility, assimilation, dating, divorce, media content, voting, lobbying, ADD children, delinquency, and attitudes toward aggression. Theory and research addressing more or less institution-wide phenomena such as the family, economy, polity, arts, or an aspect of character is broader and has tended to be more reflexive, though not holistic. Such broader and more reflexive but nonphenomenological human science may be taken as ideal typical of the human sciences.

The field of history has been particularly susceptible to ad hocery. Having all they can handle with the crucial dimension of time, modern historians, with a few notable exceptions like Spengler and Toynbee, have as a discipline largely eschewed theory for ad hoc empiricism. Historians do many things very well: they write comparatively well, they ingeniously research and document, and more often than one would expect they sense what is important and illuminatingly reveal the past with gifted intuition. Nevertheless, their work suffers from the same limitations as other ad hoc empiricism. Too often their concepts are arbitrary, their explanations unreliable, and their periodizations haphazard. Historians do not have to do comparative history, although, all else equal, it is a plus when they do. What they do have to do is select the most powerful possible concepts, interpretive strategies, explanatory tools, and periodizations. Describing and explaining historical phenomena—about every society, from every fundamental angle, and through all periods—is the core of the human sciences. For historians to do the best they possibly can with their great task, they must become better grounded.

Only occasionally does ad hoc empirical study significantly further knowledge and that only to the degree to which it is able to intuit broadly and place its work upon the larger frontiers of the advancing human sciences. Lakatos (1970, 176) is right to decry the arbitrary and patched-up research programs all too common in social psychology and elsewhere in the human sciences. Nor does mere reflexivity grant a reprieve. Absent grounding, the sectorally reflexive has fared little better than any other ad hoc empiricism. It too often mounts interesting but unproductive, unreliable, and noncumulative forays into society or the psyche in what is the analog to capricious aestheticist art. I believe that study outside the traditional disciplinary model can be more fruitful, cumulative, and grounded than it has been in the past. Lone scholars can select important topics, frame them powerfully, and produce studies of enduring value—if they use the foundations in this work.

For certain narrower questions the apparatus of rigorous science offers a way out of ad hoc sectoralism's bind, but it will not do for broader ones. Wherever significant interactions arise between sectors, the strictly disciplinary is helpless. If traditional science is nevertheless brought to bear on many-sided phenomena, it becomes unwieldy, arbitrary, and spurious, as in relatively unproductive efforts by sociologists and anthropologists to apply positivist methods to large-scale social change. The traditional scientific method becomes positively embarrassing when attempts are made to apply its rigor to highly subtle phenomena, as in various misguided efforts to address art or religion.

Profound and comprehensive aspects of events like the French Revolution, World War I, the cultural upheaval of the 1960s, and the Islamic Resurgence are outside the range of scientific rigor. The more complex human phenomena seldom make much sense and never yield consistently to our wills unless we take a subjective perspective and grasp the whole world of meaning that makes up their context. Only as we approach a holistic view does the risk of blindsiding begin to subside. Because we are many-dimensional beings for whom change on any one fundamental dimension alters kaleidoscopically the manifestations of every other dimension, because everything significant that happens to the human changes the whole structure of its being—things could be no other way. With the realm of the human we go through a metaphysical divide that renders the traditional scientific method only partly applicable. It has its place vis-à-vis the narrower matters pertaining to the human but does not apply except indirectly to the broader ones, which are holistic, interdisciplinary, and outside its range. In the end, the only way the human may be encompassed is comprehensively.

However, there are other forms of blindsiding than those stemming from narrowness and brittleness. The phenomenologist who fails to command extensive empirical knowledge of history, society, and the psyche risks blindsiding by the facts that is no less debilitating. Much of the required knowledge can only come from sectoral study.

Phenomenological and disciplinary inquiry are ultimately complementary, for phenomenology is the overarching holistic method within which the various sectoral analyses play out. The complex perspective of the whole doesn't displace such efforts but pulls them together. At home in all the special disciplines and using them as needed to put perception, thought, and action in the perspective of the whole, the phenomenologist takes over into himself all of the useful concepts, propositions, and findings of the disciplinary sciences, rejecting only those in which narrowness or overreaching violates the broader understanding of the human. For its part, disciplinary inquiry should draw orientation and frame assumptions with the help of the contextualization provided by phenomenology and its foundations while dismissing its unsound practice. Unlike the natural sciences, the human sciences need to go in two fundamental directions at the same time, one like the natural sciences and one not. Any notion of a larger incompatibility between phenomenological and disciplinary human science reflects failure to appreciate the extent to which they do entirely different things. Some are called to study the whole and others the parts. Some use the dialectic and some do not. To fully understand the human experience, all of these things need to be studied and brought together. It is not a matter of the phenomenological method versus traditional science but of two worthy approaches with different and complementary scopes and tasks. Understanding and overcoming this divide is of the utmost importance to the human sciences. As with everything, one must find the balance between these approaches.

Phenomenology and Economics

The relationship between phenomenological human science and economics is one between phenomenology and the most developed disciplinary science under its umbrella. The core of economics works with models of human action that assume scarcity (or economic need) and perfect rationality. Most at home precisely where economists must make restrictive assumptions, phenomenology moves outside the range of sectoral economics. It accepts the latter's methods and conclusions but complements it in numerous ways. Sectoral economic analysis is unable by itself to account for the institutional structures and character types that favor or disfavor growth, but studying such forms and types is a core task of phenomenology. In a similar way macroeconomists and economic historians have everything to gain from learning about the larger socio-cultural collision between industrial capitalist and neoagrarian civilizational strains that forms the larger context of the two world wars and the 1930s, for it provides many of the ultimate causes of the Great Depression. (The comparative historical sociologist who wants to get at the larger civilizational matrix that produced the 1930s must utilize ordinary macroeconomic analysis to understand the role of monetary policy and other relatively proximate economic factors in precipitating the deep slump.) Providing the general social, historical, and psychological context of economic phenomena is a most important application of phenomenology. Both phenomenological inquiry and disciplinary model building are strengthened by their mutual awareness and respect.

However, phenomenology may also directly study the assumptions made by economists. For example, an important way in which phenomenology complements microeconomics is in the study of economic wants and action directed toward the end use of acquired goods. Where disciplinary economics analyzes what rational action people engage in to satisfy their wants—and particularly to satisfy as many of them as possible under conditions of scarcity—phenomenology analyzes why people have the wants or tastes they do and what these mean. The desire for housing of various sorts, for example, prominently involves elements of myth, ideology, and aesthetics. Objective economic analysis is helpless with respect to interpreting and explaining such inherently subjective and many-sided matters. Phenomenological analysis of wants by historians, sociologists, and psychologists provides the context of consumption theory.

Phenomenology also complements economics by probing the nature of interests. Like what people desire, what they conceive to be in their interests, rationally augmenting their stock of available resources, is socially constructed by them. Phenomenology plumbs purported interests—such as those of workers and managers a century ago or of Israelis and Palestinians today—and finds them nearly as much Rorschach blots as their stated wants. To assert that people are self-seeking or pursuing their interests without going much further is frequently unsatisfactory. Invocation of interests is much more a starting than a finishing point for inquiry. A thoughtful and contextual study of the play of interests is not something foreign to phenomenology but central to it. Phenomenological analysis of how we conceive our interests provides the context of production theory. For its part, phenomenology utilizes disciplinary economics in the conduct of holistic inquiry that places interests alongside desires as central components of motivation.

Unfortunately, far too much thinking in the human sciences has proceeded as if the nature of our rational interests were a straightforward and obvious matter. In reality, determining an actor's interests can be extremely problematic. As Aristotle (1953, 182) most sensibly puts it, "the best way of pursuing one's interest is an obscure point and calls for investigation." Or, as Rousseau (1968, 72) observes, "[w]e always want what is advantageous but we do not always discern it." Unless historians and sociologists provide a great deal more information than customary, what precisely a person or collectivity's interest is remains indeterminate—a point generally obscured by hidden assumptions. We cannot uncritically assume that revolution or unionization furthers workers' interests or that protectionism or low wages further industrialists' interests.

It is not possible to specify anything about an actor's interest unless we know the time horizon over which he attempts to maximize income or resource accumulation. Whether a person or collectivity is profit- or growth-maximizing over a three-month or fifty-year time span is likely to yield utterly different solution sets from among its possible choices. Since nothing but differing wants can ever induce an actor to select between time horizons, interests are entirely context-dependent. Either being strong this year and weak forever after or viceversa may be in our interest, depending upon our relative valuation of the short and long term.

There is also the problem of how much risk an actor will accept. Higher risk strategies often confer the high-value expected outcome while carrying some risk of a low-value one as well. Once again, assumptions and parameters must be supplied that are exogenous to the analysis of interests proper. Note the frequency with which human efforts not only fail to achieve their purposes but turn out counterproductively. What was in Japan's national interest during the twentieth century prior to Pearl Harbor is a far more complex question than historians typically convey.

Additionally, we have the even more difficult issue of who the "we" are whose interests are being pursued. If we define our interests narrowly in line with our persons or families, we get one answer; if we define them more broadly, we get another. As we run through the gamut of collective identifications, including progressively larger interests as our own, each shift may change the nature of the interest-maximizing action. Once time, risk, and breadth parameters are supplied, there remains the difficult problem of analyzing what it is that will technically maximize the accumulation of power.[7]

Disciplinary economics provides invaluable theoretical insight and empirical knowledge to the phenomenologist, who applies economic analysis along with the other tools of the human sciences to all things human in conducting the phenomenology of power. Yet the phenomenologist recognizes that only certain people and collectivities under certain historical circumstances and in certain aspects of their lives lean strongly toward rational action and pursue their interests as they understand them in a fashion approximating the assumptions of economic theory. To the extent which people act rationally, phenomenology employs rational models, but it never sets aside the broader context or fails to shift to other forms of analysis as the human moves to other aspects of its being. The relationship between phenomenology and other model building traditions such as those in psychology and political science resembles that between it and economics.

Relatedly, phenomenology is neither mesmerized by quantification nor opposed to it but appreciates it in its place. As Quine (see Haack 1978, 43ff.) has taught us, in principle anything that can be done with qualitative language can also be done with quantitative language. We have so far quantified only the earlier areas to fall within what is a slowly moving frontier of quantification. As we become more developed, progressively more of our world becomes quantified. However, like many other correlates of development, such as more complex economic organization; while appropriate quantification may contribute to development, too much or the wrong kind of it will not. Quantitative and qualitative theory complement each other, and the general human scientist draws on the mathematized as he or she draws on the unmathematized.

Practicing the Phenomenological Method

Because the subject of phenomenology differs from that of disciplinary study, a different research method is required to practice it. Aristotle tells us that one must settle on the method as he or she determines what works in practice: "the idea of a simple method, a method which could be determined before even penetrating the thing, is a dangerous abstraction; the object itself must determine the method of its own access" (quoted in Gadamer 1987, 93). In order to simultaneously get at the many sides of the human, the phenomenologist primarily synthesizes others' work. In doing so he prefers to absorb broadly conceived work. The most useful materials for phenomenology's holistic inquiry are historical and ethnographic studies that present empirical reports of many aspects of the human at once, while gathering theoretically meaningful data. Five empirical works of this sort are Ibn Khaldun's *The Muqaddimah: Introduction to History,* Burckhardt's *The Civilization of the Renaissance in Italy,* Tocqueville's *Democracy in America,* Polanyi's *The Great Transformation,* and Pitt-Rivers's *Peoples of the Sierra.* Each author in his way examines his topic as a profoundly engaged outsider distilling the phenomena or people he studies to their fundamental character in pursuit of the essence or spirit expressing the whole.[8] Without explicit foundations each work is many-sided to that end. The first four are widely acknowledged to be great books.

Phenomenology is also very glad to get outstanding historical work that systematically takes a topic at or near the breadth of a socio-cultural institution or of a major aspect of the personality through different eras. Noteworthy efforts of this sort include North and Thomas, *The Rise of the Western World,* for the economic; Frye, *The Anatomy of Criticism,* Auerbach, *Mimesis,* and Bakhtin, *The Dialogic Imagination,* for literature; Hauser, *The Social History of Art,* for art; Ben-David, *The Scientist's Role in Society,* for science; Bellah, "Religious Evolution," for religion; and Baumeister, *Identity,* for individualism in the personality.

The many excellent standard histories and ethnographies of the world's major civilizational strands may also be of major value as source materials as well. Most, at least of the histories, are secondary and tertiary siftings and syntheses of the research of others. I would single out Hodgson's magisterial *The Venture of Islam: Conscience and History in a World Civilization* as among the most theoretically astute of such histories.

For the more recent past, survey research may also be of value, joining the other two sources. The concepts in such studies are often distant from those utilized by phenomenology, but they need not be. On occasion—a Piaget, Garfinkel, or Bourdieu comes to mind—a significant thinker appears in an area with such fresh insight that he must do some of his own peculiar empirical work to generate material for thought, but overwhelmingly phenomenology requires reading and synthesis from the works of others.

Much valuable comparative historical work that goes in the direction I am proposing already exists. I am thinking first and foremost of Max Weber's great work, but also, in addition to what I have already mentioned, a wonderful collection of works that includes: Perry Anderson, *Lineages of the Absolutist State;* Carlo Cipolla, *Before the Industrial Revolution;* Emile Durkheim, *The Division of Labor in Society;* E.L. Jones, *The European Miracle;* Gerhard Lenski, *Power and Privilege* and *Human Societies;* Michael Mann, *The Sources of Social Power;* William McNeill, *The Rise of the West* and *The Pursuit of Power;* Barrington Moore, *The Social Origins of Dictatorship and Democracy;* Robert Paxton, *The Anatomy of Fascism;* Henri Pirenne, *Charlemagne and Mohamed* and *Belgian Democracy;* Joseph Schumpeter, *Capitalism, Socialism and Democracy;* Charles Tilly, *Coercion, Capital, and European* States; and Immanuel Wallerstein, *The Modern World-System.* In the study of psychological development I think of such works as: Erik Erikson, *Childhood and Society* and *Adulthood;* Robert Kegan, *The Evolving Self;* Lawrence Kohlberg, *Essays in Moral Development.* Vol. 2. *The Psychology of Moral Development;* Jane Loevinger, *Ego Development;* Abraham Maslow, *Motivation and Personality;* Jean Piaget, *The Moral Judgment of the Child* and *The Psychology of Intelligence;* Jenny Wade, *Changes of Mind,* Michael Washburn, *The Ego and the Dynamic Ground;* and Ken Wilber, *Integral Psychology.*[9] What I am calling for is work similar to this and fully grounded in universalist ontology.

Standing on its ontological foundations and utilizing dialectical historicism, phenomenology is the integrated, systematic application of the full array of scholarly utensils and knowledge bearing upon the human. To practice phenomenology is to participate in the active universal as it assembles overall empirical knowledge of the human. Building upon coherent foundations, phenomenological human science promises cumulative development through time in sequential series of progressive developments instead of repeated new starts. Phenomenological human science entails much more than eclecticism and anything but dilettantism, but it is very demanding and difficult to conduct well.

Epistemic Criteria

Phenomenological theories and analyses should be scrutinized with the same four epistemic criteria as any other scientific inquiry. First, as the arguments of Lakatos and the ontology I have presented make clear, they should have range—as much as feasible over whole societies and psyches, all of history or the life course, entire institutions and sectors, and all character types. Since it is holistic, a great strength of phenomenological study is its range. As Hegel (see Forster 1998, 158–59) insists, more than just the truth, we seek the entire truth. A critical weakness of all disciplinary human inquiry is its restricted range. Second, as Hegel repeatedly emphasizes, phenomenological theories must have determinacy—they may not merely cover the range they do with vague generalizations. The more determinate, the closer the potential meeting with their subject. Rigor is one aspect of determinacy. In the past, indeterminacy has been a serious weakness of holistic study, but it is now in a position to meet this criterion and meet it well. Third, phenomenological theories and analyses must have coherence, by which I mean that their parts must be integrally related and harmoniously balanced. Hegel also emphasizes the importance of this criterion. Coherence is gotten at in part by Duhem's criterion of theoretical simplicity. The major source of coherence is philosophical groundedness. Coherence is another major strength of phenomenological theory when properly conducted.

Fourth, phenomenological human science must also have empirical corroborability. No dependable rational knowledge of the human is possible without resting upon empirical study. The criterion of empirical corroborability holds even though the empirical testing of such overarching theory, especially when extensive, can only be indirect, very long term, and cumulative. For, as Lakatos tells us, even theories of more restricted scope frequently carry a weight of anomalous findings that in time either may be explained away or accommodated with theoretical adjustments or revisions. Lakatos also makes clear that the burden of empirical anomalies a theory can bear is partly dependent upon the number and state of the competing theories. Eventually, however, there must come a reckoning. Hence large sections of Hegel's general philosophy of history (though not his particular phenomenologies of philosophy, religion, and the arts) have by now collapsed from an inability to fit history as we today much better understand it. Pointing out empirical anomalies in such a structure is like noting damaged stones in the Chartres Cathedral or fleabites on an elephant. Because it is at once uniquely holistic and empirical, innumerably many such imperfections and pricks are required to bring down a grand phenomenological structure—and even then we marvel at and learn from the ruins—but down it eventually does come if insufficiently supported by empirical study.

What satisfactorily meets the four epistemic criteria is warranted assertion about the human. Knowledge is warranted assertion, i.e., representation adequately corresponding with or having sufficient goodness of fit with reality as we are best able to present it. To speak of knowledge is not to claim infallibility but merely to take representation as suitably reliable, as adequate for being put on-line, given the circumstances. To accept theoretical or factual assertions, to hold them as true, is to judge them the best available for addressing the matters in question. Different degrees of meeting the criteria are therefore appropriate for different times. It is in this sense that we may say that what is known changes over time. Different degrees of meeting the criteria are also appropriate for different kinds of knowledge. Holistic, phenomenological knowledge must meet all four criteria, the first and third to high standards but the second and fourth to less rigorous ones than those of disciplinary science. Disciplinary science, for its part, must meet the second and fourth criteria to high scientific standards, but the first and third only to the minimal levels required of disciplinary study. Then we have everyday knowledge, assertions warranted under the circumstances of people as they conduct their lives. It meets the four criteria but only to common everyday levels. Although the notion of knowledge dichotomizes the warrantedness and reliability of representations, the actuality is a continuum from more to less warranted.

The assessment of theory arising from interdisciplinary study should be by the community of those possessing broad knowledge of the human sciences, whether or not they are professionally engaged in them. This community, like that of disciplinary scientists, will tend to converge toward consensus. If the phenomenology I propose is true science, could different portions of this community or different phenomenologists come up with different answers? The answer is, "Yes—for a time." Although their answers would often be fairly consistent, they could well differ and differ deeply for considerable periods. However, over time, a consensus will slowly develop in the holistic study I propose, and this will form a consensus that is both valuable and dependable. Not all science comes to consensus at the same rate, just as not all boats dock at the same rate. A more complex and indirect link with the empirical means that the mulling over toward consensus takes longer, and the convergence is slower.

The broad empirical knowledge I emphasize is a new kind of genuine knowledge for the human sciences not contemplated by the standard philosophy of science oriented to disciplinary science. It is a general science that extends Aristotle's notion of theoretical wisdom (*sophia*). The reigning epistemology gives fine guidance for restricted disciplinary inquiry but little for comprehensive inquiry leading toward theoretical wisdom. The traditional scientific method is very important and very valuable, but it does not apply to broader and subtler matters pertaining to the human. The standard epistemics and science have their places, but this general human science and its kind of knowledge also have a place. What traditional hard science sorts do not get is that both phenomenology and traditional science are true science and yield continuous growth of knowledge. The value of the phenomenological approach in developing true insights about human beings and societies must also be acknowledged. Universalist epistemology parallels the traditional defenses of a liberal arts education. It holds that comprehensive study is a fruitful thing to engage in. It defends the perspective of all perspectives as something distinct and valuable in its own right.

Misplaced demand for algorithms and rigor gets nowhere with the broad questions and contributes needlessly to the skepticism prevalent today. The work I propose focuses on the whole with respect to the human and seeks as much rigor as possible consistent with developing knowledge of that whole. Rigor is a good thing and so is comprehensiveness. Phenomenology demands respect for its own way of trading off the two.

A theory's range, determinacy, coherence, and validity together yield its power, of which Lakatos' "criterion" of robustness may be seen as the rate of change—although power and robustness are not properly *criteria* of theoretical excellence but the definition of it. For my theory—or, more directly, those based upon it—corroborating the Lakatosian surplus content or excess range could begin with checking for the genuineness of the discoveries of the superid and SSE with empirical research (see Lakatos 1970, 116). My unhesitating assertion would be that applying and testing such theories would generate new facts about many previously unrecognized phenomena, as the Lakatosian philosophy of science demands. In science the creative theoretical imagination is supreme, not "the universe of facts which surrounds us" (1970, 187–88). All four criteria give a paramount role in the evaluation of phenomenological work to the most serious readers able to contemplate holistic inquiries in light of broad theoretical understanding and knowledge of the world.

Studies of the sort for which I call are pointed to by the works cited above but do not yet exist to evaluate. We should ponder the above works and imagine how much more compelling they might be individually and aggregately if rendered more coherent and powerful by the foundations, framework, and method I have set forth. For the ultimate promise, one has to imagine work of the highest calibre—which is to say, Max Weber grounded, balanced, extended through all institutions, taken back to the earliest societies, and brought up to the present; and Jean Piaget grounded, balanced, applied to all aspects of life, carried throughout the life cycle, and extended crossculturally and crosshistorically.

There are many ways of working with my framework in the human sciences, with widely varying approaches and degrees of comprehensiveness. Each kind of human science stands to benefit from the foundations set forth here: phenomenology needs them to move systematically and determinately across the full range of the human, while sectoral study requires them to coherently frame, contextualize, and balance its inquiries and conclusions— all of which means restoration of the armchair to its rightful place in anthropology.

Notes

1. For examples of his applied phenomenology see Hegel 1967, 148, 203, 269, 270–71, and 277; 1975, 109; 1956, 191–92, 288–89, 294, 420.

2. Again it goes without saying there exist various partially subjective and universal views between the two that I neglect for simplicity.

3. The human doesn't require interpretation because it is textlike, but rather texts require interpretation because they are human-like in their subtlety and complexity. Sophisticated interpretation may have been first engaged in by biblical scholars and literary critics, but they have never owned it.

4. With some justification phenomenology in the human sciences is often referred to as interpretive sociology or psychology, but I prefer to call it phenomenology because that better emphasizes its holism and is perhaps somewhat less likely to slight its explanatory side. Description is only one major aspect of what it does. However, referring to the method I am describing as phenomenology has the disadvantage that it assigns it a different label than Weber's, although it is essentially his method. Neither term is perfect.

5. See Forster (1998, 477ff.) concerning Hegel's endorsement of the explanation of universal phenomena, including his own philosophy.

6. This phenomenology also avoids Rubinstein's (1981, esp. 68–90) criticisms of previous subjectivism for overemphasizing the psychological, having difficulty with power relations, neglecting social action, slighting structural phenomena, and failing to articulate the micro and macro. It can easily address such questions as what caused the rise of capitalism and why the bourgeois have such a strong sense of personal efficacy.

7. See Rubinstein (2001, 124ff.) and Haskell (1985, 342–43, 351n, and passim) concerning problems associated with determining our interests.

8. That Thomas Friedman of the *New York Times* approaches such phenomenological analysis in his best op-ed pieces is also what most makes him a great journalist.

9. See Wilber's books for further references. With his own comprehensive universalistic paradigm, Wilber (see 2000a) has already come far in the direction I recommend.

Bibliography

Anderson, Perry. 1974. *Lineages of the Absolutist State*. London: NLB.

Aristotle. 1953. *Ethics.* Harmondsworth, Middlesex: Penguin.

Auerbach, E. 2003. *Mimesis: The Representation of Reality in Western Literature.* Princeton, NJ: Princeton University Press.

Bakhtin, M. 1981. *The Dialogic Imagination.* Austin: University of Texas Press.

Baumeister, R. 1986. *Identity: Cultural Change and the Struggle for Self.* New York: Oxford University Press.

Bellah, R. 1972. "Religious Evolution." In *Reader in Comparative Religion: An Anthropological Approach,* ed. W. Lessa and E. Vogt. New York: Harper & Row.

Ben-David, J. 1971. *The Scientist's Role in Society.* Inglewood Cliffs, NJ: Prentice-Hall.

Bourdieu, P. 1984. *Distinction: A Social Critique of the Judgement of Taste.* Cambridge, MA: Harvard University Press.

———. 1988. *Homo Academicus.* Stanford, CA: Stanford University Press.

———. 2000. *Pascalian Meditations.* Stanford, CA: Stanford University Press.

Burckhardt, J. 1995. *The Civilization of the Renaissance in Italy.* London: Phaidon.

Cipolla, C. 1976. *Before the Industrial Revolution: European Society and Economy, 1000–1700.* New York: W.W. Norton.

Durkheim, E. 1997a. *Suicide.* New York: Free Press.

———. 1997b. *The Division of Labor in Society.* New York: Free Press.

———. 2001. *The Elementary Forms of Religious Life.* Oxford: Oxford University Press.

Erikson, E. 1950. *Childhood and Society.* New York: W.W. Norton.

———. 1978. *Adulthood.* New York: W.W. Norton.

Forster, M. 1998. *Hegel's Idea of a Phenomenology of Spirit.* Chicago: University of Chicago Press.

Frye, N. 1957. *The Anatomy of Criticism.* Princeton, NJ: Princeton University Press.

Gadamer, H. 1987. "The Problem of Historical Consciousness." In *Interpretive Social Science: A Second Look,* ed. P. Rabinow and W. Sullivan. Berkeley and Los Angeles: University of California Press.

Geertz, C. 1973. *The Interpretation of Cultures.* New York: Basic Books.

———. 1980. *Negara: The Theatre State in Nineteenth-Century Bali.* Princeton, NJ: Princeton University Press.

Gibbon, E. n.d. *The History of the Decline and Fall of the Roman Empire.* 6 vols. New York: Bigelow, Brown.

Haack, S. 1978. *The Philosophy of Logics.* Cambridge: Cambridge University Press.

Haskell, T. 1985. "Capitalism and the Humanitarian Sensibility." 2 parts. *American Historical Review,* 90.

Hauser, A. 1951. *The Social History of Art.* 4 vols. New York: Vintage Press.

Hegel, G. 1956. *The Philosophy of History.* New York: Dover Publications.

———. 1967. *Hegel's Philosophy of Right.* London: Oxford University Press.

———. 1975. *Lectures on the Philosophy of World History: Introduction.* Cambridge: Cambridge University Press.

Hodgson, M. 1974. *The Venture of Islam: Conscience and History in a World Civilization.* 3 vols. Chicago: University of Chicago Press.

Ibn Khaldun. 1958. The *Muqaddimah: Introduction to History.* 3 vols. New York: Pantheon Books.

Jones, E. 1981. *The European Miracle.* Cambridge: Cambridge University Press.

Kegan, R. 1982. *The Evolving Self.* Cambridge, MA: Harvard University Press.

Kohlberg, L. 1984. *Essays on Moral Development. Vol. 2. The Psychology of Moral Development.* San Francisco: Harper and Row.

Lakatos, I. 1970. "Falsification and the Methodology of Scientific Research Programmes." In *Criticism and the Growth of Knowledge,* ed. I. Lakatos and A. Musgrave. Cambridge: Cambridge University Press.

Lenski, G. 1966. *Power and Privilege.* New York: McGraw-Hill.

———. 1970. *Human Societies.* New York: McGraw-Hill.

Loevinger, J. 1976. *Ego Development.* San Francisco: Jossey-Bass.

Mann, M. 1986, 1993. *The Sources of Social Power.* 2 vols. Cambridge: Cambridge University Press.

Mannheim, K. 1936. *Ideology and Utopia.* New York: Harcourt, Brace and World.

Maslow, A. 1954. *Motivation and Personality.* New York: Harper and Row.

McNeil, W. 1963. *The Rise of the West.* Chicago: University of Chicago Press.

———. 1982. *The Pursuit of Power.* Chicago: University of Chicago Press.

Moore, B. 1966. *The Social Origins of Dictatorship and Democracy: Lord and Peasant in the Making of the Modern World.* Boston: Beacon Press.

Morris, E. 1979. *The Rise of Theodore Roosevelt.* New York: Modern Library.

Nagel, T. 1986. *The View from Nowhere.* New York: Oxford University Press.

Nietzsche, F. 1974. *The Gay Science.* New York: Vintage Books.

North, D. and R. Thomas. 1973. *The Rise of the Western World: A New Economic History.* Cambridge: Cambridge University Press.

Paxton, R. 2004. *The Anatomy of Fascism.* New York: Alfred A. Knopf.

Piaget, J. 1962. *The Moral Judgment of the Child.* New York: Collier Books.

———. 1976. *The Psychology of Intelligence.* Totowa, NJ: Littlefield, Adams.

Pirenne, H. 1939. *Charlemagne and Mohamed.* New York: Harper and Row.

———. 1970. *Belgian Democracy: Its Early History.* New York: AMS Press.

Pitt-Rivers, J. 1971. *Peoples of the Sierra.* 2nd ed. Chicago: University of Chicago Press.

Polanyi, K. 2001. *The Great Transformation: The Political and Economic Origins of Our Times.* Boston: Beacon Press.

Rousseau, J. 1968. *The Social Contract.* Harmondsworth, Middlesex: Penguin.

Rubinstein, D. 1981. *Marx and Wittgenstein: Social Praxis and Social Explanation.* London: Routledge & Kegan Paul.

———. 2001. *Culture, Structure and Agency.* Thousand Oaks, CA: Sage Publications.

Schumpeter, J. 1950. *Capitalism, Socialism and Democracy.* 3rd ed. New York: Harper and Row.

Schutz, A. 1967. *The Phenomenology of the Social World.* Evanston, IL: Northwestern University Press.

Tilly, C. 1992. *Coercion, Capital, and European States.* Oxford: Blackwell.

Tocqueville, A. 1966. *Democracy in America.* New York: Harper and Row.

Voegelin, E. 2000–2001. *The Collected Works of Eric Voegelin.* Volumes 14–18. *Order and History.* Columbia: University of Missouri Press.

———. 2002. *The Collected Works of Eric Voegelin.* Volume 6. *Anamnesis: On the Theory of History and Politics.* Columbia: University of Missouri Press.

Wade, J. 1996. *Changes of Mind.* Albany: State University of New York Press.

Wallerstein, I. 1974. *The Modern World-System: Capitalist Agriculture and the Origins of the European World-Economy in the Sixteenth Century.* New York: Academic Press.

Washburn, M. 1995. *The Ego and the Dynamic Ground.* Albany, NY: State University of New York Press.

Weber, M. 1949. *The Methodology of the Social Sciences.* New York: Free Press.

———. 1958. *From Max Weber: Essays in Sociology.* New York: Oxford University Press.
———. 1978. *Economy and Society.* 2 vols. Berkeley and Los Angeles: University of California Press.
Wilber, K. 2000a. *A Theory of Everything.* Boston, MA: Shambhala.
———. 2000b. *Integral Psychology.* Boston, MA: Shambhala.
Wittgenstein, L. 1953. *Philosophical Investigations.* New York: Macmillan.

17. Aesthetics

The Ontology of the Arts

I view aesthetics as the ontology and epistemology of the arts. Aesthetics begins with the basic elements of art (i.e., fine art): the artist or art producer, the art object or thing that is artful, and the art consumer or viewer. The artist communicates via symbolic language through the medium of her work, which the art consumer interprets. Art producers and consumers have various relationships with art objects, these "shadows of that which they were while still related to the living creative activity of the artist" (Fiedler 1957, 65). Much art comes to be embodied in or on durable media such as stone, canvas, paper, or film. Some has no durable medium, actually existing only as fleeting performance. Some art comes into being via a stored template; some is improvisational. The former may be physical or may consist of words to be read or notations and routines to guide performers. Art may therefore exist in the form of a positive or a negative, an actual, objective painting, performance, or reading or a potential but unobjectified set of images. Sculpture and painting must then be viewed, literature read, music listened to, dance watched, and drama and film both watched and listened to by the consumer. However, our primary concern lies not with the basic elements of art but with the nature of art (see Heidegger 1964, 651). The essence of art and core of aesthetics lie in a distinctive perspective of the human.

The realm of the aesthetic has three essential criteria: it is consummatory, reflexive, and ideal-dominant. We may therefore say that the basic activity of fine art is that of a society's pre-supercommunity, and, correspondingly, that persons engaged with art as art dwell in their pre-superids. As such, the arts are the nonrational analog to the human sciences. Art may therefore cease to be art and become something else by being pulled away from its characteristic pole along any of the three dimensions on which it is constituted. The object may then prove useful or valuable in other ways, but without being art. Let us consider each of the criteria defining the ideal type of fine art.

First, the arts comprise symbolic worlds speaking the figurative, intuitive language of the consummatory. As Read (1965, 18, 53) puts it, art is "a crystallization, from the amorphous realm of feeling, of forms that are significant or symbolic." The artist presents "his consciousness of . . . aspects of reality in plastic or poetic images." Artworks speak indirectly rather than directly, connotatively rather than denotatively. They forsake the unsubtle umbra for the subtle penumbra, sparking reverberations among countless allusions. Works of art evoke thoughts and feelings as our minds careen between the witting and unwitting referents marshaled by the artist. In consuming art one's mind freely associates around fields of self-consciously presented images with respect to himself, humankind, and the world. In their right-brain mode the arts provide echoes and reflections that mimic and present aspects of reality[1] indirectly and analogically rather than directly and conceptually. By moving away from its main existential home and toward the rational mode, art may become philosophy or social thought as sometimes occurs in Dostoyevsky and Tolstoy, or ideology or reporting as it sometimes does in Dreiser and Steinbeck.

Certain consequences flow from the fact that the dominant mode in which art has its being is consummatory. Because the emotional experience of art is closer to the surface than is the case in the human sciences, ordinarily art must be inherently enjoyable as we read, view, or listen to it. Art pays a good part of its way and keeps our attention by communicating in a charged, charismatic manner. Emotionality being dominant in art, we are surprised and delighted by the play element, its twists and turns of line, color, meter, and rhyme. If the poetics with which art communicates succeeds, it captivates us. If not, ordinarily it fails as art. However, this is not to suggest that we may not have to work long and hard to grasp the meaning of and appreciate a particular piece of art. Its aesthetic beauty, which is something different from surface, decorative beauty, is what meets this need to captivate. However, not only can art be ugly in the usual unreflexive sense, but much of it *is* ugly in that sense, both in form and in content, as in the German expressionism that enthrallingly conveys a sense that the world is anything but harmonious.

A consequence of art's consummatory provenience is that a high standard of artistry must accompany fine art. If it does not, our attention again flags. Fine art, in effect, must be composed by artists whose technical proficiency approximates that of full-time specialists who have mastered artistic traditions of long standing. It is this corollary to the first criterion of fine art that Weber (1969, 67) invokes in classifying certain music as "art music." When aesthetic sensibility is highly refined, works consistent with it rise to the standard of fine art. Works of crude artistry that otherwise meet the criteria of art inhabit a kind of limbo in the realm of but failing as, art.

The second criterion of art is that it reflect self-consciousness, which is what distinguishes it from popular culture and decoration. The substance of art being the content it communicates, the aesthetic wholly or partially presents the situation of persons and collectivities. Without self-consciousness one can perceive the surface of art but not fathom it. Popular culture, on the other hand, is unreflexive, ideal-dominant play that amuses but does not convey self-knowledge. Whenever art sets aside or loses its reflexivity—something that the grip of plot, heaviness of sentiment, or steaminess of sex can all do—it becomes popular culture fixed raptly on the surface. Two people side by side, looking at the same sculpture in a museum or at the same scenic view in nature, may engage on the levels of art and popular culture respectively, the one self-conscious in his relationship to the viewed object, the other not. Perceiving, thinking, and communicating about the objects, people, and nature around us in the self-conscious manner of the arts means doing so in poetic language that says things about life, society, and our place in the world. If something is created in this mode, it is art, irrespective of whether it is consumed or viewed in the same mode. Art objects may exist as art but be taken in another way.

Popular culture, entertainment, and decoration themselves actually appear on a range of levels of self-consciousness. The most elementary is exemplified by forms that are substantially oriented to the physical, such as slapstick, juggling, or bearbaiting. The next more developed popular culture is squarely pre-community and pre-id-oriented. The most developed popular culture moves into middlebrow, remaining predominantly unreflexive though having become partially reflexive, albeit somewhat narrowly and formulaically so. Popular novels may fall in either of the two more developed categories. Popular humor may fall in any of the three, as may folk art or music. Moreover, particular works of popular culture and popular art may often traverse the line between the unreflexive and reflexive. Storytelling, painting, poetry, film, spectacle, and mime frequently move back and forth between the unself-conscious and self-conscious and between entertainment and art. We can find aesthetic aspects in bullfighting and football just as we find diverting aspects in serious drama and music. Film moves back and forth across the line as it dwells alternately on meaningless suspense or pure form. Nudes in a single painting may have varying degrees of aesthetic and decorative interest. Despite the range, popular culture falls predominantly in the second category above, i.e., it is oriented to the human but unreflexive, which may be taken as ideal typical of it. Between art and popular culture lies middlebrow, which extends between more developed popular culture and less developed fine art.

When middlebrow becomes relatively self-conscious and refined, attempts to distinguish it from art become tendentious.

The need for entertainment is to popular culture as the need for beauty is to art. Art is about more than the passive enjoyment of agreeable, familiar forms; popular culture is not. The need for entertainment and decoration is the slack motivation of the *popolo,* for whom the self-consciousness of the aesthetic is too strenuous. In consuming entertainment the pre-id naïvely takes in the wonder of juggling, the frolic of folk music, the lunacy of television comedies, or the spell of folk sagas. Decoration and background music in their surface pleasantness emptily fill space and time. Where prolonged education is required to appreciate art, anyone can enjoy popular culture—popular culture panders. When one deletes the reflexive meaning from art, what remains is entertainment and decoration, which are formulaic because of their need to put at ease and amuse in the absence of reflexivity.

Nevertheless, entertainment is a universal aspect of life and a genuine need for all in relaxation. Even those dwelling predominantly or frequently in their superids or the aesthetic have their diversions. Historically composed variously of bons mots, puns, witticisms, clever skits, entertaining stories, and gourmet food, their entertainment remains largely parallel to—if more refined, complex, and self-conscious than—everyday popular culture. Kant (1951, 148) refers to these forms as the pleasant or charming arts.

In actuality art, too, comes with varying degrees of reflexivity. Where popular culture takes away from ordinary art by removing its reflexivity, highly self-conscious art adds to it by imparting additional reflexivity. Highly reflexive and ordinary art respond to distinct valid needs and are not in competition with each other. In highly reflexive art the play of form is compounded and a higher need for beauty emerges. To the extent to which this austere metaneed arises, as in Umberto Eco's novels, the need for ordinary beauty in art recedes. Because many art consumers are not highly reflexive, they cannot relate to the highly reflexive. When highly self-referential art, music, and literature is also academicist, it becomes suffused with looking not at self and society but at artists and writers looking at self and society. In such cases a subtle, though academicist, higher motivation can also come into play that we may describe as a work's "interest," which, however, represents another sort of intrusion of the rational into the nonrational.

The third criterion of fine art is that it be ideal dominant. To the extent which real-world considerations intrude into it, art doesn't become bad art but ceases to be art at all. Business, political, salacious, and other such considerations drop art and its consumption from the ideal to the real world where it becomes advertising, importunement, enticement, etc. In addition to the gap in reflexivity, a difference between finding a figure in a painting sexually appealing and aesthetically engaging is that in the former the experience of the perspective is real while in the latter it is ideal. The real-world "relation of desire is not the one in which man stands to the work of art" (Hegel 1975, 36). To achieve good form in elegant manners or in a well-designed commercial product is to represent, even with refinement, but to do so in a real-dominant mode and therefore not as art. Kant is right to insist that art be disinterested.[2] Thus the full autonomy, as Adorno (1997, 211–12) describes it, or detachment and indifference as Bourdieu (1984, 34–5) does, that something must achieve to become art—in which sense "l'art pour l'art" is required of all art.

As it ranges on the reflexivity dimension, art also ranges between the ideal and real, although, insofar as it strictly remains art, it necessarily remains predominantly in the former. It may cross the line into the real in some religious art, socialist realism, family-planning posters, and literature of social protest. De la Croix's partisan paintings move between art and politics while Goins's posters move between art and business, even as the latter also do between art and decoration. While architecture should be treated as an art form, it is to some extent a special case requiring relaxed criteria, for most architecture remains predominantly real due to the high costs involved. In addressing architecture as fine art, one is therefore ordinarily isolating the aesthetic aspects of buildings having salient practical purposes.

In addition to being unself-conscious, popular culture tends to be less ideal than art. As Bourdieu (1984, 32, 34) says, in the popular "aesthetic" there is an "affirmation of continuity between life and art" which fine art denies. "[P]opular entertainment secures the spectator's participation in the show" in an atmosphere of general festivity. Very much in the popular direction, the viewing of competitive sports often occurs amid revelry and hearty laughter. However, to the extent that the real-world play aspect becomes pronounced, what goes on ceases to be culture.

Comparable issues arise regarding the historical lines between magic and art and between rustic forms and art. In early archaic Egypt the freer and more fluid "syncretistic" style of pottery was among the very first in which art began significantly leaving behind the world of magic. Where the geometric style it replaced had consisted of manipulable signs predominantly aimed at the needs of magic, its flexible new symbols, unsuitable for magic, were primarily directed to emerging aesthetic needs (Raphael 1947, 116–17). Fine art appeared historically as the real-world concerns of magic that lay behind primitive "art" gave way to ideal-world ones of pure appreciation of form, while at the same time unreflexive folk expression gave way to reflexive civilized expression in a twofold transition that occurred in the visual arts before it did in literature. The birth of the arts at the onset of archaic society in the Middle East coincided with the formation of the world's first true upper class, a priestly one insulated from the influence of popular culture.

The object of the aesthetic perspective may be a clear-cut, designated work of art, or it may be anything else through which the aesthetic is suffused. The aesthetic may be viewed, interpreted, and enjoyed in a person or people's lifestyle as in formal artworks. Insofar as the pre-superid lies behind human forms, the same essential phenomena are involved as in art. If we label as art a created object which previously had been of some other use, we attach something to it that had not been there before (Frye 1957, 345). We declare that it be perceived aesthetically and direct attention to it as such, suspending its prior ontological status—although the process can quickly become tedious. Nature, too, may be approached aesthetically (see Adorno 1997, 61–78), which entails viewing it as a work of art. Detachedly, reflexively, and in the consummatory mode, one may find aesthetic beauty in a mountain, meadow, or tree. Doing so, however, is far more tenuous and indeterminate than when we so view the artificial. The focus of self-consciousness can only be on selfhood, something about which the natural world is finally mute.

Art may be technically proficient, beautiful, and even moral, but it can never become high art, which is to say, great art, without presenting universal truth. High art poetically addresses the many-dimensional reality of the whole. Where ordinary fine art restricts itself to the sectoral, high art plumbs the depths of existence and reflects the poetic universal. Universal art overcomes many oppositions and communicates wisdom, as Aeschylus does in the *Eumenides*. The tone of high art, like that of everything else from the universal, is oracular and conveys the sound of the depths. Although high art must retain the artistry of ordinary art, no amount of technical proficiency in itself qualifies as greatness. He may have been verbally gifted like no other, but what makes Shakespeare great is that he raised himself to the universal. Goethe is great and Sherwood Anderson not, primarily because of their respective degrees of universalism. While its most characteristic mode is the symphony, large canvas, tragic drama, or other grand form, high art by no means expresses itself only in such a full manner. Many of Prokofiev's short piano compositions powerfully evoke fleeting aspects of the universal as do Sappho's lyric poems, Shakespeare's sonnets, Rembrandt's portraits, and Chekhov's stories. Contrary to the claims of Hegel (see 1975, 1:70, 101) and Heidegger, art is not inherently universal; it must work up to the universal. Only then does it reach the same ground as religion and philosophy and parallel the universalism of phenomenological human science. Only high art merits the grand accolades Schopenhauer and so many others have directed to art in general.

High art cannot exist any more than ordinary fine art can without emotional appeal, but where the motivation behind sectoral art ordinarily is beauty, that behind universal art is sublimity. As Hegel (1975, 1:339) says, "[i]n the sublime . . . the finite appearance expresses the Absolute. . . ." The universal is the source of the great thoughts and inspired emotion of the noble mind prominent in Longinus' (1965, 8–9) view of the sublime. Sublimity, like aesthetic beauty, is inherently rewarding, but sublimity goes beyond beauty to a sense of reverence in the presence of boundlessness in the many-sided acknowledgment of the way things are. Great art requires the infinite reverberation of the sublime. As one approaches the sublime—in *Oedipus Rex, King Lear,* the Belvedere torso, *David,* the Brandenburg Concertos, Beethoven's symphonies, the Parthenon, or Proust in certain aspects—to the extent which the percipient is both aesthetically and universally aware—appreciation is transformed into awe.

If to many the notion of the sublime carries an archaic ring today, that does not indicate any deficiency in the concept but our loss. For the sublime being derivative from the universal, the concept's rapid decline in usage charts the fall of the universal through realist, modernist, and postmodernist art and literature.

The Application of Art to Life

Although removed from the real world, the arts are applied in lifestyle and manners in much the way the human sciences are applied in social policy. Works of art mimic reality, but they also invite reality to mimic them, presenting what might be as well as what is. If never their dominant concern, from their onset the arts have imparted charged meaning to styles of life and images of society, shaping the aspirations of millions. In this subordinate role, beauty's charisma inspires love and identification, putting forth new ways that compel imitation. To the extent which people possess and dwell in aesthetic awareness, the style of personal and collective action becomes for them the application of art to life.

Due to the relative inaccessibility of the arts, their most direct influence is on the lifestyles of the upper and upper-middle classes and particularly on their more leisured segments, the most creative of whom significantly draw on the arts and literature. (The pre-superid and superid may be joined in extreme cases in which life becomes art, as perhaps in the creatively stylish life of an Oscar Wilde or Isadora Duncan. Nevertheless, lifestyles rarely rise to the level of art because of the exceeding difficulty of combining the requisite perspective, artistry, resources, and single-minded attention to the task.) The styles of elegant Ionian gentlemen and chivalrous medieval nobles were inconceivable without the prior aesthetic consciousness from which both lifestyles drew. The increasingly refined aristocratic manners of the late Middle Ages and early modern period again owed everything to courtly fine art and the sensibility that developed with it. To the extent to which the upper and upper-middle classes have cultural power their influence then reaches indirectly through other classes. To the extent they do not, the reverse process occurs from popular culture. In either case most stylistic content ordinarily comes proximately from concrete models within people's ken. In the arts and in life, people's ubiquitous mimicry of the forms around them is highly subject to consensus.

Crucial to the well-being of the human is that the arts, along with all other social and cultural institutions, slowly be worked into harmony with the larger society in order that their influence be as beneficial as possible. As this process occurs, the aesthetically beautiful and the edifying converge, and virtue becomes stylish. Narrow pursuit of the arts without regard to the needs of the larger society and culture is finally no different from single-minded pursuit of any other sectoral activity. Aestheticism, absent any regard for its larger impact, is as grotesque as Frankensteinian science, beggar-thy-neighbor trade policy, or bare-knuckles politics and runs equally counter to morality. However inordinate and misguided his response, the growth of pure aestheticism in the fifth and fourth centuries BCE is what prompted Plato's bitter attacks on the arts (Hauser 1951, 1:99). As the human becomes more holistically worked, a balanced concern for the many aspects of life grows in the arts. Moralizing the aesthetic need not be heavy-handed and detract from art, any more than humanizing research need diminish science or restraining competition need mar business or government. Purely on its own, art becomes one more sectoral perspective unable to appreciate or respect any other.

The Epistemics of the Arts

The central thrust of the arts with their connotative language is ultimately the same as the central thrust of the human sciences with their denotative language, the elucidation of the human and its situation. Although they use a nonrational mode of presentation and concrete images and intimations in place of concepts and propositions, artworks nevertheless suggest the general. Where the human sciences generalize, artworks put forth concrete models of reality in the consummatory mode with varying degrees of fancifulness.[3] Where a theorist might generalize about certain negative effects of capitalism, Dickens's novels intimate the same point, among many others, with the doleful occurrences in his characters' lives. Works of art and literature tacitly suggest theory, as the human sciences tacitly convey myth. As Goodman (1978, 104) says, "[f]iction . . . whether written or painted or acted, applies, . . . albeit metaphorically, to actual worlds." The consummatory knowledge in the arts is haunting and fleeting. It conveys a sense of recognition of and familiarity with things pertaining to the human. In its way, from poetry to architecture, art mimics and speaks about everything concerning life, its orderliness, seriousness, boldness, warmth, nobility, and tragedy. In Goodman's (102) words, "the arts must be taken no less seriously than the sciences as modes of discovery, creation and enlargement of knowledge in the broad sense of advancement of the understanding. . . ." This astonishing vehicle not only conveys knowledge but does so in a unique and irreplaceable manner.

Just as a crucial and neglected aspect of the human sciences has to do with getting at the whole by means of rational language, a crucial and neglected aspect of the arts has to do with getting at the whole by means of nonrational language. Not only must the arts intimate the truth, but insofar as possible they must intimate the whole truth. They must convey the truth about profound questions and ultimate concerns. Hence the need for a renewed universalism in the arts to parallel the phenomenological human science described in the last chapter. Artists, like their cousins in the human sciences, must again raise themselves to the universal. The aim must again be to produce high art.

In literary and art criticism the indispensable initial task is the interpretation or "reading" of works, singularly and plurally, in what is essentially a subtle form of perception and description. This activity entails getting at two kinds of meaning. Most important, it requires a successful decoding by the art critic or consumer of the intended or "nonnatural" meaning conveyed by art, for the conduct of which, acquisition of the nonconceptual languages of the arts is a prerequisite. However, there may also be an interpretation of the unintended or "natural" meaning conveyed by them, one often reaching into the artist and his context (see Grice 1989, ch. 14, 18). In either case, the content of literature and art cannot be simply or straightforwardly described rationally; it must be deftly interpreted to be drawn into rational discourse. Even the elementary analyses of individual works of art in literary and art criticism entail a hermeneutic effort. A more demanding aggregate criticism then interprets or reads artists, schools, styles, phases, movements, and eras in the arts. However, aesthetic knowing is a different and complementary kind of knowing that demands pursuit in its own language, not constant translation into rational discourse.

The central task of criticism should then be to assess the value of the art's intimations. In spite of the radically different form taken by artistic truth, the ultimate standard for the arts, as for the human sciences, is truth. Truth content alone "is the justification for aesthetics," as Adorno (1997, 128, 212) says—leading him to his famous judgment that between Bach and Beethoven the latter must ultimately receive the nod because of his supreme truth content. All truth being correspondence with reality in the broadest sense, with what is, the higher responsibility of critics lies in assessing such congruence in works of art. Yet all assessment of the proffered truth of art necessitates the prior grasp of what it says, only after which may there be evaluation of the warrantedness of its intimations.

As in the critique of theory, the highest task of literary and art criticism is not just determining whether particular works get some truth right but also assessing the extent to which great works of art get large sweeps of it right. The preeminent task in evaluating art and literature is the probing of high art and literature for the universal truth they carry. This task is not something essentially different from the other aspects of criticism—it is merely carrying them out holistically in determining what artworks or art currents get how much right across the manifold of all that is. The message is the architecture, not the bricks. In such judgments one is dealing with large matrices rather than individual equations, so to speak. In the appropriate shorthand one sometimes starts from nothing and adds whole dimensions gotten right, but she must often talk of limitation and bias, starting from the whole and subtracting entire dimensions botched or blurred.

Accordingly, to a large degree, art may be deemed ultimately of value to the extent that it manifests the same four qualities as those used to evaluate knowledge in the human sciences, namely range, determinacy, coherence, and validity. Art needs to be oriented as broadly as possible and to say powerful, coherent things about the way things are that bear up in experience. Its family resemblances must work, and its intimations must have insight. When art and human science contradict each other, at least one of the two is wrong.

If the preeminent aspect of art is that which conveys meaning, not to be slighted are those many significant aspects of art that do other things. These are its illocutionary moments, the things art has to do in order to speak, beginning with its play element. Technique itself is without truth content and uninterpretable in the way in which art's truth content is discerned. What the criterion of artistry demands is commentary describing and explaining what is going on. In music the evocative overhead is particularly pronounced, for which reason music carries comparatively less rationally describable truth content than the other arts. The novel represents the opposite extreme. What art says is evaluated in one way, what it does is evaluated in another, according to how well it works. The additional standard for evaluating art that must join the four epistemic criteria is the excellence of this artistry. The critical exploration of artistry, the methodology of the arts, although very important, must finally be secondary to evaluating artistic meaning. Many more artists are able to achieve technical refinement than get to the essence of things and rise to the universal.

Who ought to evaluate artworks and art currents and shape canons are, above all, those best able to assess the truth of art and particularly its universalistic truth. This is the community of those broadly educated in the arts, and notably the most thoughtful part of it. With his customary rudeness, Nietzsche (1974, 141) indicates one important group for judging art when he says that the rich and idle are the ultimate appraisers of value. Those engaged full time with the arts, including artists, critics, dealers, and performers among others, who variously overlap with the first community, should and will be another important group evaluating art. From among those professionally engaged, the generalists in the arts, including great artists and such critics as the earlier-mentioned Auerbach, Bakhtin, and Frye form a crucial subset. From among the professionally engaged, the various specialists should also have a say, since they always best understand its technical aspects. Yet because they are often more susceptible to sectoralism, they may not be the best judges overall.

Taken comprehensively, criticism and theory in literature and art become synonymous with the human science of art and literature. Where traditional criticism engaged in interpretation but not explanation, the broadened criticism of the postmodernist period reads aesthetic forms while the corresponding theory goes on to explain them in a melding of criticism and sociology pioneered by the Frankfurt School. Literary and art criticism and theory bring to the other human sciences an immersion in the arts and possession of a far richer and more developed tradition of interpretation than any previously practiced by the social sciences and psychology. This tradition has taught the other human sciences to read aesthetic forms wherever they appear—not solely in artworks—for the meaning in the arts is also present less concentratedly in much that we do. In such forms as the dreams accompanying economic progress, the fantasies accompanying political history, or the imageries accompanying family formation, substantially submerged myth and suggestion have always floated amid the predominantly rational topics engaging the human sciences. In addition to being described and explained rationally, lifestyles, consumption patterns, social policies, and even warfare must be read as we would read poems and buildings (see Geertz 1973, ch. 1; 1983, ch. 5, 6; Foucault 1979, ch. 2). Sensitivity to the poetic is vital to all human science. The incorporation of literary and art criticism and theory into the human sciences opens this wide expanse of the aesthetic to them. At the same time the explanatory power of the social sciences and psychology benefits literary and art criticism and theory. Their merger into the larger human sciences makes possible the comprehensive interpretation and explanation of all things pertaining to the human.

Notes

1. I will clarify and defend what I mean by reality in this sense in the next chapter.

2. Although he is off-key in singling out *interestedness* as the problem when that is only one of two equally significant means by which art strays from the ideal, the other being by affectedness, being pulled over the line into the real by desire.

3. This function is every bit as significant in Beowulf or de Kooning as in Crane or Courbet. In other words, truth content is decisive in other forms of art than "realism," if not as vividly so.

Bibliography

Adorno, T. 1997. *Aesthetic Theory.* Minneapolis: University of Minnesota Press.

Bourdieu, P. 1984. *Distinction: A Social Critique of the Judgement of Taste.* Cambridge, MA: Harvard University Press.

Fiedler, C. 1957. *On Judging Works of Visual Art.* Berkeley and Los Angeles: University of California Press.

Foucault, M. 1979. *Discipline and Punish.* New York: Vintage Books.

Frye, N. 1957. *The Anatomy of Criticism.* Princeton, NJ: Princeton University Press.

Geertz, C. 1973. *The Interpretation of Cultures.* New York: Basic Books.

———. 1983. *Local Knowledge: Further Essays in Interpretive Anthropology.* New York: Basic Books.

Goodman, N. 1978. *Ways of Worldmaking.* Indianapolis, IN: Hackett.

Grice, P. 1989. *Studies in the Way of Words.* Cambridge, MA: Harvard University Press.

Hauser, A. 1951. *The Social History of Art.* 4 vols. New York: Vintage Press.

Hegel, G. 1975. *Aesthetics: Lectures on Fine Art.* 2 vols. Oxford: Clarendon Press.

Heidegger, M. 1964. "The Origin of the Work of Art." In *Philosophies of Art and Beauty,* ed. A. Hofstadter and R. Kuhns. New York: Modern Library.

Kant, I. 1951. *Critique of Judgment.* New York: Hafner.

Longinus. 1965. *On Sublimity.* Oxford: Clarendon Press.

Nietzsche, F. 1974. *The Gay Science.* New York: Vintage Books.

Raphael, M. 1947. *Prehistoric Pottery and Civilization in Egypt.* New York: Pantheon.

Read, H. 1965. *Icon and Idea.* New York: Schocken.

Weber, M. 1969. *The Rational and Social Foundations of Music.* Carbondale: Southern Illinois University Press.

18. *Overcoming Skepticism and Radical Relativism*

Knowledge, however, and particularly knowledge of the universal, encounters fierce opposition today. In addition to that from disciplinary science which I answered primarily in Chapter 16, there are two more general forms of doubt. On the one hand, we have the general skepticism that denies all knowledge, whether of nature or the human. On the other hand, we have the radical relativism that most often directs itself against knowledge of the universal, although it also attacks other forms of knowledge. Let us address these challenges in turn.

Skepticism and the Real World Problem

Skepticism is the systematic negation of knowledge, the doctrine that it is impossible for us to know anything dependably. The main contemporary forms of skepticism as it pertains to the natural world are doubt about our perceptual and cognitive capacities. Some skeptics go so far as insisting that we have no reliable way of distinguishing between wakefulness and dreaming. However, it is also instructive to consider the corresponding negativism of action. Where one who says we can't perceive or understand anything is a skeptic, one who says we can't *do* anything or make a difference in what we do is a fatalist. The skeptic is essentially an intellectual fatalist who holds that what will be perceived and thought will be perceived and thought, that we don't amount to much intellectually. The fatalist, for his part, is essentially a skeptic with regard to action and its consequences.

   Much of the discussion of perceptual skepticism has manifested itself as the real world problem, which is philosophy's and above all bourgeois philosophy's major concern with whether the things we perceive are real. For more than two thousand years in much of the West one began philosophy with first philosophy. In the various capitalist societies and those influenced by that system, philosophers have instead tended to begin with the real world problem, with the prevailing position having been one degree or another of perceptual skepticism. The doubt has generally focused on whether we can know that what we perceive actually exists.

This skepticism has arisen in part from excessive bonding by bourgeois and bourgeois-influenced philosophers with rigorous method. Those one-sidedly bent on the procedural, particularly as in the rigid application of logic, can never achieve more than a local and tentative comfort with knowledge and are therefore chronically vulnerable to skepticism, as has been apparent since the onset of the modern world. To the degree that one attempts to restrict herself to rigorous disciplinary methods while pursuing questions out-side their range, she is going to get skepticism. For language in its various forms to have become a Holy Grail for some has been in effect to exalt the heuristic in such a manner. That doesn't mean it is not possible to know, only that, in their awkward methodism, strict analytic philosophers have been lim-ited in their ability to know beyond sectoral questions narrowly focused on the possessions of language, logic, and mathematics and leave an atmosphere of doubt (cf. Taylor 1989, 75–90).

Skeptical antirealism has also stemmed in part from individualism. Not only do the bourgeois tend to radically separate themselves ontologically from other people, but they also tend to radically separate themselves from the natural world. An important result of this is the modern proclivity to see knowledge as lying inside and reality outside the person, setting the stage for a salient distinction between appearances and reality. Bourgeois philosophy negates the traditional epistemic in which one is simply immersed in reality. That view, nested in the collectivist experience of traditional agrarian soci-eties like ancient Greece and Rome, left no such gap between reality and the person.

A third source of antirealist skepticism, complementing the others, is the modern decline of holism which has contributed to the ascent of narrowly proceduralist tendencies. That the notion of appearances would then become more salient vis-à-vis small pieces of reality wrenched from the world for analysis in contrived puzzlement is understandable. Where holism is a stronger leaning, the emphasis on context is greater, undercutting the ten-dency to antirealism.

Drawing on phenomenology, modern universalism overcomes skepti-cism. Rising above rigorism, individualism, and decontextualism, it considers the broad context of what we perceive and think, noting that by our very nature we encompass and are about what is in the natural world plus what is in the world of the human over and against it. As Heidegger, Merleau-Ponty, and Taylor hold, our very being is "Dasein-in-the-world," and we have intense, real contact with the things around us that presumes at least moderately effective perception, thought, and action with respect to those things. Everything that we are about is an overcoming of the opposition between mind and world, a coproduction that occurs informally in the conjectures and refutations of everyday life and systematically in those of science. As Searle (1983, 159) says, "There can't be a fully meaningful question, 'Is there a real world independent of my representations of it?' because the very having of representations can only exist against a Background which gives representations the character of 'representing something.'" By our nature, the source of our knowledge of things is "our *experience* of them" (Merleau-Ponty 1962, 23). Paraphrasing and extending Husserl (1982, 51), things are simply there for us, on hand for us. Consciousness doesn't *have* the power of attributing meaning to sense data, of organizing experiences into "an identifiable unity when seen in different perspectives," of "breathing spirit into them"—it *is* that very power (Merleau-Ponty 1962, 121). By virtue of being human we get at the thing-in-itself (see Sokolowski 1974, 246). Universalism notes the distinction between appearances and reality without disproportionately emphasizing it.

Adopting skepticism raises crippling problems. For one, doing so is flagrantly incoherent. One of Stroud's ways of dealing with the conundrum in *The Quest for Reality* is amusing. He doesn't boldly assert propositions—he can't. Instead he speaks softly, he intimates, he hints, he speaks provisionally and tentatively. But one doesn't escape the problem by tiptoeing. Suggestions, whispers, and allusions all still bear propositional content rendered just as incoherent by the self-contradiction of skepticism as are plain assertions.

Stroud (see esp. 2000, ch. 3) attacks our perception of reality by attempting to undermine the notion that color is real, arguing that, no, what we perceive as color physicists have concluded to be nothing more than appearances in ourselves caused by the wave-lengths across the visible spectrum of light. Color perception is therefore not real. But this claim is like saying that the ordinary perception of weight is not real because physicists have discovered the concept of mass and can finely measure it. That more technically refined and exact scientific ways of conceptualizing color or mass or sound or smell exist takes nothing from the basic reality of such everyday perceptual phenomena; it merely sharpens them. Color perception becomes random only in the color blind. Discriminatory color vision, along with certain color characteristics in us and many plant and animal species, would never have evolved were color not real.

Seriously maintaining that there is or can be no reality independent of our experience of it is something quite different from acknowledging that we can only know reality via experience gained in approaching it—from postulating that the real world exists but treating it as the hypothetical manifold toward which our knowledge tends to converge. For holding that external things might come into being and cease being with our consciousness is an incoherent solipsistic and idealist projection. To each separate consciousness, at least in a state of extreme insularity, we know that things may seem that way, but we also easily note the steadiness of everything else around us through the cycles of wakefulness and sleep and birth and death of particular human beings. Infants at the peek-a-boo stage are endearing; philosophers artificially propounding the same view of the world are absurd. Yet there is no way for a thoroughgoing skeptic even to get past sensation to arrive at perception in the first place. "How do you know that door is real?" —"That *what* door is not real?!" The conversation quickly becomes Beckett's *End Game* or *Waiting for Godot*.

Skepticism in its avowal of utter meaninglessness is a paralyzing inner conflictedness in which there is no reason to get up in the morning, get dressed, and take nourishment. Its fatalism about knowledge shares the weaknesses of all fatalism. People get nowhere with obsessions about whether things are really there. Above all, skepticism, to the extent practiced, neutralizes its adherents from making a constructive difference in their own lives or those of others.[1] Traditionally the Roman Catholic Church, when sometimes encountering people so afflicted with the minutiae of whether they might have committed sin that they were unable to get on with life, wisely treated such phenomena as unbalanced "scruples" in need of correction. Enshrouded in darkness, Kafkaesque epistemic paralysis is no way to lead one's life. Over and over again the skeptic goes to the door in uncertainty and turns back. What the skeptic begs for is therapy: "You aren't sure the door is really there? Tell me what you would like to do if you were able to go through the door?" Only when we get bits of substantive reply and listen carefully to them do we begin to fully understand. Skeptics sometimes apologize for having found no other way—a disconnect between consummatory and instrumental knowing that cries out for ministration. Universalism again begins with first philosophy rather than with appearances because general skepticism is nonsensical.

Not surprisingly, however, the ultimate target of skepticism is often knowledge of the universal. Skeptics almost always give a wink to everyday knowledge and often another to scientific knowledge, but they never do to knowledge of the universal. When skepticism moves from the natural to the human world, it largely transforms itself into radical relativism, directs its artillery at universalism, and becomes formidable.

Radical Relativism

Breathtakingly nihilistic and powerful after having gathered momentum for more than a century, radical relativism has swept everything before it since the 1960s, spreading the rejection of universalism in philosophy, religion, and morality with its barbed skepticism and cultural slurs. I am thinking, for instance, of such arguments as "We know about several thousand different religions, each fervently believed in by its adherents. Who are we to say that our one religion is right and the others wrong?" and of ironic ways of conveying similar messages. Radical relativism demolishes naïve manifestations of universalism by confronting them forcefully and mockingly with the effects of profoundly divergent contexts. Radical relativism has permeated the human sciences in the postmodernist period to such a degree that young people have entered them at some peril.

All forms of radical relativism come down to epistemic doubt. Ethical relativism reduces to epistemic questioning because its underpinning is the assumption that we cannot reliably know what is truly moral. Cultural relativism with its injunction that we not judge other cultures is but an extension of ethical relativism and similarly grounded in the assumption that moral standards are necessarily culture-bound and arbitrary. Aesthetic relativism is based upon the belief that we cannot know well enough aesthetically to judge. Conceptual and ontological relativism are related to the epistemic as narrower portions of it, concepts of various sorts being part of the apparatus of knowledge. Nevertheless, radical relativism is more dangerous than general skepticism in no small part because it is less extreme, granting that we can know that human beings and their actions exist and that we can to some degree describe and explain what they do. If it did not, it could not be what it is and talk about what is related to what.

Radical relativism or radical historicism centers on two implicit or explicit propositions: that all socio-cultural and historical variations are contingent and situationally determined, and that all are therefore arbitrary.[2] Such relativism takes all claims of knowledge and all injunctions based upon them merely to reflect particular viewpoints no more justified than any other. Rorty (1982, 166), for example, defines (radical) relativism as "the view that every belief on a certain topic, or perhaps about any topic, is as good as every other." In its romping negation radical relativism attacks all knowledge and meaning—exempting only its own thinnest of reeds. The implicit or explicit conclusion is that we therefore cannot judge between the various competing human forms. Hence, Goodman's (1978, 96, 107) emphasis on "the multiplicity of right world-versions" and "countenancing unreconciled alternatives." Not only are philosophy, religion, and morality not spared by radical relativism, but their universalism and absolutism form its central target.

Denying above all that we can know or judge universally, radical relativism or radical historicism is "the doctrine of the necessary and total parochiality of human reason" (Page 1995, 48–9). As Margolis (1987, xii) puts it, "[n]o one can escape his local history." Radical relativism therefore denies the possibility of reasoned debate and selection between rival traditions (MacIntyre 1988, 352). To radical relativism, human beings cannot intellectually grasp and reconcile difference. Rorty (1989, 22) in his languid and skeptical Wittgensteinianism wants us to reach "the point where we no longer worship *anything,* where we treat *nothing* as quasi-divinity, where we treat *everything*—our language, our conscience, our community—as a product of time and chance." Radical relativism self-consciously denies the efficacy of contemplation. In place of a story of convergence toward the universal Rorty (1989, 67, 73–76) holds that searching for any reality with which our notions might converge, and particularly any corresponding with the universal, is futile. He wants people "to stop asking for universal validity." Radical relativism essentially argues that sectoralism is our unavoidable lot and renounces its overcoming on principle.

However much we may reject other aspects of the doctrine, radical relativism's often unstated first proposition that human variations are situationally determined, namely its basic socio-cultural and historical relativism, is unexceptionable. Subject to certain limits, all human patterns *are* shaped by their socio-cultural and psychological settings. Historicity and situatedness are givens with respect to humans and their forms, and they demand explication as such. Properly understood, relativism in and of itself is nothing more than a benign way of situating or positioning things in existential space and time. One cannot make distinctions or move around in the many-dimensional space of the human without the language of relativism. Relativism in this necessary employment is the very lifeblood of the human sciences, and its relentless contextualizing is essential to any sophisticated understanding of human forms and patterns, including those of philosophy, religion, and morality. The indispensability of a basic socio-cultural and historical relativism, however, has not been apparent to sectoral absolutists, who, unable to cope with situational variation in beliefs and standards, have either arbitrarily rejected as much relativism as possible or cowered in mute terror of it. But the absolute must be built up as the overcoming of relatives, not asserted arbitrarily. Such feeble conservative opposition as there has been even to a basic socio-cultural and historical relativism has dogmatically and unconvincingly clung to narrow and dated embodiments of the universal in strained efforts to preserve a semblance of stability. Relativism per se can only be opposed by the naïve.

Nevertheless, there are limits to this basic socio-cultural relativism, for many human patterns are shaped powerfully by what exists independently of them and only partly by socio-cultural and historical context. For example, knowledge is often explained by the way things actually are, rather than by social or psychological factors. Thus in contemporary physics the nature of physical reality rather than socio-cultural context is responsible for a very great deal, although to what precise degree it is impossible to know. In many areas of business and technology that abut the natural world, a similar convergence occurs upon actual physical parameters. In a comparable way, if for the most part less perfectly, there is a convergence of socio-cultural knowledge on reality. Much of our knowledge about the human is explained not by the situated and empowered leanings of a class or person but by the overcoming and absence of such leanings, i.e., by the approximate balance of the inquirer allowing her to approach what is actually there. As social forms in their aboutness converge on reality, how things actually are becomes a more prominent feature in their explanation. As against what we might know about physics or government a century or millennium from now, it is likely to appear retrospectively that today's knowledge has significant distortions brought on by leanings of which we are unaware that will by then be better overcome. The imperfection of current knowledge does not alter the judgment that an important element shaping what we know remains the way things are independently of us. Other kinds of important limits on explanation in the human sciences are posed by physical and biological factors that also explain much about us. One way in which relativism may become radical is by disrespecting these kinds of limits, as is done by certain postmodernist practitioners of the sociology of science.

The main conceptual problem with radical relativism lies with its second proposition, that all the different human forms are therefore arbitrary, that they are all randomly and meaninglessly varied, such that no one of them could claim special privilege. The assumption of general arbitrariness is the central source of the doctrine's radicalism, and it is false. While there is a certain arbitrariness in all *sectoral* positions, and no particular one of them can be privileged, there is nothing arbitrary about the positions of the universal, and those coming from it *are* privileged. As I have amply demonstrated in the preceding chapters, there is system, not randomness, to the different positions of the human, one that the universal presents. Contrary to Rorty (1989, 50), there is a "way to rise above the language, culture, institutions and practices one has adopted and view all these on a par with all the others." Relativism or historicism per se is not a problem; radical, antiholist relativism *is* a problem.

In their failure to grasp the universal, radical relativists assume that the only absolutes are dogmatic, sectoralist ones vulnerable to relativizing. For this reason it is axiomatic to radical relativists that something cannot at once be contingent and universal or infinite (see Page 1995, 28, 80). Hence, as Page says, radical historicism rejects absolutes by invoking "the historicity of the knowing subject." Kracauer (1995, 218) works on this assumption when he says, "once one enters into a relationship with the absolute, historicism immediately becomes impossible; and . . . conversely, where historicism reigns, access to the absolute is unavoidably cut off." Heidegger shuddered for decades over the same specter. Margolis (1986, 40) is another who believes that historicity casts a pall over reason. Rorty (1989, 45–49, 76, 88) is one more who avers that because all our positions are contingent, they are necessarily tenuous. To him, we are nothing more than "centerless webs of beliefs and desires," "sentential attitudes . . . phrased in some historically con-ditioned vocabulary . . ." In this spirit, he suggests that taking something from the metaphysical tradition from Plato to Kant "is just the characteristic mark of the discourse of people inhabiting a certain chunk of space-time." True enough, except for the "just," for large portions of it also happen to be valid. The history of philosophy, religion, morality, and statesmanship demonstrates them all to be caused, but whether something is caused has zero bearing on either its truth or its universalism.

All of this is aside from the fact that radical relativism is made preposter-ous by its inherent inconsistency. "In effect, [radical] relativism consists in declaring it to be true that there is no such thing as truth, or in declaring it to be absolutely true that nothing but the relatively true exists. . . ." (Schuon 1984, 7). It may not be strictly illogical to exempt one's belief in skepticism from that very skepticism, but it is exuberantly incoherent to do so.

Radical relativism culminates in the anorexic suspension of judgment. Yet because one cannot live on such a diet, and radical relativists, like others, have to judge, they do so evasively and sheepishly. Often this is done in part by jury-rigging another assertion, that everything is to be tolerated which does not "objectively" harm us or our property. Virtually no one who purports to be a radical relativist applies the doctrine across the board to suspend judg-ment about objective harm to human beings, even though any who do not are again being flagrantly incoherent. Holding everything to be arbitrary and the world absurd, radical relativism cannot consistently support tolerance by the different views of each other, for what could privilege its own positive value? However contortedly, radical relativism often at least calls forth a cer-tain minimalist good sense in extending this one value.

The Return of the Absolute

The key to overcoming radical relativism lies in recognizing that an entirely different kind of relativism is also possible—a holistic relativism in which all variations are respected but sublated—one long practiced by universalists but philosophically developed by Hegel. As Schuon (1984, 62) says, "full com-prehension—in light of the Absolute—of relativity dissolves it and leads back to the Absolute." Thus we have two strikingly different forms of relativism (and historicism), a radical, destructive, meaningless, and incoherent relativism and a moderate, constructive, meaningful, and coherent one. As ontology and method progress, we don't banish relativism but incorporate it within universalism, rendering the differences of humankind well understood and well respected. Philosophers frequently but wrongly equate the notion of relativism with radical relativism (there having been so little holistic relativism that what there has been has often passed unnoticed). Subscribing to a universalistic relativism in service of the absolute, I am both relativist and absolutist.[3]

Holistic relativism is a comprehensive situationalism that categorizes the types of philosophical, religious, and moral positions among others under a well-developed universal. Applying such relativism to ethics, for example, we note the deeper sameness in surface difference, the worthy ways of caring for the whole represented by different moralities in different contexts. One cannot ask for a general determinate answer to the question, What is moral? For each particular set of circumstances, however, there exists a determinate moral solution. Instead of taking them to be arbitrary, universalism holds different moralities to possess large, albeit varying, degrees of universalism and validity, while partly reflecting different sectoral proveniences. What is good, right, and/or virtuous in every particular situation becomes absolute, but always for specific groups and circumstances that continually change. When the reference shifts, some of what had been Moral becomes Immoral, while some of what had been Immoral becomes Moral. With a mere change of reach, character, or resources, morality must be adjusted to enhance well-being under new conditions. It is not so much that the appearance of what is moral changes around us, as radical relativists would have it, as that what is absolutely moral changes. With holistic relativism one can even address and respond to general moral ascent or decline, and can do so because he is watching all forms of morality simultaneously. Holistic relativism supports a robust situational absolutism. Most of the world's historic philosophies, religions, and moralities are understood by universalism to be beneficial and to complement each other—where they do not, it seeks to critique and reform them that they might. In holistic relativism it is "different strokes for different folks"—some suited to certain conditions and some to others but with varying degrees of validity.

The meaninglessness, tumult, and agony so widespread in the world today arise largely from the unavoidable rigors of the socio-cultural marketplace presented by our historical circumstances, but they also arise increasingly from a skepticism that seeks to bar the working which rebuilds the whole, a skepticism preferring to rigidly lock in sectoral forms. For the skeptics, lacking either a sense of the whole or the desire to reconcile, have looked at the variations and pronounced conversation between them meaningless. The real problem has never been relativism per se, only the skeptical radicalization of relativism. In its exaltation of skepticism we again see the hollow-ness of the postmodernist framework.

When Hegel (1967, 246ff.) tells us that, misguided though it be, skepti-cism already represents the first dialectical step, foreshadowing the onset of a larger self-consciousness of difference, he refers to that ancient skepticism which highlighted the need to look for the equally plausible opposites to our assertions, not to the dogmatic, self-refuting skepticism of the modern world (see Forster 1989, ch. 1). The direct step past sectoralism and toward the universal is to note the plural perspectives and aims of humankind without rejecting those that are different, a stance in which perplexity is natural. Responding to pluralism in tentative, cautious, open-minded suspense of belief is progressive—going on to deny in principle that we can know is not. Doubt that becomes dug in and fortified in systematic, self-conscious resist-ance to the universal is a trap blocking reconciliation.

Radical, skeptical relativism in its fundamental leaning against reconcilia-tion is the epistemological analog to conflictualism. Radical relativism per-ceives ubiquitous unbridgeable differences among socio-cultural forms and considers the peoples, experiences, and settings behind them as fundamen-tally incommensurate. By declaring conversation between the variations meaningless and disallowing talk of essential sameness or of reconciliation, radical relativism turns mere difference into intractable, seemingly essential difference. If people can't know things universally, they can't resolve con-flicts. Refusal to accept that opposition can be overcome effectively takes glar-ing and open contradiction and essential difference to be the norm between people. In this cultural contradictionism it is the war of all against all in which commonality and morality are but illusion. Yet many conflicts around the world and within psyches actually do get resolved. Sweden and Norway almost came to war in 1905 before backing away and slowly reconciling their disputes. Britain almost came to revolution in the early 1830s before the king relented, permitting the Great Reform and significant democratization to go forward. Traditional Japan freely accepted marked religious diversity and crossfertilization in a spirit of tolerance. Aside from their preposterousness, attacks on such achievements as essentially no different from any other out-comes have appalling practical implications.

Here we come to a three-way parting of the trails. The first, that of naïve sectoralist absolutism, is no longer passable. For one who is aware and acknowledges difference and pluralism, there remain two choices. She may deny the possibility of reconciliation and go down the path of radical rela-tivism, or affirm the possibility of reconciliation and go down the path of uni-versalism. Before one treads too far along the path of radical relativism she needs to think long and hard about how it could possibly be the right one, and what kind of world it would lead to if taken. That leaves one sensible course.

The universalist understands not only that we can know but that we can know the most difficult, ultimate, and universal things, though such knowledge can never come to those blinded by superstition, enthralled by method, or conflicted by skepticism. Universalism retains and furthers radical relativism's sophisticated, savvy receptivity to diversity while overcoming its skepticism about reconciliation. Although this work refutes radical relativism in the abstract, the decisive overcoming must occur in more concrete empirical work built up in reoriented human sciences as the major socio-cultural variations are sublated intellectually—and in the real world as the tangible oppositions of humankind are patiently reconciled by those dedicated to the whole.

Coda

Where the sectoral has fixed horizons, the universal soars among horizons, steady in its transcendent weightlessness. It shocks some that we speak only metaphorically of foundations and the truth is more evanescent. All "grounding" is but the best intuition of the most adept celestial mariners—their highest ascent and nothing more. With the universal we glide above fixed ground, overcoming the pitching horizons in the rarified atmosphere of high peaks and perfect freedom. Are not the heaviest atoms mostly empty space and the heaviest planets mostly frozen hydrogen? There too the gymnasts know a world of tumbling where others stand fixed. Those with the universal have neither real solidity nor any need of it. From their lofty realms, they rotate the horizons, fast-freeze the ambrosia, and the world is again whole: *all that was air becomes solid*.

The balanced cutting between perspectives is our overcoming of the postmodernist chaos—as, millennia ago, it was the overcoming of the early agrarian chaos. For those able and willing to rise above particularism, the world *is* again whole—only now this is not a simple traditional whole but a complex modern one. With its many-sided coherence this first large glimpse of the more harmonious world we all will one day inhabit has the sure and vibrant feel of the liberal, humane, metropolitan system for our time. It embraces diversity and complexity with Foucault, Derrida, Jameson, Rorty, Lyotard, Olalquiaga, and the other riotous postmodernists; only now, through the cacophonous din, one begins to hear a distant and classical but curiously new melody.

Yet one will always hear from the sophomores, "But that's just your view!" That's not *just* my view or my social category's view but the only coherent one and the only one that includes and overcomes all others by distilling the cumulative wisdom of philosophy and the human sciences for contemporary conditions. But let us not be unduly concerned—such protests are no more than tapping the ground on the way to a world of Meaning.

Notes

1. Thus Hegel (1956, 318) aptly speaks of the immobility and aimlessness of skepticism, of its "counsel of despair."
2. I take these to be effectively equivalent to Page's (1995, 80) two axioms of philosophical historicism: "(I) *The axiom of historical contextualization:* History, construed as a wholly contingent process, provides the ultimate framework within which to justify any human claim to have understood the truth or to be doing the good." and "(II) *The axiom of reason's finite historicity:* The powers of human understanding are necessarily finite, as determined by the contingent, historical nature of human existence."
3. I consider this to be substantially parallel to Hegel's epistemological defense of the absolute against skepticism (see Forster's excellent account in 1989, ch. 7, 8).

Bibliography

Forster, M. 1989. *Hegel and Skepticism*. Cambridge, MA: Harvard University Press.

Goodman, N. 1978. *Ways of Worldmaking*. Indianapolis, IN: Hackett.

Hegel, G. 1956. *The Philosophy of History*. New York: Dover Publications.

———. 1967. *The Phenomenology of Mind*. New York: Harper and Row.

Husserl, E. 1982. *Ideas Pertaining to a Pure Phenomenology and a Phenomenological Philosophy*. The Hague: Martinus Nijhoff.

Kracauer, S. 1995. *The Mass Ornament*. Cambridge, MA: Harvard University Press.

MacIntyre, A. 1988. *Whose Justice? Which Rationality?* Notre Dame, IN: University of Notre Dame Press.

Margolis, J. 1986. *Pragmatism without Foundations*. Oxford: Blackwell.

———. 1987. *Science without Unity*. Oxford: Blackwell.

Merleau-Ponty, M. 1962, *Phenomenology of Perception*. London: Routledge & Kegan Paul.

Page, C. 1995. *Philosophical Historicism*. University Park: Pennsylvania State University Press.

Rorty, R. 1982. *Consequences of Pragmatism*. Minneapolis: University of Minnesota Press.

———. 1989. *Contingency, Irony and Solidarity*. Cambridge: Cambridge University Press.

Schuon, F. 1984. *Logic and Transcendence*. London: Perennial Books.

Searle, J. 1983. *Intentionality: An Essay in the Philosophy of Mind*. Cambridge: Cambridge University Press.

Sokolowski, R. 1974. *Husserlian Meditations*. Evanston, IL: Northwestern University Press.

Stroud, B. 2000. *The Quest for Reality*. New York: Oxford University Press.

Taylor, C. 1989. *Sources of the Self: The Making of the Modern Identity*. Cambridge, MA: Harvard University Press.

19. Reunifying the Human Sciences under Philosophy

Human studies have found themselves in a great impasse in our times. On the one hand, philosophers, apprehending the brittleness of the old forms of universalism under modern conditions but unable to imagine or justify new ones, have largely withdrawn from their universalistic past other than as antiquaries and technicians. On the other hand, human scientists, unable to bring even a semblance of coherence to their sprawling fields, have largely ceased looking for order. In each case technical achievement and an enormous proliferation of results have been accompanied by a growing sense of bafflement and discouragement about the resulting disarray. The vacuum in contemporary philosophy is intimately related to the conceptual chaos in the human sciences.

Philosophy and the human sciences have both been substantially stymied for the same reason—because they have been separate from each other. Philosophy has been stymied because it has been unable to engage the human sciences. Under the spell of scientism, philosophers abandoned economics in the eighteenth century and withdrew from the other human sciences in the nineteenth, retaining only their lustrous colony in political philosophy. Philosophers themselves became convinced they had little any longer to learn from or say to the emergent human sciences. Sundered and stripped of their legacy, they retained only the right to rove about as methodological police, dutifully echoing the growing methodism of the larger society and the disciplines. To philosophy's disinheritance has been added in the postmodernist period a most uncharacteristic anti-holism effectively barring its reacquisition of universalism. A ghost of its former self, philosophy for more than a century has barely recognized itself.

For their part, the social sciences and psychology have been in such disorder because there has been no coherent modern philosophy from which they could draw. The subject fields, distancing themselves from philosophy in their skittishness about any taint of metaphysics or abstraction, have willingly restricted their scope and hobbled their theory. Conceptual chaos and the aimless profusion of incommensurate findings have been the result. The binds in philosophy and the human sciences comprise a vicious circle in which the incoherence of each is the chief barrier to the other. Yet each has also been whole in ways the other has been partial, and each can supply what the other has been lacking. The two predicaments possess a single solution: the merger of philosophy and the human sciences.

Where we begin their reintegration is not with the methodological thrusts of either. From philosophy's side we start with Hegel, and, from that of the human sciences, with the most general of the special fields. As it turns out, the human sciences, largely in continental Europe, have maintained a significant universalism of their own throughout the period of their independence, especially evident in grand sociological theory from Comte, Durkheim, and Weber to Parsons, Habermas, and Bourdieu, but also in its analogs in psychology and anthropology. This tradition, which has steadfastly maintained its own claim to study the human comprehensively, has already carried out significant integration of the human sciences. Effectively taking itself to be general human science, it has worked with most social and cultural institutions and with most aspects of character. Where traditional philosophy, though universal, has been empty without most of the dimensions and sectors of the human; social thought, though comprehensive, has been incoherent without the universal.

A watershed is reached as philosophy and the modern human sciences are joined conceptually. Alone among philosophies, a universalism wielding dialectical historicism and phenomenology takes seriously the calling of philosophy to shed light on the whole while engaging the world determinately. How philosophy regains its sense of the whole is and can only be by embracing the great variations in the world as it acquires and integrates the theory and methods of the human sciences—while not only reviving but developing its traditional universalism. In doing so determinately and empirically it overcomes the opposition between itself and the human sciences. Under today's conditions in which social and psychological thinkers know so much that is vital to generalizing about the whole, philosophy has no alternative but to master the knowledge of the special sciences below it—as many of them as possible and as profoundly as possible. Among other things, that mastery means going beyond philosophy's traditional conceptualism to embrace description and explanation. In this undertaking it makes the most sense to begin with the broadest generalizing tendencies in sociology, psychology, and anthropology because they are the most strategic bases for movement into the other fields.

In this universalism the most basic metaphysics, even first philosophy, becomes part of empirical science. The concepts upon which such universalism is built largely emerge from the theory of the human sciences—for their determinacy is not gratuitous. At once philosophical and sociological, this universalism is inspired by and must be corroborated by empirical work, precisely as is necessary at the foundations of physics. Ultimately one evaluates even the most abstruse ontology on the basis of how well it fits the facts. Kant notwithstanding, even existential space is an empirical concept about which there is nothing a priori. Not only does the universal arise "out of the manifold detail of concrete existence," as Hegel (94) tells us, but it is corroborable. It goes without saying, however, that corroboration of such an all-encompassing theory is necessarily extremely indirect and can only occur in very long-term cumulative experience. That does not mean there is no empirical corroboration—merely that the usual problems in the indirect assessment of large theoretical structures are compounded. The span may be great but the linkage is valid. That the myopic technicians of science become anxious about such linkages detracts not at all from the latter's effectuality or importance.

Here the rarest meditation and most disciplined empirical inquiry complement one another as essential aspects of the same great enterprise of knowledge. When the universalist is deep in contemplation, he is simultaneously in touch with the most general framework and the empirical results of the sciences; he can see from the foundations to the facts. Contemplation does not contradict natural or human science but enables its highest assembly and furthest reach. Not Hegel's (cf. 1967, 70) but our time is the one in which philosophy is raised to science and science to philosophy. The implications of this reintegration cascade in many directions.

When a sociologically and historically sophisticated phenomenology, grounded in a mature ontology, is directed back upon philosophy itself, philosophy undergoes yet another dramatic transformation. For the first time one understands why different societies and times have the philosophies they have, just as she understands why they have the economic systems or popular cultures they have. When the most powerful human science is directed back upon philosophy, it describes and explains movements toward and away from the universal by particular philosophies and types of philosophy. By knowing who diverse philosophers are and what their experiences have been, one understands why various philosophies get some things right and some wrong, and what social and psychological circumstances make possible the balance possessed by true philosophy. Philosophy in its partial self-knowledge has but dimly apprehended its own social conditions. Like every other social or cultural institution, philosophy can only be fully understood if seen to be socially constructed and to varying degrees bearing the characteristic distortions of its milieux. Accordingly, an early priority of modern universalism must be to carry out a powerful comparative historical phenomenology of philosophy itself.

Not only is it not a problem that the universal itself be determined, but the human science providing such knowledge turns out to be therapeutic and equilibrating for philosophy and the other institutions of the whole. Revoking the substantial de facto exemption of philosophy from socio-cultural self-scrutiny leads not to radical relativism but away from it—precisely as comparative religion leads not to atheism but to universal religion. Philosophy's demure self-privileging has borne more than a little resemblance to that of naïve religion.

A phenomenology grounded in dialectical historicism arrives with the epochal merger of philosophy and comparative historical analysis. What Nietzsche says about ethics, that it is impossible without the assistance of sociology, is extended to all of philosophy, as he himself began doing with piecemeal aphorisms. Fittingly, universalism contains the first comprehensive ethical philosophy to bridge the moral forms of all social classes determinately. A similar synthesis is promised in every other branch of philosophy as it comes to know itself. For every philosophy, we enter the mind of its creator and ascertain the social and psychological sources of the leanings and resources with which his work has been built. Bringing the total experiences and situations of philosophers into its gaze, phenomenology analyzes and comes to understand why they were able and willing to overcome certain oppositions but not others, together with the consequences of this unevenness. Only when philosophy looks back upon itself with coherent human science at its command can it again know itself and be whole. Philosophy does not have to be academicist, scholasticist, proceduralist, and narrow as it often is today—nor will it be once it examines itself to the extent now possible and necessary. Having the broad outlines of a world that is again authentically whole means for philosophy the displacement of an entire constellation of priorities and problems together with the assumption of new responsibilities reminiscent of those carried by the traditional philosophies of Aristotelianism, Stoicism, and Confucianism, although now in a dynamic global context.

If modern universalism leaves philosophy a radically different enterprise, it no less radically alters the human sciences. Chaotic, conflicted, fractious, and directionless on their own, as they build upon universalism, the human sciences can and will begin the sustained development that has so far substantially eluded them. The fundamental concepts of the human sciences, from culture and society to harmony and conflict to institution, class, and character, are philosophically grounded and the oppositions beneath their multiple paradigms overcome in these pages. Just as chemistry could at last develop in the late eighteenth and early nineteenth centuries once its foundations were soundly in place, the human sciences are now primed for development. Universalism opens a large territory for progressive research programs in all of them, setting the stage for their sustained cumulative growth.

The paradigmatic ascents of the human sciences will take place within an overarching paradigm encompassing them all. Not estranged from any theory in the human sciences, universalism incorporates the whole range of valid approaches. As universalism spreads and these are recast upon its foundations, not only their compatibility but also their mutual enhancement will become increasingly evident, making it possible that universalist subparadigms be achieved in all of the human sciences in the coming decades. The human sciences will not be unified mainly in rigorous chains of concepts and propositions, at least not in the foreseeable future, although as such work becomes grounded in universalism and better placed in context it too will become more coherent in the aggregate. The unification of the human sciences will take the form primarily of broadly conceived comparative historical and developmental inquiry that congruently draws upon a common, grounded framework. The emerging synthesis will represent in effect the maturation of the philosophy of history and philosophical history. In the practice of this profoundly interdisciplinary study, the scholar will have one foot in philosophy and one in the human sciences, carrying out general human science in work that is the rational counterpart of high art.

What I envision is an integral relationship between phenomenology and all reflexive inquiry in the human sciences, together with a loose umbrella relationship with unreflexive inquiry. In the coming decades, theory of the sort I have grounded and am calling for is capable of directly subsuming the human sciences insofar as they are reflexive. It would not directly subsume them insofar as they are unreflexive—for that would both overreach its purview and interfere with their needs to explore rigorously within the confines of limiting assumptions—but would instead provide them grounding, orientation, context, and a coherent umbrella. History, anthropology, most of sociology and political science, a good part of psychology, and such portions of economics as economic history and development theory should now be carried out together. Scholars and students need to push the limits of their abilities to cover as much of this expanse as possible and orient themselves to it in their work, and cultural institutions need to be restructured to facilitate this joint practice. Neoclassical economics, behavioral psychology, and the other largely unreflexive studies of the human should be left substantially on their own, although universalists will want to probe, critique, and adjust their assumptions comparatively. The one set of fields may be directly administered, as it were, while the other should be accorded significant autonomy. As the human sciences become aware that a most difficult stream has been forded and they have achieved solid ground, they can begin the process of concerting themselves and discovering a new coherence and productivity.

For more than two hundred years we have accepted the erroneous justification for the proliferation of the human sciences that we know so much it is impossible any longer to manage all knowledge of the human from a single field. It is not that we now know so much but that the larger bourgeois world leans toward specialization, feeling most comfortable developing knowledge the way it manufactures durable goods—objectively, formulaically, compartmentally, and with strict incentives. In their characteristic myopia, insecurity, and rigidity the bourgeois of all stripes shy away from the universal knowledge that transcends their narrow worlds. Yet the human is inherently multifarious, and we cannot truly know it without knowing it comprehensively.

Directionless by themselves, the human sciences will become at once the inspired subsidiaries and indispensable resources of philosophy. This grounding means for the human sciences the conceptual wherewithal to make their work count, a degree of clarity of which they have lost all recollection. As philosophy increasingly comes to see again the unity of the fields it had supposed not to have any, it will notice them to be but extensions of itself.

This work is a blueprint for the unification of the human sciences to reintegrate the secessionist social sciences and psychology—once known as "moral philosophy"—just as one day the natural sciences will be reintegrated. In moving from philosophy through the various subject fields we move along a web of diminishing abstractness into the general theory and methodology of the human sciences, philosophy having "its being essentially in the element of that universality which encloses the particular within it," precisely as Hegel (1967, 67) says. For in Husserl's (1960, 1) words, the particular sciences "are only non-selfsufficient members of the one all-inclusive science, and this is philosophy." All that we know ultimately depends upon both simultaneously. "Only within the systematic unity of philosophy can they develop into genuine sciences." Outside the single partial example of ethics, however, we cannot expect a mature universalist human science for some time to come. Beyond the comparative historical analysis of philosophy itself, a considerably larger collection of works would be required to build the human sciences in the phenomenological vein required to more fully effect this unification. The synthesis of philosophy and the human sciences is possible and necessary because everything human is intrinsically related to everything else and can only be fully understood in a comprehensive way. The human sciences are and always have been all of a piece.

****

This determinate and modern universalism simultaneously represents a significant cultural closure of the modern world. Looming beyond the countless intellectual tasks to which it points are the immense practical tasks of the universal in harmonizing and developing the world. Now that we have knowledge of the fundamental nature of the human we may more concertedly bring wholeness to the world, overcome conflict, and release human potential. Upon these foundations the cosmopolitan world within which people might lead their lives in harmony and fulfillment must be painstakingly assembled. Toward this end it is a matter of the highest priority that there be greater exposure to universalism in general education. Although I have not developed this aspect of it here, universalism is also a philosophy one may live by.

While our world is no longer an idealistic one waiting to be molded by philosophy, universalism may give insight and encouragement to those who all along have been holistically addressing the many-sided problems of the world, even while resisted by major ideologies and undermined by philosophy. Nevertheless, like religions, philosophies do ground societies, and this neo-Hegelian universalism's conceptual framework can help bring about the more harmonious and developed world for which we all hope. This philosophy and the human science based upon it have central roles to play in developing the universal society already forming around us.

Dedicated men and women striving for their entire lifetimes on issues of global import are out of the postmodernist world and into the more universalist one to follow. Yet not only are they still modern; they are the culmination of everything toward which the modern has been tending for five centuries. The new universalists will by no means forget the many concerns for inclusiveness and social justice that have dominated postmodernism. Indeed, they will implement them on a scale previously unimagined. What they will overcome, however, are the particularistic resentment, endemic conflictualism, and nihilist chic of postmodernism—all of which find themselves refuted on the ground, so to speak, by the events of and following September 11, 2001. In a comparable way 1848 signaled the impending demise of an early bourgeois epoch that still had some time to run before social conditions would allow its decisive overthrow.

The coming era of universalism will also be dominated by a different kind of philosopher, one who is no longer a gamesman smitten by the academicist ethos of university administrators, one who may still teach at a university but who will not be a careerist—either finding a program or institute that supports serious long-term effort or working part time and taking frequent leaves from a position that does not. In either event, with full time or nearly full time to herself and leisure her mode, she will contemplate large portions of all that is and extend, round off, and perfect universalist philosophy, completing the building of a balanced view of the world for the global civilization now taking form.

Understanding that the social conditions most productive of universalist philosophy include a massive collision of cultures during the tumultuous mingling of previously separate traditions, leading up to the formation of a unified state—as occurred in Greece, China, and India 2200 to 2500 years ago—we note the same underlying demand bearing the same great need again to be in place. The epochal philosophical syntheses of the past have come at times like ours in which people felt acutely the pain of pluralism and chaos. This time it is not a number of regional cultures flowing into a single continental civilization but a number of continental cultures flowing into a single global civilization. We know that we achieve balance less easily than did our predecessors, but we offset that with a far more developed reflexivity and historical awareness. The universalist philosopher of this and the next century, aware of his responsibility to humankind, will be consumed with the noble task of participating in philosophy's second great period of classicist universalism, in which all of the major oppositions of the world are overcome intellectually, helping to prepare the way for a universalistic world civilization in which we may be one with each other and one with nature. He will have come full circle to the first classicists, but now with the entire world and a much more complex whole as his reference. As Heraclitus' work announced the arrival of the first great classicist phase of philosophy and its ascent of the universal, this one announces the arrival of the second, again conducting philosophy as in ancient Greece, China, and India. With it comes the opportunity to build on the highest of all classicist peaks for several generations, leaving a collective monument for all times—to the many-sided Oneness that we are.

Bibliography

Hegel, G. 1967. *The Phenomenology of Mind*. New York: Harper and Row.
Husserl, E. 1960. *Cartesian Meditations*. The Hague: Martinus Nijhoff.

Appendix/Glossary

First Philosophy

The first category is being. In its most general sense, substance is the set of all that is. Neither substance nor being can be conceived without the other. Substance exists; existing is what substance does in being. What exists has substance within space and time. For something to exist means for it to lie within space and time. Space and time comprise the arena of existence—not mere relations but the framework of existence. Form is configuration or structure in space and time. What exists obtains its form through its distribution in space and time. All properties are characteristics of form, which is to say, they are ultimately spatiotemporal. Substance, form, space, and time are the bedrock categories upon which all other categories stand.

I follow Aristotle (see *Metaphysics*, V:6 and IV:2) in defining a thing as a portion of the manifold of substance of which we may say that it is one or a unity. Some things are countable in discrete units; some, like sugar or air, are aggregable as stuff. Things have different levels of generality. A hierarchy of "thinghood" displays layers of genera—as with protons, nuclei, and atoms, planets, solar systems, and galaxies—all including the same substance (see 1941, 998a20-b13).

As things vis-à-vis temporality, events make up portions of the temporal flux that form unities (cf. Kant 1965, 172). That they are concrete things having substance and form is what particular supernova explosions or continental drifts have in common with other things. As things have form in space, they also have form in time. For example, volcanic eruptions are sometimes discrete and explosive and sometimes continuous and mild. Particular events, like all things, have different levels of generality—there are eras and epochs in which large sets of events take place. Processes are general occurrences in time.

What exists in space and time is composed of matter-energy.

The Three Realms

There are three realms: inert things, living things, and the **human**. By the human I mean mind or spirit. Persons are human. Collectivities of persons are also human.[1] In this work I am concerned with the human.

The realm of inert things is one of matter and energy, and their form consists of patterns in physical space and time. Space-time is the range or field in which substance and form exist. It therefore constitutes the broadest framework of existence.

Much scientific debate has taken place about the distinction between inert and living things. However, it seems to me that living things are essentially inert things with an ability to sense their surroundings and instinctively respond to them.[2] Living things are alive.

The realm of the human differs from that of the biological in that it possesses **consciousness** or mind. Hence the *thereness* of the human. In addition to being alive the human is conscious. Consciousness encompasses the totality of mental processes (Husserl, 1982, 64).

Representation and Meaning

To Schopenhauer (1969), consciousness is comprised of representation and "will." The representation is the cognitive aspect of consciousness, and the "will" is the motivational aspect of it.[3] Consciousness is a flow of representation that orients and motivation that pushes, the two sides of our most fundamental being. Any being with representation and motivation is human.

To represent is to bring something before the mind (see *Webster's Third International*), to present it to consciousness. **Representation** in one sense is what is brought before the mind, in another, bringing things before the mind.[4] The human uses representations in relating to its surroundings, enabling it to apprehend and respond flexibly to substance and form across a vast manifold of meaning. Humans are beings that represent things instead of merely processing information. To represent is to mean or to give meaning, variously (to) the world to which representations refer or the world they are aimed at bringing about, whether or not these exist or take place. The symbols the human uses in representation go infinitely beyond the signals of the merely living. Representation differs from mere information in that it forms a whole universe within which meaning arises. With the step to the human, the purely instinctual, meaningless patterning of fixed biological routing becomes dynamic, learned representation.

To mean something in the corresponding sense is to present it or have it presented to consciousness—one's own or someone else's. By **meaning** I understand both intended and unintended meaning, or more fully a broader parallel to Grice's (1989, 220 and especially 291–92 but also his ch. 14 and 18 in their entireties) "nonnatural" sense of meaning as conventional, in which to say that *A* means something by *x* is approximately equivalent to saying that "*A* intended the utterance of *x* to produce some effect in an audience by means of the recognition of this intention"—and his natural sense of meaning as neither conventional nor intended.

In the first basic use of representation the human mimics the world—past, present, or future. The most elementary version of this merely describes phenomena in any of the three realms. A more complex use of such representation relates why things occur. In the other basic use people mimic not the world but potential action by themselves with which they might transform the world.[5] In this employment, representation takes the form of **routines**, which are blueprints or templates that guide or route what we do. With routines we can perform or make what we choose with results we have foreseen. These blueprints for action are applied representation, knowing-how-to as opposed to simple knowing.[6] We don't passively model the world with such routines but actively change it. Providing the form to which action is contoured, routines are constructed or borrowed to route action through obstacles toward realization of our aims.

The outcome to which routines impart form may be as fleeting as a gesture or as enduring as a monument. Routines may be as simple as an impish child's vague notion or a manual worker's rule of thumb, or as complex as a nation's business strategy or an art movement's aesthetic imperative. Routines may be constructed well before action or they may arise as designs-in-action almost simultaneously with action. They may be formal or informal, polished or unpolished, complete or incomplete, and on-line or off-line.

Routines, however, can never guide action by themselves. They must always be accompanied by ordinary representations in the form of putative facts serving as markers to position or adjust the routines. As we adjust the paper model of a shirt to the wearer's size and material's limits before cutting fabric, we recall a partner's location and stage plan before performing a dance, and make instantial assumptions and set parameters before casting scientific predictions. When we create routines, we construct empty forms, but we then impart reality to them through action that endows them with substance in more or less enduring fashion. Routines are analogous to the rigid patterns of behavior in the biological world, except that we construct, select, and revise them.

Motivation

The energy moving the human through time takes the form of **motivation** rather than genetically determined impulsion. Things matter to us, or Dasein cares, as Heidegger (1962, 235–41) says—for which reason all of our representations are cathected. We attach desirability across the manifold of representations of actual or imagined things, past, present, and future. Anticipations, experiences, and memories of the things that matter to us are emotionally charged possessions, emotion being the sensation we feel in association with all that we like or dislike, and which we judge as pleasant or unpleasant and experience an inclination to approach or avoid. Emotion comes as raw feeling from within, which we must mentally process, as we must process sensation from without. Of all the things we like, those upon which we set our minds are wants. Wants are likes that impel pursuit. Responding to our wants (or needs in the sense of wants), we select among routines by projecting the alternative outcomes to which they lead and determining the preferred scenarios. These become our goals or aims. Motivation arises in the tension between what we want and what we have, between expectations and reality. The greater the gap between expectations and reality, the greater the motivation—up to a point, beyond which it again begins to fall.

Intentionality

Central to the human is the *aboutness* or referentiality of representation and motivation, its *intentionality*[7] (cf. Searle, 1983, 1ff.). The essence of human being, as Husserl makes clear, lies in its aboutness. Humans are beings whose being encompasses reference *to* and concern *with* things. Consciousness is *about* things (Husserl 1982, 200; Merleau-Ponty 1962, 37). Where there is *intentionality* there is meaning, and vice-versa. Yet just as information in the biological world consists ultimately of matter-energy and form, or matter-energy in its spatiotemporal framework, so ultimately does meaning. Both are always embodied or housed. At the lowest level, representation and motivation are material forms physically present in our brains or in such places as books or computers.

Intentionality includes *being* and *doing*. Some of what the human is about is relatively static, as manifested in a particular character. Those with different kinds of character are regularly *about* different things with their lives. Some of what the human is about is dynamic. We do or occupy ourselves with different kinds of things. Perception, thought, and action make up the elementary moments of *doing*.

Perception and Thought

By its nature as conscious being in the world the human perceives the world, thinks about it, and acts with respect to it. **Perception** is the registering or taking in of things in themselves that exist or occur in or around us. In perception something is given to us originarily. Perception is an adverting to and seizing upon of an object against a background (Husserl, 1982, 5–6, 70–71). "The perceptual 'something' is always in the middle of something else, it always forms part of a 'field'" (Merleau-Ponty 1962, 4; see also Smith 2002, 134–38, 153). The interpretation of which perception essentially consists yields knowledge of the existence of things (Smith 2002, 37, 40). **Thought,** on the other hand, is a recalling, creating, judging, or combining of representations of things in themselves that are in or around us. Thought consists broadly of generating or searching for alternatives and screening them. Unlike perception, which directly engages what exists, thought is a hermetic processing or manipulating of or from representations that have been taken in. Thought works what it is given, using representations to operate upon representations.[8]

Action

Another fundamental attribute of the human is that it is capable of **action**.

An act occurs when we intentionally (in the everyday sense) cause something to happen (see Weber 1978, 1375; cf. 4). In action we are pushed by our motives along tracks laid down by our representations toward achievement of our aims (cf. Weber 1958, 280). Moving between future and present, the human transforms the potential into the actual, what exists only in ideality into what also exists in reality. Action is analogous to motion in the physical world and behavior in the biological one.[9]

A basic feature of action is that it is embedded in hierarchies, simultaneously part of many different events on different levels of abstraction. Searle (1983, 98–99) refers to this as the accordion effect, giving the example of Princip (which I abbreviate slightly and punctuate), who in a single act "pulled the trigger, fired the gun, shot the archduke, killed the archduke, [and] struck a blow against Austria. . . ." (Its unintended consequences then went on to start the war, begin the thirty-one-year crisis, and seal the fate of neoagrarian society.) Searle's point addresses the ambiguity concerning the scope of an act.

The limits of an act are governed by the limits of its two essential components, its *intentionality* and its causation. A particular act in the fullest sense is the most inclusive way in which the actor intends to make a difference with action, incorporating all of the component elements leading up to it. Thus, as Schutz (1967, 62) says, at any level, "[t]he unity of the action is constituted by the fact that the act already exists 'in project,' which will be realized step by step through the action." However, Princip's *act* was to strike a blow against Austria, not to start World War I, since the latter was an unintended side-effect. Had he fired the gun and missed, the act would have been a failed assassination attempt, reaching only part way up the hierarchy of intention (and making much less of a difference). However, *an* act also may be taken to be any less inclusive portion of a larger act of which there were intended effects.

The Phases of Doing

We may be said to be doing and experiencing something every moment of our waking hours, but we are not acting in every moment, for **doing** is engaging in an *intentional* process and having *intentional* experience, only some of which is intentionally causing things to occur. Perception, thought, and action are phases of doing. Perception and thought form a kind of *pre-*action that Homeric language beautifully expresses in saying that a word or thought "completes itself" in overt action (see Snell 1982, 142). When one has engaged in the needed perception and thought, they may be utilized in action. Hence the theoretical primacy Searle (1979, 135) accords to perception among the forms of *intentionality*. Perception and thought necessarily precede action in any given cycle of doing, though not necessarily by much. Moreover, action may bring new representations into being which may then be utilized in further action.

Perception is receptive, action is active, and thought intervenes between the two. It may be helpful to think of this as an input-throughput-output sequence. Where multiple humans are present, the input frequently entails being acted upon communicatively and the output communicatively acting upon others—being done to and doing to. The component parts of a complex act may be extensive, as when we engage in systematic strategic planning in the thought phase; or they may be momentary and half-conscious, as when we turn on a light upon entering a room. Those of complex perception or thought may also be extensive, with many subordinate perceptions, thoughts, and acts. Perception or thought, like action, may be considered on any level we wish. With the human and meaning come perception over and above elementary sensation, thought in place of automatic response, and communication in lieu of mere signaling.[10] All doing is accompanied by experience.

Possessions

Possessions, those things we have under our control or ready-at-hand, constitute a fundamental ontological category that cuts across the realms of being. We may possess that which is human, biological, or merely inert. Scholars have directed relatively little attention to the categories and types of possessions, but they are very useful for study in the human sciences.

Our **bodies**, which link the physical, biological, and existential realms, are developmentally the first things we control. As Hegel (1952, 43) says, if the body "is to be the willing organ and soul-endowed instrument of the mind, it must first be taken into possession by mind." Our own personal domesticated animal, the body is our most elementary possession, housing, serving, expressing, and giving satisfaction to our psyches. Yet the relationship between mind and body is even more intimate and subtle than this, for our minds have large genetic components—a substantial portion of all we are is biologically inherited. As with computers and even more so with us, the line between what is inherited and what is learned is by no means simple. However, the body is not the only possible housing for the human; our material infrastructure could be very different from what we know today. All we can say is that mind is by nature materially embedded.

In addition to our bodies, possessions include fixed and movable objects as well as real property. When we act, the intended effects may or may not bring into being and under our control what we desire. When they do, production has occurred, and the resulting possessions are artifacts. In production, things are formed with routines and tools, driven by resources at our command. Possessions may also be obtained from others or found. Additionally possessions include representations and motivation in our minds. We act with material and mental possessions on material and mental objects, utilizing accumulated reserves of motivation. Where tools are possessions seen in light of their extrinsic value, treasures are possessions seen in light of their intrinsic value.[11]

What *we* are, where our *thereness* lies, is primarily (in) consciousness, personal and collective, but other senses exist in which we may be taken to extend through all that we control or all that we care about, including portions of the physical and biological realms as well as other persons and collectivities.

Language as a Possession

Language may also be considered as a possession. **Language** is the symbolic infrastructure of the human. Languages are conveyances for carrying meaning (Wittgenstein 1953, 107). Their symbols enable us to wield, store, and communicate representations so that we may mimic things and orient ourselves. Everything that is can be represented with language and everything that can be done can be done with language. This is the principle of expressibility basic to speech acts theory which holds that "whatever can be meant can be said" (Searle 1969, 19; see also 1968, 415). There can be no aboutness without language. Thus, as Wittgenstein (1953, 18) says, "[i]t is only in a language that I can mean something by something."

However, in addition to verbal languages, we have also the most diverse kinds of nonverbal languages: languages of music, painting, and sculpture; and languages of gesture, worship, and dance. The broad definition above includes the language or dialect of French Impressionism as it does body languages. Wittgenstein, Chomsky, and many others underappreciate the importance of nonverbal languages. The rigorists of all persuasions tend to be impatient because little is known about most kinds of nonverbal languages (not counting those of mathematics, logic, and programming which are but specialized variants of verbal language), but impatience should not drive ontology.

While very important, language is only the "material" out of which representations are fashioned, not those representations themselves. Many recent thinkers view language as itself the content of our thought instead of merely the possession with which we think. Just as the study of materials is of significant but limited use in technology, the study of language is of significant but limited use in the study of the human. Saying that culture is *just* language is no more helpful than saying cathedrals are just bricks and mortar, or human beings just quarks and leptons. Language carries representations and influences them in so doing, but studying language is not a substitute for studying the human, only a significant complement to it. Although language is worthy of study, owing to its very serviceability, one may study the human or anything else very effectively with, but without foregrounding, language.

Power

Power is a very basic concept in the human sciences. That philosophers have done so little with it ontologically is a rather glaring and telling omission. Russell (1938, 35) is a partial exception, having organized one of his popular works around the concept. I start from his definition of **power** as "the production of intended effects," but that is no more than a suggestive beginning, for which reason on this basic concept I must provide most of my own groundwork.

For a fuller understanding of power, one must distinguish between the stock and flow of power. Russell defines power rather awkwardly as a flow and does not clearly make the distinction. We should instead view power as a stock, as the ability or potential to produce intended effects. Power, in other words, is the capacity to bring about intentionally a series of causal linkages, leading to the realization of goals. What we have the power to bring about constitutes potential reality under our control. Power takes many different forms, from a country's ability to defend itself militarily to a youth's ability to obtain social invitations, from a religious group's ability to propagate its view of the world to a person's ability to control her own impulses. Not power itself but the *exercise* of it is a flow, the actual or kinetic production of intended effects. For power to be exercised, the action must actually bring about the intended consequences: the causation has to be in the intended direction, and it has to achieve the intended result. The exercise of power does not displace other forms of causation but is superimposed upon and operates through them. The exercise of power on a continuing basis constitutes **control**, and when this is established, domination. What we intend is also in the great majority of cases what we want. Hence, my definition is effectively equivalent to holding with Lasswell that power is the ability to get what we want, and its exercise, the getting of what we want.

Resources, tools, or "capital," those things we have the ability to control seen in light of their instrumental value, are utilized in the exercise of power. Human capital, in the form of representation and motivation, what we know how to do and how much motivation we have with which to do it, is a crucial source of power. Beyond wielding ourselves, it is the ability to wield money, factories, equipment, and other humans that confers specific forms of power, thereby enabling us to realize the goals and expectations we entertain. We may speak interchangeably of a political boss's power over his associates or of them as his resources or capital.

Power may be viewed qualitatively or quantitatively, depending upon need.[12] The quantity of power, essentially its existential amplitude, is best captured as its value. The quantity of power, so expressed, is how much people want its effects after considering how much they must forego to obtain them. Quantity and value in power, as in goods and services, are a function of supply and demand—how much of something would be available at what cost and how badly people want it. Such costs are considered broadly, for in some circumstances monetary values come to be assigned to power and its corresponding resources while in others they do not. The exercise of power of which action consists has costs. In action we necessarily exercise some power and consume some possessions, leaving altered balances of resources. Our action always uses power and has results that return varying amounts of power. For this reason we ordinarily ignore those technical powers a person has that it would be absurd for him to exercise, such as a poor man's power to stay for a brief while in the Four Seasons, consuming his life savings, or anyone's power to throw a pie at her boss. What ordinarily counts is the power we have that is profitable or rational to exercise. But when rationality recedes, at least short-term power may go up steeply. While peasants typically have only negligible ability to change the conditions under which they labor, they do have the power to strike back in anger against their lords.

Influence

Influence, on the other hand, is the ability to bring about effects, irrespective of intentions. The exercise of influence is the production of the intended plus the unintended effects of our action. Influence too may be viewed qualitatively or quantitatively. While Princip did not have the power to start the war, he did have the influence to do so. Since in time we inevitably lose control of the effects, all power eventually turns to influence, as all possessions eventually turn to detritus. The concepts of power and influence are often misused in scholarly and general discourse.

Collectivity

The exercise of interpersonal control joins two or more actors into a single larger entity and brings into being a new form of the human, **collectivity**. In the simplest collectivity, *A* perceives, thinks, and communicates, and her representation becomes realized in *B*'s action through the exercise of control. Elementary specialization takes place in which *A* thinks across a larger range but her acting is restricted, while the reverse is the case for *B*. Coming under each other's control to varying degrees, persons form various kinds of collectivities in which they conduct their action jointly in cooperation or coaction. To the extent to which a collectivity's members cooperate and merge in their action, the collectivity becomes a thing in its own right. Control rather than mere power must be present for this to occur. Collectivity is actually only *there* to the extent to which cooperation and merger occur or are set up to occur. Hierarchies of control with multiple layers of collectivity may come into being around stocks and flows of power and resources. Collectivities are altered whenever the power around which they are formed changes.

Collectivities are disaggregable things. "There *are* things, especially things composed of parts that may be reassembled temporarily into other things and then taken apart again to enable the reconstitution of the original object, that thereby lead a discontinuous existence" (Hamlyn 1984, 74). When they come into being, their component parts remain things in their own right, but at the same time these parts gain an added identification as parts of a larger thing. The intermittent existence of collectivities in which their members come together for a time, leave for a time, and do the same with other collectivities is somewhat analogous to the building block constructions of children. However, a collectivity is more than a mere collection of individuals. The atomist may not view collectivities as things in their own right, but they are quite as real as we. If they are not things, what are they?

Collectivities, like persons, are human; they possess consciousness made up of representation and motivation. They perceive, think, and act. They display what Husserl (1960, 107) refers to as communalized *intentionality*. To the extent to which persons become parts of collectivities, they have representation and motivation and do things as parts of collectivities and for them—they wield possessions, exercise power, and feel emotion for them. The being of collectivities is realized through their members. Collectivities are superimposed upon persons and reveal emergent properties of their own.[13]

Satisfaction

The achievement of goals and fulfillment of expectations bring varying kinds and degrees of satisfaction, the favorable emotional state to which our nature draws us. **Satisfaction** is contentment with what holds concerning that about which we care. Satisfaction, like other *intentional* states, is always about something. Satisfaction, like power, may be viewed as a stock or flow, respectively satisfaction overall and satisfaction accruing at a particular time—always vis-à-vis that in which one is emotionally invested. Again like power, it may also be viewed qualitatively or quantitatively: there are particular kinds of emotional response to things about which we care, and there is the emotional assessment of these.

Power and satisfaction, our twin elementary possession balances and bottom lines, derive respectively from our tools and treasures. As power is the ability intentionally to bring about outcomes, satisfaction is the ability to be content with outcomes. As power may also be seen as the ability to get what one wants, satisfaction may also be seen as the ability to want what one gets.

This view of the human is at once structural and teleological. Because the human simultaneously has to do with representation and motivation, a teleology is at least tacit in every structural metaphysics directed to the human, and viceversa. Teleology is properly rejected from physics; it is vital to the human sciences.

Environment

For the human there is also that which is around it, its **environment** or the "world." The environment includes human, biological, and physical elements. In action the human surveys environing conditions and wields resources toward the best possible fit with the exigencies that hold, seeking to realize its aims. In so doing it slowly transforms environment into possessions and detritus, the former being portions of what was once environment now under control, and the latter being portions of the environment affected by unintended side-effects. All else equal, as power grows, the human reaches progressively further into the social and natural environment with increasing effects, foreseen and unforeseen. Looked at from the point of view of the human, we move from the three realms to the view that there exist the human, its possessions, and its environment.[14]

Notes

1. Made up of persons, collectivities manifest many of the same fundamental properties as persons. Both Plato and Heidegger make the core reference to being, but Plato above all emphasizes the ontological parallels between persons and collectivities.

2. In life, external stimuli prompt chemical, electrical, and mechanical reactions in a realm of beings processing information by way of programmed feedback loops. Biological things are natural cybernetic systems that sense their surroundings and adapt to them by instinct. The physical energy of the inert world, harnessed by instinct, impels cells, organs, and organisms in accordance with genetic instructions. In mutual adjustments between living things, signals are emitted and sensed, and the automatic signal of one unit becomes the sensation and automatic response of the other. At the gross organismic level we may speak of instinct responding to stimuli as behavior.

3. Unlike Schopenhauer, however, I mean *Darstellung* rather than *Vorstellung* by "representation." For this reason my intention is usually more accurately rendered by "presentation" or "re-presentation" than by "representation." Out of consideration to the general reader, however, I use "representation" with the attached caveat.

4. We must be careful not to confuse the noun and verb forms of this word, which would result in "act-object" or "process-product" ambiguity (see Searle 1968, 422).

5. The distinction is adapted from Austin and Searle (see p. 58, n.1).

6. On the notion of knowledge see the section on epistemic criteria in Chapter 16.

7. Because this term is easily confused with intentionality in the ordinary sense, I italicize it and its cognates.

8. On perception and thought see also the section on the phases of doing that follows.

9. Just as the emergence of living things does not displace physical ones but superimposes new features upon them, so the emergence of the human does not displace either earlier realm but superimposes new features upon them. Nor are living things composed of different elemental substance than the inert—everything human is still biological and physical, just as everything biological is still physical—they simply organize it on a higher level. Human beings are animals that act and have meaning. The result is greatly more complex emergent phenomena among things and occurrences composed of the same elemental stuff.

There is only one kind of elemental substance, matter-energy that physically exists. Yet in the higher, emergent realms of being, physical things manifest structural and dynamic patterns which must be treated so differently that it is *as if* they were of a different substance—until, that is, natural science becomes sufficiently developed to incorporate them. Thus, while ideas are ultimately physical configurations in brain cells or some other housing, they cannot satisfactorily be studied on that basis at present. Purely as an expedient—and for a time, albeit possibly a very long time—we must treat them as if they were of entirely different substance, although they are not. Therefore, what makes the life sciences distinct is that although the phenomena they treat are not ultimately different in substance, many of them will not be fully reducible to elementary physical processes for the foreseeable future. Even more so, the human sciences will not be fully reducible to the biological for the foreseeable future. The distinction between the realms of the inert, the living, and the human then is not one of most fundamental substance but a pragmatic and provisional world-picture acknowledging a situation with a three-leveled human—physical being, body, and consciousness—that will nevertheless hold for a very long time.

This I believe to be the moderate and wise position on the debate about substance. Traditionalists have argued for "dualism" (i.e., radical metaphysical separation between nature and the human, opposing the inert and living to it) because all meaning seems to dissolve in the monist world of natural science. On the other hand, the monists have rightly argued that ultimately there is nothing else present but matter and energy. Yet the monist case is one in which metaphysics has outrun science because one can still do only extremely limited work in the human sciences on its basis. (Failure to grasp the implications of this limitation is the central weakness of Searle's social ontology in *The Construction of*

Social Reality.) Mind is *not* a unique elemental substance, but it *is* a strikingly different emergent phenomenon. One must put up with imperfect groundedness—and without deceiving himself. We essentially proceed as if there were three different substances. To speak of three realms of substance, then, is to have it both ways, to concede monism theoretically and take it back practically—for a very long time. The reason is that such large transitions separate the realms that it will be too long to wait for a "monist" world. (This is to disagree with those who hold that substances do not have to be simple, but it is to disagree more strongly with materialists like Chomsky, Dretske, and Searle who are willing to suffer the Ptolemaic complexity and rank inadequacy of monist scholarship in the human sciences to achieve spurious consistency with metaphysical foundations.)

Human inquiry can and must proceed on a provisional basis until in the remote future natural science arrives in a serious way in the realm of the human. However, all meaning will by no means then dissolve into mechanistic equations—that occurs only as a consequence of today's crude scientific tools. A natural science that were truly able to incorporate the human sciences would be so radically different from any current natural science as to moot all objections today imaginable. My provisional approach, in effect, allows effort based upon each assumption to go forward in competition until further knowledge should give us grounds for changing the judgment upon which it rests.

10. An important implication of my distinction between the realms of the human and the biological is that the line between humans and animals has been too sharply drawn, for the human begins long before homo sapiens. Some of the essential features of the human are fairly well developed in significant parts of the animal world. Searle (1983, 5) convincingly argues that at least higher animals possess *intentionality*. Some of the id's development—and the id, I would argue, is human—came already with lower mammals in particular; and it is more developed in most mammals, as for example in grief among elephants or play among rhesus monkeys. The emotional lives of the higher mammals don't resemble the human; they *are* "human." In other words, we are not the only ones to have significantly "escaped" the biological world—the higher mammals have also partly done so. (And it is because to some degree they are "human" that the higher mammals have greater value in their own right than worms or barley.) With the appearance of fully human beings, rational capacity and the ability to communicate went up dramatically. But emotionality—and fully human beings themselves dwelt overwhelmingly in emotionality until the very recent past—was so highly developed in other mammals, and our emotionality is so kindred to theirs, that it seems untenable to deny the elements of continuity. Many of our simple representations would also seem kindred to theirs.

Moreover, while I have used the expression "fully" human for convenience, we have by no means yet completely made the transition between the biological and human realms. Our sexual desire retains a good deal of the instinctual, as does the desire for aggression in some. Most of us most of the time add considerable human content to sexual wants, but their biological impulsion and direction remain pronounced. Various other quite specific biological needs continue to carry not inconsiderable force in our lives—residues of a biological epoch, one might say, that we are rapidly leaving behind. After registering the above reservation, I would feel most comfortable with the position that mammals are partly human and we for practical purposes fully so. Like the physical and biological, the human is an ideal type.

However, I only bring up the issue in passing and as an adjunct to other matters because I restrict my concern in this work to persons and collectivities. Since it would be awkward to refer constantly to our simpler mammalian cousins (and our more complex artificial successors), I take the human in practice to be coextensive with fully functioning human beings and collectivities.

11. The distinction is more fully treated in Chapter 1. See Simmel (2004, 209–11) for another relatively comprehensive understanding of tools capable of including the state, laws, and money.

12. On the one hand, there is the question of the specific ability of a given actor or set of actors to bring about particular intended effects in particular situations, with no necessity to compare that to the specific abilities of others. For example, the customary power of a U.S. senator allows her to veto federal judiciary appointments in her state, or the power of schoolyard ruffians in a particular location allows them to bully their classmates with particular acts of intimidation. Often it helps to view power qualitatively in such ways. On the other hand, for many purposes it is how much the intended effects matter that counts, not the specific effects that might occur—for which reason we must often speak of the magnitude of power. (Qualitative and quantitative approaches to power correspond to Marx's use value and exchange value.) For example, we may be concerned with how much overall political power the French aristocracy held and exercised during the eighteenth century. Or we may be concerned with the changing levels of informal social power exercised by women in their families between the 1950s and 1980s in the U.S.

13. The relationship between persons and collectivities is considered in greater detail in Chapter 6.

14. This brings us close to a Heideggerian "Dasein-in-the-world-with-tools-ready-to-hand."

Bibliography

Aristotle. 1941. *Metaphysics.* In *The Basic Writings of Aristotle,* ed. R. McKeon. New York: Random House.

Grice, P. 1989. *Studies in the Way of Words.* Cambridge, MA: Harvard University Press.

Hamlyn, D. 1984. *Metaphysics.* Cambridge: Cambridge University Press.

Hegel, G. 1952. *Hegel's Philosophy of Right.* London: Oxford University Press.

Heidegger, M. 1962. *Being and Time.* New York: Harper and Row.

Husserl, E. 1960. *Cartesian Meditations.* The Hague: Martinus Nijhoff.

———. 1982. *Ideas Pertaining to a Pure Phenomenology and a Phenomenological Philosophy.* The Hague: Martinus Nijhoff.

Kant, I. 1965. *Critique of Pure Reason.* New York: St. Martin's Press.

Merleau-Ponty, M. 1962, *Phenomenology of Perception.* London: Routledge & Kegan Paul.

Russell, B. 1938. *Power: A New Social Analysis.* New York: Norton.

Schopenhauer, A. 1969. *The World as Will and Representation* Vol. 1. New York: Dover Publications.

Schutz, A. 1967. *The Phenomenology of the Social World*. Evanston, IL: Northwestern University Press.

Searle, J. 1968. "Austin on Locutionary and Illocutionary Acts." *Philosophical Review* 57.

———. 1969. *Speech Acts: An Essay in the Philosophy of Language*. Cambridge: Cambridge University Press.

———. 1979. *Expression and Meaning*. Cambridge: Cambridge University Press.

———. 1983. *Intentionality: An Essay in the Philosophy of Mind*. Cambridge: Cambridge University Press.

———. 1995. *The Construction of Social Reality*. New York: The Free Press.

Simmel, G. 2004. *The Philosophy of Money*. London: Routledge.

Smith, A. 2002. *The Problem of Perception*. Cambridge, MA: Harvard University Press.

Snell, B. 1982. *The Discovery of the Mind*. New York: Dover.

Weber, M. 1978. *Economy and Society*. 2 vols. Berkeley and Los Angeles: University of California Press.

———. 1958. *From Max Weber: Essays in Sociology*. New York: Oxford University Press.

Wittgenstein, L. 1953. *Logical Investigations*. New York: Macmillan.

Index

SAN FRANCISCO STATE UNIVERSITY SERIES IN PHILOSOPHY

This series is designed to encourage philosophers to explore new directions of research in philosophy. The underlying premise of the series is that contemporary philosophical research is impeded by an understanding of the intellectual division of labor according to which philosophy is conceived of as separate from the natural and social sciences, the arts and humanistic disciplines. Science is impoverished by the neglect of immediate attention to the metaphysical and moral questions posed by scientific developments. The arts and humanistic disciplines are also impoverished by a lack of sufficient attention to the philosophical implication of innovation in each of these areas. Philosophy for its part is in danger of grinding away on outdated problems posed by the scientific and artistic developments of past centuries. The usual remedy for this situation, inter-disciplinary work, typically falls far short of the needed re-integration of philosophy, the sciences, the arts and humanistic disciplines. The pressing problems of contemporary civilization, particularly the problems that concern the relationship between science, technology and ethical and political values, we believe, can only be adequately explored by a re-integration of philosophy with other fields. Our series seeks to call attention to itself by meeting high standards of scholarship and producing work of unquestionable merit. Works in our series should contribute to the re-integration of philosophy with the natural and social sciences, technology, the arts or humanities by challenging philosophical pre-conceptions that block the re-integration of philosophy with other disciplines.

For more information about this series, please contact:

Anatole Anton
Dept. of Philosophy
San Francisco State University
1600 Holloway Avenue
San Francisco, CA 94132
(415) 338-1596
aanton@sfsu.edu

To order other books in this series, please contact our Customer Service Department at:

(800) 770-LANG (within the U.S.)
(212) 647-7706 (outside the U.S.)
(212) 647-7707 FAX

or browse online by series at:

www.peterlang.com